Competition Policy in the European Union

Second Edition

**Michelle Cini
and
Lee McGowan**

palgrave
macmillan

First edition 1998
Second edition 2009

Published by
PALGRAVE MACMILLAN

Palgrave Macmillan in the UK is an imprint of Macmillan Publishers Limited, registered in England, company number 785998, of Houndmills, Basingstoke, Hampshire RG21 6XS.

Palgrave Macmillan in the US is a division of St Martin's Press LLC, 175 Fifth Avenue, New York, NY 10010.

Palgrave Macmillan is the global academic imprint of the above companies and has companies and representatives throughout the world.

Palgrave® and Macmillan® are registered trademarks in the United States, the United Kingdom, Europe and other countries.

ISBN-13: 978–0–230–00675–1   hardback
ISBN-10: 0–230–00675–2   hardback
ISBN-13: 978–0–230–00676–8   paperback
ISBN-10: 0–230–00676–0   paperback

This book is printed on paper suitable for recycling and made from fully managed and sustained forest sources. Logging, pulping and manufacturing processes are expected to conform to the environmental regulations of the country of origin.

A catalogue record for this book is available from the British Library.

A catalog record for this book is available from the Library of Congress.

Contents

List of Boxes, Tables and Figures   viii

Preface   x

List of Abbreviations   xii

1   **Introduction**   1
   Competition and competition policy   2
   Introducing the European competition regime   6
   Organization of the book   9

2   **The Evolution of the European Competition Regime**   11
   Origins and influences   11
   From coal and steel to EEC   16
   The first fifteen years: 1958 to 1972   21
   From recession to stagnation: 1973 to 1981 25
   Towards a 'new' competition policy   29
   More recent trends and developments   35
   Conclusion   39

3   **The Institutions of European Competition Governance** 41
   The Parliament and the Council   42
   The European Commission   44
   Organization and functions   45
   The European Courts   54
   National actors and European networks   59
   Conclusion   61

4   **Restrictive Practices Policy**   63
   Article 81: regulating restrictive practices   64
   Policy practice   74
   Assessing restrictive practices policy   82
   The age of aggressive enforcement: the situation after
      2004   89
   Conclusion   96

5   **Monopoly Policy**   **98**

Article 82 in context   99
The Commission's analysis: demonstrating and
    establishing 'dominance'   101
The Commission's assessment of 'abuse'   111
Assessing monopoly policy   119
The modernization of Article 82   123
Conclusion   126

6   **Merger Policy**   **127**

The origins of European merger control   128
Towards a coherent merger regime: procedure and
    practice   131
The recast 2004 European Merger Regulation   140
Assessing merger policy: politics and political
    sensitivities   147
Conclusion   159

7   **State Aid Policy**   **162**

Organization, powers and decision-making   163
Towards a cohesive state aid regime   176
Policy content   182
Assessing state aid control   191
Conclusion   197

8   **Theoretical Perspectives**   **199**

Can neo-functionalism account for supranational
    competition governance?   201
Exploring Europeanization   207
Conclusion   213

9   **Conclusions**

Modernization and decentralization: policy and
    organizational reform   214
Decentralization and Europeanization: from delegation
    to network governance   217
Liberalization: competition v. competitiveness revisited   223

International cooperation and the centrality of the
  EU–US relationship   225
The future of European competition policy   226

Guide to Further Reading   229
References   232
Index   245

List of Boxes, Tables and Figures

Boxes

2.1 The Treaty of Rome provisions 17
2.2 Regulation 17 19
2.3 *Grundig–Consten* 22
3.1 The Competition Commissioners 46
3.2 The Structure of DG Competition (2008) 50
3.3 Human resources (staff numbers): DG
Competition (2006) 53
4.1 Article 81 67
4.2 Block exemptions regulations 73
4.3 The lifts and escalators cartel 90
5.1 DG Competition *v.* Microsoft 109
5.2 The *AKZO* and *Tetra-Pak* Cases 116
6.1 Notices in force to assist understanding of the
principles and aims of the Merger Regulation 141
6.2 The merger review timetable 143
6.3 Statistical overview of mergers, 1990 – January 2008 148
6.4 Locating the politics of EU merger policy 149
7.1 State aid provisions of the Treaty of Rome 167
7.2 State aid decision-making procedures 173
7.3 State aid roadmap: 2005–07 181
7.4 Northern Rock 187
8.1 Europeanization dynamics in EU cartel policy 208
8.2 Europeanization dynamics in EU merger policy 212

Tables

4.1 Selected fines under Article 81, 1994–2004 83
4.2 The fourteen largest fines 85
4.3 Commission cartel decisions, 2003–07 92

4.4   Cartel fines (not corrected by Court judgments)
      2003–08   93
7.1   The trend in the level of state aid in the EU member
      states, 1997–2006   179
7.2   Number of registered aid cases in 2005   192
8.1   Tracing the expansive development of EU competition
      policy   203

Figures

8.1   Competition policy as spillover into other sectors   206

Preface

It has been more than ten years since we completed the first edition of *Competition Policy in the European Union*, and a great deal has changed in the EU competition regime since that time. As will become apparent in the chapters that follow, some commentators even go so far as to claim that a 'revolution' has taken place in the policy since the mid 1990s (Wilks 2005b). Others, however, prefer to emphasize the deepening of trends that have been apparent in the regime since the neo-liberal turn of the 1980s (Wigger 2008). Whichever reflects better the recent transformation of the policy, there is no doubt that for those of us interested in this topic, we are living in interesting times.

Yet beyond the disciplines of law and economics, competition policy is little understood. Political scientists rarely focus their attention upon it; and even those working in the field of European Studies seem to underplay its importance as a European policy – even if they are prepared to acknowledge in passing its distinctive supranational or federal credentials. But this point is not a new one: we said as much in the Preface to the first edition. Yet there are indications that the tide *may* be turning. In updating this text we hope to encourage even more work in this area, and provide a point of departure for new scholars who may in future decide to engage in research on competition policy.

Before moving to more substantive issues, however, there are a few stylistic points we need to address. First, with regard to the numbering of treaty articles, this book uses the post-Amsterdam (post-1999) numbering only. Thus, we refer to Article 81 when we discuss restrictive practices policy. We only mention its former incarnation (as Article 85) in historical context where to use the current numbering would make no sense. However, a word of caution is needed given the uncertainty over the ratification of the Lisbon Treaty following its rejection in the Irish referendum of June 2008. Should the ratification of the Treaty proceed at some point in the future, the numbering of the treaty provision would change once again. Readers can access a table listing each of the different numbering systems at Palgrave Macmillan's website: www.palgrave.com/politics/eu

Similarly, in 1999, DGIV (Directorate-General Four) of the European Commission became DG Competition (or DG COMP). We use DGIV in Chapter 2 as we chart the historical evolution of the policy. Otherwise, we refer to DG Competition throughout.

Finally, we would like to thank family, friends and colleagues for their forbearance as this second edition was being completed. Our gratitude also goes to the series editors, Neill Nugent and Willie Paterson, and – of course – to all at Palgrave Macmillan, and to Steven Kennedy in particular.

MICHELLE CINI
LEE McGOWAN

List of Abbreviations

ABA	American Bar Association
BEUC	European Bureau of Consumers' Unions
BKartA	German Federal Cartel Office
CEECs	Central and East European Countries
CET	Common External Tariff
CFI	Court of First Instance
CLP	Competition Law and Policy Committee
CMLR	Common Market Law Reports
CMLRev	Common Market Law Review
DG	Directorate-General (of the Commission)
DGI	Directorate-General 1 (external relations)
DGII	Directorate-General 2 (economic and financial affairs)
DGIII	Directorate-General 3 (industry)
DGIV	Directorate-General 4 (competition)
DGVII	Directorate-General 7 (transport)
DGXIII	Directorate-General 13 (telecommunications)
DGXVI	Directorate-General 16 (regional policies and cohesion)
DGXVII	Directorate-General 17 (energy)
DTI	Department of Trade and Industry
EC	European Community
ECJ	European Court of Justice
ECLR	European Competition Law Review
ECN	European Competition Network
ECO	European Cartel Office
ECR	European Court Reports
ECSC	European Coal and Steel Community
EEA	European Economic Area
EEC	European Economic Community
EFTA	European Free Trade Association
EP	European Parliament
ERT	European Roundtable of Industrialists
EU	European Union
EUMR	European Union Merger Regulation

EURATOM	European Atomic Energy Community
FTC	Federal Trade Commission (US)
GATT	General Agreement of Tariffs and Trade
GNP	gross national product
G8	Group of Eight (industrialized countries)
ICN	International Competition Network
IEM	International Energy Market
ICI	Imperial Chemical Industries
IT	information technology
ITO	International Telecommunications Office
KPN	Dutch Post Office
LS	Legal Service
MEP	Member of the European Parliament
MMC	Monopolies and Mergers Commission
MTF	Merger Task Force
NAFTA	North Atlantic Free Trade Association
NCAs	National Competition Authorities
NTB	non-tariff barrier
OECD	Organisation for Economic Cooperation and Development
OFGAS	Office of Gas Supply
OFT	Office of Fair Trading
OFTEL	Office of Telecommunications
OFWAT	Office of Water Supply
OJ	Official Journal
PHARE	Poland-Hungary Aid for Economic Reconstruction
PTO	Post and Telecommunication Office
R&D	Research and Development
SEA	Single European Act 1986
SEM	Single European Market
SG	Secretariat-General
SME	small and medium-sized enterprises
ToA	Treaty of Amsterdam 1997
ToN	Treaty of Nice 2001
TEC	Treaty Establishing the European Community
TENs	Trans-European Networks
TEU	Treaty on European Union (Maastricht Treaty) 1992
UK	United Kingdom
UNCTAD	United National Conference on Trade and Development

UNICE   European Employers' Association (now Business Europe)
US(A)   United States (of America)
WTO   World Trade Organization

Chapter 1

Introduction

European competition policy is one of the success stories of the European integration process. This is not to say, however, that the policy always works effectively; that it is always transparent and legitimate; nor indeed that its constituents and stakeholders universally approve of the framework which structures the policy, the procedures that govern its implementation, or the way it is enforced from day to day. Nevertheless, European competition policy is perhaps the most supranational of all EU policies and has become something of a flagship for the EU. For that reason alone it is important for students of European integration and EU politics, among others, to engage with this policy area.

But there are other reasons too. Competition among firms is central to the effective functioning of market economies. Competition policy therefore constitutes a crucial instrument of regulation for governments (or in our case, the EU) keen to ensure that a competitive environment persists. This is particularly important since firms may wish to dominate or fix markets, undermining competition in the process. However, competition policy may serve a variety of ends, and even where the stated policy goal is the maintenance or encouragement of competition, there are a number of different ways such a general ambition may be translated into a workable policy and subsequently enforced.

Where the regulator is not a government but a supranational institution, the formulation and implementation of competition policy is yet more complex. In the case of the European Union, which is the subject of this study, it is the European Commission which takes the lead both in shaping and in setting the policy, and also in establishing the parameters within which it is applied in practice. Even though certain aspects of policy enforcement have been decentralized, and despite the fact that the Commission now sits within a network of competition actors and institutions to which it has delegated some of its earlier responsibilities, it remains the dominant player in the European competition policy game.

This short introduction offers some basic information about

1

competition, competition policy and, more specifically, European competition policy, providing a contextual foundation for the chapters that follow. The first section begins by examining the meaning of competition, and then goes on to unpack what competition policy is. The second section introduces the key elements of European competition policy, and focuses on four themes that highlight the ways the policy has evolved since the 1980s. The final section explains the organization of the book.

Competition and competition policy

The belief that economic competition is a good thing is something of an act of faith in countries where the economy operates on the basis of free-market principles. The commitment to competitive markets is rarely questioned, although the pervasive pro-competition rhetoric reflects more of an aspiration than a reality.

Competition has been defined as the 'struggle or contention for superiority, [which] in the commercial world ... means a striving for the custom and business of people in the market place' (Whish 1989:3; see also Bishop and Walker 2002; van den Bergh and Camasasca 2006). However, it is not always clear whether it is competition itself, or the function that competition is said to perform, which justifies its status as the most important organizing principle in the capitalist world. Theoretically speaking, in the language of neo-classical economics, this function is explained by the theory of perfect competition, where many small firms compete in the supply of a single product and where no one firm can affect prices or conditions of sale. The theory demonstrates how, in conditions of perfect competition, consumer welfare is maximized. It also shows how this leads to allocative, productive and distributional efficiency, allowing goods and services to be supplied in exactly the form and quantities desired by consumers and at the lowest cost possible. At the same time, monopoly, where there is only one supplier, is shown to restrict the supply of goods and services, and to charge higher prices. Thus, while competition 'magically and surreptitiously orders society's resources in the optimal way' (Whish 1989:7), monopoly is deemed to be the epitome of inefficiency.

However, even Adam Smith, with his talk of the 'invisible hand' of the market, recognized that competition was an abstract notion which could not exist in its purest form in the real world. Moreover, competition may even create as many problems as it solves. But although there can be some uncertainty about the merits and demerits of competition, there is all the same an acceptance within market economies that the advantages of competition generally outweigh the disadvantages. Rather than relying on some abstract notion of perfect competition, however, the looser concept of 'workable competition' has become the benchmark by which markets are assessed (Clark 1940; Sosnick 1958). This is theoretically a much vaguer notion, but one which is much more grounded in the real world. Competition within markets – even workable competition – should not be taken for granted, however. As Doern and Wilks (1996:1) have affirmed, '[n]either competition nor the market is inevitable or natural. Markets have to be created through processes of social change and public regulation' and while there is indeed some consensus that competition is a good thing, there is little agreement about what 'workable competition' implies in concrete policy terms.

Competition policies allow for the development of a regulatory framework within which governments can maintain or encourage competition. Such policies are clearly based on an assumption that enhanced economic performance will ultimately result from such an approach. Competition policies are deemed to be necessary, as firms (and indeed governments) sometimes behave in a manner which is harmful to competition. They do this for a number of reasons. Industrial actors often perceive competitive pressure as a constraint upon their freedom of manoeuvre. Competition causes uncertainty, and anti-competitive behaviour is one way of making the future more predictable. In addition, firms may also be keen to increase or maintain their profit margins. By acting collusively or by abusing a dominant market position, they may be able to charge higher prices and reap substantial gains. Competition policies are therefore drafted to prevent, deter or persuade firms from acting in such a fashion. They are negative policies, in the sense that they seek to *prevent* rather than to *promote* certain activities, so that it is by limiting the extent of anti-competitive practice, rather than by more positive means, that competition is encouraged.

So far, it has largely been taken for granted that the rationale behind *competition policy* is a desire to promote *competition* and thus consumer welfare. This may not always be the case, as competition policies can serve a multitude of different ends. While almost all policy-makers will happily agree that there is a need for structures and procedures which protect and maintain competition, the many different policy options on offer demonstrate the potential for disagreement over the objectives and functions of these structures and procedures, and in particular over the extent to which cooperation rather than competition ought to be encouraged. This is what makes the formulation of competition rules so controversial. Rules may be drafted in such a way as to leave few options open to the policy-maker, though this is rare. More often than not, a variety of objectives are pursued within a single competition regime. These may be objectives that are at times mutually incompatible. Likewise, the practical implementation and enforcement of competition policy often leads to controversy, when the implications of policy decisions become highly politicized. Discretion in decision-making can be contentious, but so too can the absence of discretion in cases where outcomes resting on an 'objective' technical analysis are politically unacceptable.

It is possible to identify a number of objectives that are often associated with competition policies. These are:

- *Consumer welfare.* This is a technical function of competition policy which assumes a direct and formal relationship between the promotion of competition and improved economic performance.
- *Protection of the consumer.* This involves the defence of the individual against big business, usually for moral or political reasons.
- *Redistribution of wealth.* This is an attempt to inhibit a small number of firms from accumulating a large amount of wealth, an inherently political objective which implies that monopolies and cartels are undemocratic.
- *Protection of small and medium-sized enterprises.* This does not just imply the protection of infant industries, but also assumes that a large number of small firms in a market is in itself a good thing.
- *Regional, social and industrial considerations.* These reflect the frequent use of competition policy as an instrument working for non-competition policy ends, such as the development of regions in decline, the reduction of unemployment or the attainment of a global presence in a particular sector.
- *Market integration.* This is a particularly European phenomenon

in which competition policy is used to break down privately constructed barriers to trade between the EU member states, thus contributing to the creation of a Single European Market (SEM).

- *Promotion of competitiveness*. This has become particularly important since the end of the 1990s, with the introduction of the Lisbon Strategy in 2000 (and especially in its post-2005 form) which subsumes competition policy within a broad framework of economic development.

Just as there are many different competition policy objectives, so there is no one competition policy. As anti-competitive practices take a number of different forms, various of corresponding policy responses are required.

- Firms may engage in restrictive practices such as the setting up of **cartels**. These agreements, which may be informal and unwritten, might involve setting prices above the market price (price-fixing), or carving up a market so that each firm acts as a monopolist in its part of the market (market-sharing). Agreements can involve similar firms, that is, direct competitors within a market (horizontal agreements or restraints), or firms operating at different stages in the production/distribution process (vertical agreements or restraints). Vertical agreements could take the form of exclusive distribution ties, for example, where suppliers are allowed to buy their products from only one approved source. Restrictive practices policy or some form of cartel policy is often developed to deal with such cases.
- The existence of a monopoly (one firm dominating a market) or an oligopoly (a very small number of large firms dominating a market) may also have a detrimental effect on competition. In such cases, dominant firms (either on their own as monopolists or together as oligopolists) can abuse their position, using their market power to cut prices and drive out competitors (predatory pricing) or to charge high prices where consumers have little alternative but to pay up. Monopoly policies exist to deal with behaviour such as this.
- Mergers and joint ventures may have anti-competitive implications because they could lead to a situation where a monopoly or oligopoly is formed (a process of *concentration*). Merger policies thus allow authorities to assess the potential impact on com-

petition, and to decide whether the merger should be allowed to go ahead.

While these three elements are the building blocks of most competition policies, there is no agreement over what exactly a competition policy should include or on what basis decisions should be taken. Definitions of what a competition policy is, and the distinctive characteristics of different policies, vary therefore from regime to regime. In Japan, for example, trade associations and holding companies have been a particular cause for concern; while in the EU regime, as we see below, subsidy control (state aid policy) falls under the rubric of competition policy.

Introducing the European competition regime

European competition policy can be segmented into four main sub-policy areas. Restrictive practices policy focuses on the regulation of cartels; monopoly policy is directed towards the abuse of a dominant position by firms in a particular market; and mergers policy, a relative newcomer (since 1990), has mergers and acquisitions (M&A) as its target. Finally, state aid policy is of a different order and deals with the potentially anti-competitive effects of national grants of subsidy to industry within the context of the EU's single market. It might also be possible to further differentiate the policy by highlighting the EU's strategy towards particular types of firm – for example, what in EU-speak are referred to as 'services of a general economic interest' (SGEIs), such as rail transport or electricity, although this is not the approach adopted in this book.

While this study sticks to the above distinction and includes chapters on restrictive practices policy, monopoly policy, merger policy and state aid policy, it also acknowledges that the EU – and more specifically the Commission – has sought to make these four aspects of European competition policy more coherent. One way it has sought to do this has been by reorganizing, between 2002 and 2004, the department (or 'Directorate-General') in the European Commission responsible for most competition matters (DG Competition). With some exceptions (see Chapter 3) this reform created units which deal with various aspects of competition regulation, structuring their workload in terms of cases and markets, rather than 'type' of competition policy.

Even without this organizational innovation, there have been various trends in competition regulation within the European Commission since the late 1980s, which have affected all aspects of the institution's work in this policy area. Four particularly notable trends serve as intellectual threads that weave their way through the chapters of this book. These are 'modernization', 'Europeanization', 'decentralization' and 'liberalization'. Although these do not constitute a conceptual framework for the book, they do represent recurring themes. And although it is in the concluding chapter that a spotlight will be cast on the threads, both individually and in terms of how they relate to each other, it is worth considering, albeit with some brevity, what is meant by these concepts within this study.

Modernization was the label given to the Commission's competition policy reform of the mid 2000s, which primarily related to cartel and mergers policy; but which has also since 2005 been adopted as a mantra for state aid reform. The reforms were driven by calls for changes in the substantive analysis that constituted competition decision-making, in part emanating from the European Courts who had frequently criticized the Commission for inadequate economic reasoning in their competition decisions; and by pressure to reduce the administrative burden that the ex-ante notification requirement placed on the Commission, and which was likely to be exacerbated by the accession of twelve new member states in 2004 and 2007. The use of the word 'modernization' is not neutral, however, and has certain normative connotations. At its most basic level it concerns bringing the policy, assumed to be out of date, up to date. But in addition, modernization is often associated with new public management (NPM) ideas, which denote a shift from traditional forms of public administration towards a more varied role for civil services, within which the boundaries of public and private are blurred, in which effectiveness trumps public service values, and where what counts as policy is what can be measured and quantified. As such, modernization suggests the overturning of traditional ways of working and the introduction of new basic assumptions which can be controversial, not least as they may lead to a new configuration of winners and losers, in our case as a consequence of competition enforcement.

The second theme which runs through this book is Europeanization. This is a widely used and very fashionable concept in the field of European Studies which is contested, in the sense that there is no agreement on what Europeanization means or how it might be used (whether as a research agenda or a theory, for example). In this study Europeanization is generally used in two interrelated ways. Both imply a top-down (or perhaps a horizontal) process, in which EU rules and norms are either imposed or diffused across the Union. In the first case, the imposition of EU rules, aside from in the early years of the policy, has been a consequence of rounds of enlargement, the last of which were in 2004 and 2007. In this case, applicant states wishing to join the EU had to adopt the *acquis communautaire*, a core part of which were the competition provisions and supporting legislation. In the second case, the mechanism of change is less tangible and comprises a diffusion of norms and ideas about the operation of market economies, and more specifically of competition and competition policy. Here, the Commission seeks to promote a sharing of experience and to provide guidance on how to interpret EU competition rules so as to prevent the fragmentation of the system.

Decentralization in this study refers to a process begun in the early 1990s and continued with the modernization reforms, whereby aspects of competition enforcement were removed from direct Commission control and granted to national competition authorities and domestic courts. Decentralization may be understood, therefore, as delegation of authority from supranational-level principals to nationally based agents. However, decentralization can also imply a pluralist dispersal of decision-making which has normative connotations. In other words, the assumption may be that to decentralize – or to deal with matters of policy at the lowest possible level – is a good thing. This is a characteristic embedded in EU policy-making through the formalized use of the subsidiarity principle.

Finally, liberalization, meant in its economic sense here, has become closely associated with European competition policy, as it implies an opening up of sectors that have traditionally be devoid of competition, and – for various reasons – have been exempt from competition regulation. In this context, therefore, liberalization points to the widening scope of the competition regime. While exemptions are still possible, sectoral exceptions to the general competition rule are few and far between. Liberalization is not the same as privatization, however, as it is neutral on the question of state or private ownership, even if the Commission might keep a closer eye on state-owned firms, and assume that they ought to behave much the same as if they were in the private sector. Where exceptions are made, they are for SGEIs, as noted above. This does not mean that anti-competitive conduct is tolerated without question in these sectors; just that specific rules may need to be formulated to cover the specific context within which these firms operate and to encourage reform in a pro-competition direction.

Whether we are discussing modernization or liberalization, Europeanization or decentralization, the context in which the study of (European) competition policy takes place is always the negotiated relationship between state and industry. This relationship is not a given, but reflects particular assumptions at particular points in time about the public sphere and the private sphere, and the responsibilities that each owes to the other within liberal-democratic market economies. There is no doubt that competition policy is a matter of economics, just as it is a matter of the law. What is often forgotten, however, is that the reasons for having a competition policy, the form that policy takes – both substantively and procedurally – and how the policy is implemented and enforced are all at the core questions of politics. A political dimension demands that we stand back from the micro- and mesoanalyses of the competition economists and lawyers to address broader questions of state, economy and indeed society. This latter point may at times seem like background information as we launch into our chapters on the policy detail. But the reader should remember that while others will push the boundaries of the political further in their analysis of competition policy (see Wigger 2008, for example), the motivation behind this book (both in its first edition and in this current edition) was to contribute to an emerging political and policy literature on the European competition regime.

Organization of the book

The chapters that follow begin with an account of the evolution of European competition policy. Thus Chapter 2 identifies the origins of the policy as well as the various stages in that evolution, times when different dimensions of competition regulation were in the ascendant. It also accounts for the increasing importance of the policy in the mid 1980s, its metamorphosis at that time, and some of the more recent developments associated with the modernization agenda of the 2000s. Chapter 3 examines the institutional framework which governs the EU competition regime, and touches on key elements in competition decision-making. It focuses in particular on the European Commission, and on the network of domestic bodies which now, together with the EU institutions, comprise the EU's quasi-federal system of competition governance.

When identifying the main components of a competition policy, restrictive practices (or cartel) policy and monopoly policy spring immediately to mind. These two central strands in the EU's policy fall under Articles 81 and 82 of the EEC Treaty and are dealt with in Chapters 4 and 5, respectively. In each chapter, an account of the legal framework goes hand in hand with an assessment of policy substance, which is illuminated by a number of key case examples. Chapter 6 then explores the evolution, the characteristics and the decision-making elements of EU merger policy which has existed as a discrete element of the EU's competition regime only since 1990. Chapter 7, which focuses on the Commission's state aid policy, also explores historical, substantive and procedural matters in this unique area.

Chapter 8 introduces a theoretical perspective into the study of competition policy, something often lacking in the literature in this field. Finally, Chapter 9, which presents the conclusions to the book, identifies key themes dominating the current debate on EU competition policy. It does this by assessing the policy's reform agenda, using reform as a window on to current policy trends and controversies. This final chapter also considers the challenges likely to face the European competition regime in the years to come.

Chapter 2

The Evolution of the European Competition Regime

The history of European competition policy makes a truly fascinating story, involving the incremental emergence of a body of
case-law, close-knit inter-institutional relations, and both institutional passivity and institutional activism on the part of the
Commission's Directorate-General for Competition. Moreover,
there is a broader tale to be told, involving DG Competition's reac-
tion to and interaction with its external political, legal and economic environment. In charting the chronological development of
European competition policy from the early 1950s to 2007, this
chapter highlights both the internal dynamics of the policy and the
exogenous factors that have influenced its effectiveness over the
last six decades. The chapter begins by examining the origins of
competition policy, then introduces briefly the legal provisions of
the first European competition policy, that of the European Coal
and Steel Community (ECSC). The rest of the chapter concentrates
on the European Economic Community (EEC) rules, first identifying the legal provisions that have shaped the policy, and then
providing an overview and analysis of its evolution. The chapter
concludes by focusing on the revitalization of the European competition regime over the course of the 1980s; finally, it summarizes
more recent developments and priorities since then.

Origins and influences

Ever since Adam Smith remarked that '[p]eople of the same trade
seldom meet together, even for merriment and diversion, but the
conversation ends in a conspiracy against the public or in some
contrivance to raise prices', the problem of how to maintain and
restore competition has preoccupied lawyers, economists and
policy-makers. It is only fairly recently, however, that the control
of anti-competitive practices by means of statute, rather than a

common law, has become the norm (Hunter 1969:3). In the Western European context, competition policies are largely features of the post-1945 policy environment. In many other parts of the world, it is only since the 1980s that the regulation of competitive behaviour has been taken seriously.

The United States (US) experience was somewhat different, however, and as such it is tempting to assume that US anti-trust is the model upon which all later policies are based. While there is some truth in this, it is important to remember that competition policy is shaped as much by domestic considerations, such as historical traditions which have a bearing on the role of the state, and cultural attitudes towards industry, as it is by external policy-borrowing. Contrasting the American model against other European models demonstrates this point.

The American anti-trust (or competition) tradition, embodied in the 1890 Sherman Act and in subsequent legislation, began as an attempt to defend the individual entrepreneur against large companies (or trusts). At the end of the nineteenth century, huge enterprises, especially the railroad companies, swallowed up small firms at a frightening rate. Anti-trust legislation was brought in to check that trend. The Sherman Act, which was agreed in 1890, introduced a prohibition on restraints of trade and monopolization. The Act was not simply a legislative text. It also embodied the values on which America was built: individualism, fairness and free enterprise (Whish 1989:16). As free and fair competition was viewed as the economic embodiment of political freedom and democracy, surrender to the unaccountable economic power of the monopolist would have undermined the ideological foundations of the American state (Neale and Goyder 1980:16). This does not mean that the American approach to concentration was unquestioningly hostile. Rather, it tended to focus on the need for balance, and on the fostering of a positive pro-competition ethos.

Initially the US anti-trust regime was firmly identified with the promotion of free competition and small business. It seemed, as a result, that competition was being encouraged for its own sake, rather than for the efficiency gains that it could bring to the US economy. This approach to anti-trust was vehemently criticized from the 1950s onwards by the Chicago School of economists who argued that the only justifiable rationale for anti-trust policy should be the maximization of consumer welfare through enhanced economic efficiency. As a result of the Chicago School's increasing influence, the emphasis of US policy gradually changed over the 1970s and 1980s, especially after Ronald Reagan's arrival in the White House in January 1981 (Fox 1981:442). A reconstitution of the Supreme Court, and a broad policy commitment by the Reagan administration to the rolling back of the state, confirmed that the US had shifted its approach to 'restrictive' business practices. With more emphasis placed on market impact, the policy increasingly came to operate along efficiency-orientated lines. Horizontal cartel cases were targeted and there was an effort to introduce more sophisticated economic analyses within anti-trust investigations. Although these changes now seem firmly embedded in the US regime, the debate about the function and practice of anti-trust policy continues. Given that the issue is essentially an ideological one, reflecting normative understandings about the role of the state in industrial affairs, this should come as no surprise.

By contrast, the British system was not shaped by any considerable anti-trust movement, and while restrictive practices were not uncommon in the UK, there was a feeling that they were no particular cause for concern. The tolerant British attitude towards cartels and concentration, particularly in the 1920s and 1930s, stemmed at least in part from the belief that British industry was generally much more exposed to international competition than the US, and as such, had little need for US-style legislation. Unlike the Americans, British public opinion was not preoccupied with notions of concentrated power. Social protest, which was certainly a feature of the times, rarely seemed to focus on the power wielded by big business. Indeed, it was not until the post-1945 period that the monopoly problem and the benefits of competition really appeared on the political and social agenda. This change of attitude among policy-makers occurred largely with an eye to pre-empting inflationary pressures and encouraging productivity.

Although the British competition regime is constructed on a solid legislative base, it has often been criticized for its complexity and incoherence. Both the legislative framework and policy practice have frequently been deemed arcane and opaque. As an administrative rather than a judicial system, UK competition policy allows for far-reaching political and administrative discretion in competition cases, with a 'public interest' element used to justify decisions taken on non-competition grounds. With each case decided on its merits, the application of the policy is often unpredictable (Wilks 1996:139). A more competition-orientated approach, in line with

Thatcherite thinking, was introduced in the mid 1980s, though this policy change took place within the existing legislative framework. Plans to reform the UK's competition regime were proposed in the late 1980s, but these came to nothing at this point. The Labour government elected in 1997 revived the issue of competition reform, and introduced new legislation in 2002 in the form of the Enterprise Act, drawing on its experience of EU competition policy (ironically just as the EU itself was about to undergo reform in a rather different direction) and on the US model, which relies heavily on the use of criminal sanctions.

In the German case, another unique competition policy model, the motives for competition legislation were very different from those in the UK, largely because of their historical context. With Americans assuming a direct link between cartelization and National Socialism, just as they saw a direct relationship between competition, the free market and democracy, it is hardly surprising that one of the main strands of US policy in Germany in the immediate post-war period 1945–49 was the decartelization of German industry.

But there was also support for this particular policy line within West Germany. Influential in the establishment of the German social market economy, the ordo-liberal school, a group of economists and lawyers, combined elements of classical liberalism and social democracy to form a system which was often considered to lie halfway between laissez-faire and central planning (Braun 1990:177). Many ordo-liberals would dispute this, however, given their unequivocal commitment to market mechanisms. Nevertheless, in contrast to advocates of a *laissez-faire* approach, ordo-liberals rejected an absolute faith in the self-regulatory capacity of the market. It was argued that the dangers inherent in central planning – state capture by big business and cartels, and the abuses of power so well remembered under National Socialism – could also be present when the market (or the firm) was given a free rein. For ordo-liberals, then, 'although the market captures an important aspect of freedom, it does not itself constitute a *Weltanschauung* [ideology]'(Barry 1989:108).

While it is clear that West Germany's competition rules, enacted in the late 1950s, were at least in part a response to US policy in the years up to 1953, with the US clearly stipulating that the decartelization law imposed on the West Germans during the Allied Occupation had to be replaced by German laws of a similar kind, it became almost impossible to distinguish the ordo-liberal from the American anti-trust influence on German policy. To a large extent the ordo-liberals were able to feed off American demands for the breakup of German industry.

Attempts to incorporate an ordo view of cartels into German law met with stiff opposition from German industry. An early 1948 draft of the German competition law, the Jösten draft (Wagner 1956:66–72), was extremely tough in its condemnation of anti-competitive practices. Yet by the time it was enacted in 1957, it had been substantially watered down. To describe the German law as either ordo-liberal or US-style would therefore be inaccurate. The competition objective was partially sacrificed when confronted by the very business interests the law was intended to control. Instead, German competition policy became a tool of economic efficiency instead of a means of ensuring the liberty of the individual.

Although the landmark Law Against Restraints of Trade (1957) amounted to a watered down version of the US model, this became a solid base on which a rather different type of competition regime was to be constructed. With the German competition framework still closely tied to the notion of a social market economy, which had competition as a basic principle, a tough competition policy was and still is judged to be essential for a prosperous economy. As such, competition policy has taken on what amounts to a symbolic function within the social market model, which makes the system almost impossible to challenge. The application of a rather inflexible (or neutral and objective) approach to competition policy has meant that the competition criterion is rarely challenged and the pragmatic public interest dimension which has characterized the UK and other systems is almost entirely absent.

These three competition models and the differences between them emphasize an important point: that there is no one agreed set of competition policy objectives and very little consensus on how best to organize a system of competition enforcement. Each system is shaped very distinctively by the historical and cultural environment in which it operates. Yet it is also clear from these examples that these regimes are far from being set in stone. They have demonstrated at least a potential for dynamism, in terms both of the functions they perform and of the structures and procedures that frame their systems of enforcement. This dynamism allows for the possibility of adaptation to changing industrial, social and political circumstance, and as a result opens the door to a process which involves the cross-fertilization of ideas, overt policy-bor-rowing, and even, ultimately, the convergence of what began as a set of very different competition models.

From coal and steel to EEC

Although the 1951 ECSC Treaty was a West European initiative, American influence in European affairs at this time was still exten-sive. While the precise involvement of US representatives in the drafting of the coal and steel provisions is unclear, there are cer-tainly remarkable similarities between Jean Monnet's Memoran-dum, which fed directly into the ECSC Treaty, and the US provisions in the 1890 Sherman Act. There is indeed some evidence to suggest that the precise wording of the ECSC competition provi-sions was insisted upon by US representatives (Berghahn 1986:118). Even so, it seems that there was no attempt to impose an entirely alien regulatory framework on the Europeans. Moreover, in more recent historical research of the period, Leucht (2008) has highlighted the importance of informal transatlantic policy networks of academics, civil servants and politicians in shaping the provisions of the Treaty during the inter-state negotia-tions. This she contrasts against an assumed process of Americanization which focuses solely on national governmental elites.

The first competition regime of the European Community (EC) thus emerged in embryonic form in 1952. The ECSC Treaty sought to inject competition into the coal and steel sectors. It did this in order to achieve both economic and political ends and, as a result, the competition provisions were fairly tough. But while Articles 65 and 66 which then underpinned the policy on restrictive coal and steel agreements and concentrations echoed the competition rules subsequently spelt out in Articles 85 and 86 (now Articles 81 and 82) of the 1957 EEC Treaty, it is clear that by the late 1950s these regulatory structures were not considered appropriate for use in other European markets. The EEC competition provisions ended up, therefore, as a watered-down version of the ECSC rules, largely because of disagreements among the member states on whether to include anti-trust provisions, and what form they should take (Seidel 2008) – though at the same time they were much wider in scope than their precursors (see Box 2.1).

Box 2.1   The Treaty of Rome provisions

European competition policy is based on Article 3(f) (now Article 3(g)) of the EEC Treaty which seeks to ensure that 'competition in the Common Market is not distorted'. One of the ways this principle is implemented is through the application of what the Treaty called its 'rules on competition'. These were found in Part 3, Title 1, Chapter 3 of the Treaty, in Articles 85 to 94 (later numbered 81–89). The provisions cover the Commission''s control of restrictive agreements (or cartels); its regulation of anti-competitive monopoly behaviour and public sector firms; and its oversight of nationally granted state aid. These components of the early EEC competition policy are in fact policies in their own right.

- The Community's restrictive practices policy, which is now governed by *Article 81* (formerly 85), prohibits agreements or concerted practices between firms which are likely to prevent, restrict or distort trade within the Community. It is an effects-based system which means that an agreement will be prohibited if it is likely to *affect* interstate trade. Article 81 also spells out the exceptions to the general rule.
- Monopoly policy is governed by *Article 82* (formerly 86). This provision regulates monopolies where their behaviour is likely to affect trade between the member states, prohibiting 'abuses of a dominant position' within a market (the definition of which often proves contentious). The focus of the Commission investigation rests on the notion of an 'abuse', that is, on the conduct of the firm and not just on its structure.
- *Article 86* (formerly 90) deals with the specific case of public sector and other firms that are granted special rights by the member states. The Treaty recognizes that these firms may be entrusted with particular tasks that justify some restriction of competition. However, the Commission has increasingly sought to apply the competition rules in full.
- State aid policy is governed by *Articles 87–89* (formerly 92–94). This element of the European competition policy is very different from its direct control over firms. The state aid provisions prohibit subsidies granted by national or subnational authorities if they are likely to distort competition between the member states. The exceptions to the rule are crucial, as they imply a positive (social, regional or pro-competitive) dimension to the policy which has in practice proven extremely controversial.

The Commission has also had since 1990 a Merger Control Regulation, although there was no provision for the control of mergers in the EEC Treaty.

While the state aid provisions of the EEC Treaty included a procedural dimension, the absence of procedural rules covering what are now Articles 81 and 82, the anti-trust provisions, meant that there was some delay in implementing the Treaty. In the intervening period, it was intended (under Articles 84 and 85 of the EEC Treaty) that domestic courts would make use of Articles 81 and 82. This came to nothing, however, as national courts were reluctant to use these new and untried legislative instruments. Given the lack of domestic experience in competition enforcement at that time, this should come as no surprise (see Chapter 3).

When European competition policy first appeared, the founder member states, excluding Germany, had only very weak competition rules compared with those envisaged in the EEC Treaty. Belgium and Luxembourg had no legislation, and the Dutch had only a rather weak Economic Competition Act drafted in 1956. In Italy, monopolies and restrictive practices were governed by the Civil Code, while under French law there was detailed but very weak regulation of restrictive business practices. Germany, then, was the only country with a tough competition regime.

Initially, prior to the agreement of a procedural regulation, national governments were expected to apply the EEC competition rules themselves. However, this proved unsuccessful (Seidel 2008). In any case, the Council was under pressure to agree a procedural regulation before the expiry of a three-year time limit written into the Treaty, but the negotiations were complicated and at times acrimonious. However, in spite of initial resistance from the French, the Regulation was ultimately agreed unanimously, in part because it was tied, as part of a package deal, to the establishment of the Common Agricultural Policy (Seidel 2008) When the Regulation was finally agreed in 1962, it became clear that it had been drafted in such a way so as to ensure that control over the policy remained in the hands of the Commission. Thus the Commission sought to create a *common* competition policy, and not just a coordinated one. This approach sowed the seeds of what would later become a highly centralized regime, the EC's 'first truly supranational policy' (McGowan and Wilks 1995:142). The Council negotiations that led to the agreement in 1962 of what is now known as 'Regulation 17' were intense, with the Commission determined to prevent the establishment of a weak and ineffective system of enforcement. 'Regulation 17, based on a German model of notification, evaluation, and exemption, effectively centralized enforcement and marginalized the national authorities' (Wilks and McGowan 1996:231–4). However, the Commission's success proved ultimately to be a double-edged sword, as the Regulation soon caused administrative gridlock.

Although the text of Regulation 17 included assurances to the business community that legal certainty was a priority, the centralization of control, coupled with the malleability of the original treaty provisions, meant that predictability was at least partially sacrificed once the Regulation was in place. Discretion and flexibility became the enforcement watchwords. In spite of, and perhaps because of this, Regulation 17 became the cornerstone of the European Union's (EU) restrictive practices and monopoly policy. Even in the early 1960s the authors of the Regulation understood the importance of procedures. Regulation 17 did not create a set of rules that would apply in all cases, but it did detail the rights and powers granted to those involved in and affected by the policy (see Box 2.2).

However the enactment of Regulation 17 brought with it a host of practical problems. The effect of the Regulation's notification requirement, which obliged all firms to notify their agreements to the Commission within certain specified dates, had been underestimated. By the deadline for multilateral agreements in November

---

BOX 2.2   Regulation 17

Regulation 19/62 set out:

- The notification requirements (Articles 4 and 5).
- The rights of the member states and of third parties within the investigation process (Article 19).
- The upper limits of fines and penalties (Articles 15 and 16).
- An institutionalized consultation mechanism for national governments (the Advisory Committee) (Article 10).
- The conditions under which individual exemptions were granted (Articles 6 and 8)

The investigatory powers of the Commission in the practical administration of the policy (Article 14).

1962, approximately 900 notifications had been received by DGIV (now DG Competition). And in the case of bilateral agreements, the number of notifications lodged reached an incredible 34,500 (Goyder 1993:50).

The notification problem was the single most important issue in the first years of the policy. As the majority of agreements notified under the Regulation were vertical agreements (see Chapter 4), it was understandable that the DG would begin its work by focusing on this aspect of policy (Hawk 1985:336). Although this provided a justification for the development of a policy towards vertical restraints, there have since been doubts about the effect of such agreements on market integration. It is now believed that the policy would have been likely to have had more of an impact on European competition had it focused first on horizontal agreements.

The initial emphasis, which was largely on exclusive distribution, was therefore caused by a procedural misjudgment. The policy's first set of priorities were reactive as a result. With procedure dictating policy, there was little possibility of DGIV being able to assert itself in any coherent way. Fortunately however, the problems initiated by Regulation 17 could also be resolved by the self-same Regulation. Even so, the support of the Council of Ministers was necessary for a solution to the notification problem to be found.

The solution which emerged in 1963 rested on the exemption of entire classes or groups of agreements. As it was recognized that the large majority of agreements notified would in any case be exemptible under Article 81(3) once DGIV officials found the time to examine them, the challenge was to find a way of wiping these agreements automatically from the backlog. Although officials could have opted for a negative clearance route (making a statement that a group of agreements did not in fact distort competition and as such did not fall under the treaty provisions), it was the advent of the block exemption regulation that was hailed as the answer to DG Competition's prayers – even though at the time this was merely a tool to prevent something that should not have happened in the first place (Korah and Rothie 1992). Nevertheless, the Treaty provisions did seem to allow for this development.

The purpose of the block exemption was twofold: it would not only reduce the size of the backlog, but also help to persuade industry to abide by the competition rules. It was said that '[t]he great advantage of the group exemption . . . would be that undertakings would have an incentive to frame their new agreements in terms that complied with it' (Goyder 1988:58). But although the Council recognized the importance of this form of regulation and agreed to it in principle, it refused to proceed until the Commission had gained some experience in handling relevant cases, so that the regulation was not drafted in a legal and political vacuum. Several cases dealt with over the course of 1964 provided the necessary experience in the fields of exclusive distribution and exclusive purchasing, allowing the first enabling regulation to be drafted and agreed by the Council in 1965.

It was the Exclusive Distribution and Purchasing Regulation issued in 1967 that opened the floodgates to a fully fledged DG Competition block exemption policy. The Regulation was issued by the Commission under delegated authority from the Council of Ministers. By agreeing to this course of action it is ironic that the Council further strengthened the position of the Commission at its own expense. Ever since, block exemption regulations have been used to enable competition policy priorities to be highlighted and administrative overload to be minimized. The block exemption instrument has thus become as much a form of policy statement as a direct instrument of control and policy management.

The first fifteen years: 1958 to 1972

The first fifteen years of the EC's competition policy were characterized by the cumulative and incremental development of a coherent set of policy priorities. These were to provide the Commission with a solid foundation upon which to build an activist policy. However, institution-building was also crucial at this stage (see Box 2.1). While the setting up of the organization involved the establishment of the Competition DG (until the late 1990s known as DGIV), one of the first of the Commission services, and the appointment of Hans von der Groeben, an economic liberal, as Commissioner responsible for competition, officials also set to work drafting background studies that would inform later policy priorities, consulting widely and holding numerous meetings and conferences.

During the early 1960s, European competition policy was synonymous with restrictive practices (including cartel) policy. At this stage, the role of the European Court of Justice (ECJ) was minimal.

This was soon to change, however, as legal judgments began to 'fill out' the law, contributing to the emergence of a fully fledged policy. *Grundig–Consten* became the first of many landmark ECJ judgments (see Box 2.3).

In contrast to restrictive practices policy, both the Commission's state aid policy and its monopoly policy were largely neglected. Not until the mid 1960s was there much discussion of concentration. It was the publication of the Commission's *Memorandum on the Problems of Concentration in the Common Market* in 1966 that proved a turning-point (Woolcock 1989). Before the mid 1960s one of the Commission's main aims had been the encouragement of large European firms as a means of promoting European industrial competitiveness. As Article 82 seemed to be at odds with this policy, it remained an empty threat, even after 1966. Although the first formal Decision of the Commission in an Article 82 (dominant position) case was taken in June 1971, this hardly marked the emergence of a fully fledged policy.

Both state aid policy and monopoly policy were thus marginalized until the Competition DG had developed a comprehensive policy on horizontally and vertically restrictive agreements. Both the institutional and the environmental context of policy development fed directly into the EC's competition priorities, shaping their evolution

---

BOX 2.3   Grundig–Consten

In this case, a German firm, Grundig, had appointed Consten as its sole distributor of electrical appliances in France. Meanwhile UNEF, a competitor of Consten, was buying up Grundig products in Germany and reselling them to French retailers. This was possible because of the abolition of quotas in the sector in 1961. After an injunction in the French courts brought by Grundig, UNEF complained to the Commission. The negative decision against Grundig was upheld (in part) in the ECJ.

The case, with other more minor ones, was crucial in raising morale within the Competition DG. It was also important in highlighting the role that would in future be played by the European Court. The Court was well placed to use its judicial discretion as an instrument of flexible enforcement when faced with hard competition cases, as well as when defending the cause of market integration.

well into the 1970s and 1980s. Internal procedural factors, together with a wider integrative environment (both pre- and post-1966), forced DGIV into reactive mode. Even with some experience and growing internal institutional self-confidence, it was not possible to transform this reactive policy into an activist one.

While the legislative approach to competition policy allowed for cases to be dealt with either individually or en masse depending on their anti-competitive potential, charting the early evolution of policy purely in visible legislative terms offers an incomplete picture of the DG's activity. The legislative approach outlined above went hand in hand with what has been identified as 'pseudo-legislative action' (van Gerven 1974:38). This involved the use of informal processes to create simplified administrative channels through which policy objectives could be achieved. These rather arcane informal processes have since emerged as a parallel to the more open and formal decisional mechanisms that are part and parcel of the administrative life of DG Competition.

Informal channels of decision-making are unlikely to produce anything other than incremental policy developments. Indeed, the drafting of Notices and other non-binding guidelines, the gradual construction of a body of case-law, and an increasing reliance on informal settlements, all point to the creation of a policy of small steps. Both formal and informal decision-making has contributed to this evolutionary process. The gradual development of the policy has allowed Competition DG staff to develop a certain policy expertise. Incrementalism should not therefore be considered a bad thing for the policy, but a necessary stage in its evolution.

The administrative culture of DGIV in the 1960s was very different from what it would become later, as it was based at least in part on a pro-consumer ethos. Even though only two officials dealt specifically with consumer affairs at this time, an identifiable consumer culture provided evidence of a public interest dimension within the policy (Goyder 1988:121). At this stage, the emphasis on the powerless consumer facing abuses from powerful industrial actors or cartels was directly inherited from the American populist tradition. Indeed, the very fact that both consumer and competition functions were vested in the same Commission department suggests that the competition objective was focused directly on consumer benefits. At this time, it was generally believed that the promotion of competition would be all the consumer policy the Commission would need, and that the benefits of competition would 'trickle down' to the consumer. This cultural perspective diminished, however, when responsibility for consumer relations was transferred out of the Competition DG in 1967.

The commitment of Competition DG officials to consumer protection went hand in hand with a prevalent anti-business ethos. Officials perceived themselves, at least rhetorically, as defenders of the weak. In practice, the rhetoric did not always match up to the practical application of the policy. There was, in addition, little prestige in working for the Competition DG at this time. This is not surprising given the irrelevance of the policy until after 1968. Competition policy was and continues to be a policy supplementary to (though essential in) the creation of a common market, as it provides a mechanism for removing mainly private barriers to trade between the member states, driving forward market integration.

The customs union was not completed until 1968. Before that date, supranational subsidy control and indeed even European-level restrictive practices policy seemed rather anomalous. However, with the establishment of a Common External Tariff (CET) and with the removal of intra-EC quotas and tariffs at the end of the 1960s, it was timely for emphasis to be shifted towards non-tariff barriers to trade (NTBs). These would include, alongside the more conventional governmental NTBs (such as differing technical, fiscal and administrative standards), government subsidies used unfairly to advantage national industry, and private restrictive practices established by the firms themselves.

The question of a European-level industrial policy was raised for the first time at this juncture. While there was no specific treaty base upon which a Community industry policy could be constructed, this was no barrier to policy formulation. But while industrial affairs were at the forefront of the drive to create a customs union and then a common market, these negative moves – to remove tariffs, quotas and, later, non-tariff barriers to European trade – were not considered as industrial policy *per se*. Positive, interventionist elements of a strategy for industry were blatantly absent from the Community's policy armoury.

Only in the mid 1960s, with a growing concern in Western Europe about foreign direct investment and a wave of US takeovers did European-level interventionism become likely. While the US had earlier encouraged the emergence of a tough European competition regime, this was now used against them, as the Europeans began to apply their rules extraterritorially. This opened the door to the trade disputes that would henceforth dog transatlantic relations. There was at the same time little agreement over the creation of a European industrial strategy. Calls for a policy which would encourage the creation of large-scale European firms were treated cautiously by the Commission (Swann 1983:136). Nevertheless, a number of memoranda, first on industrial concentration (1965), and later on industrial policy (1970) and science and technology policy (1970), suggests that the issue of supranational industrial interventionism was at the very least being discussed.

With this in mind, the Commission began to address problems of technological innovation (or the lack of it) by setting up a working party for science, technology and research policy. This produced an influential report in 1967, advocating a number of areas for Community involvement. By 1970 and the publication of the seminal *Colonna Report* (Swann 1983:138), the Commission was toying with a number of more dirigiste policies, including the active encouragement of transnational firms through the facilitation of cross-border mergers, and the promotion of job creation through the encouragement of growth industries. Even so, the common market remained the basis of Commission policy.

Ironically, momentum on the competition policy front also increased as a consequence of the slowdown in supranational political activity at the end of the 1960s. Quasi-legislative activism through judgments of the ECJ seemed inversely related to the Council's increasingly minimalist approach towards policy-making and regulation. It was as though the ECJ had stepped in to fill the political vacuum left by the Council. The delegated quasi-judicial policy-making of the Commission combined with the judicial activism of the ECJ to provide an alternative to the conventional legislative route. The intergovernmental emphasis that was prevalent in the EC during the 1970s had less of an impact on the evolution of European competition policy than it did in other policy areas.

From recession to stagnation: 1973 to 1981

Although the policy of the 1960s was largely reactive, the benign external economic and political environment was conducive to the gradual emergence of a pro-competition, pro-consumer policy. While its own internal procedures shaped policy content in the early years, developments after 1973 were much more affected by the external economic environment of the time. Although the internal procedural problems were well on their way to being resolved, the recession that followed the oil crisis of 1973–4 ushered in a new and more reactive policy. The Commission as a whole coped badly with recession, and DGIV was no exception.

Throughout the 1960s, competition policy had followed a smooth developmental path. There were signs, even so, of inherent contradictions in the Commission's policy towards industry. Attempts to get a fully fledged European industrial policy off the ground had, perhaps surprisingly, borne fruit in 1972. The Communiqué issued at the end of the Paris Summit of that year called for the establishment of a single industrial base within the Community. Reference was made to industrial sectors in decline and the need to provide assistance to ensure that such industries could be restructured under acceptable social conditions.

On the basis of two reports issued by the Commission in 1973, the Council adopted programmes which would provide the basis for future action on the industrial policy front. Indeed, '[t]he beginning of 1974 represented a high point in the willingness of the Community to contemplate positive action in the broad field of industrial 'policy' (Swann 1983:141). Yet, when it came to translating this into concrete and coherent policy, the results were rather paltry. A number of proposals were drafted, but very little was agreed. The negotiations seemed never-ending and inconclusive. There were a few achievements, most notably on the science and technology front, but even here coordination rather than supranational action provided the main thrust of the 'positive' elements of the would-be European industrial policy.

This is not surprising given the economic conditions of the time. The tendency of national governments to turn in on themselves during recession, and the consequent emphasis on national rather than European industrial strategies, meant that the Commission could do little but encourage cooperative ventures. One of the key areas of activity during this period involved the management of sectors in decline. Here the Commission had really only two policy instruments at its disposal: the use of state aid control to place limits on subsidies granted by member state authorities, and the use of import quotas to defend European industry from external competition. It would be difficult to claim that either of these could compare with the industrial policy tools at the national governments' disposal.

As recession hit hard upon European industry, the Competition DG's position was increasingly ambivalent. There was some tolerance of temporary crisis cartels and the Commission's annual reports on competition policy even began to see the reduction of inflation as one of the direct objectives of its competition policy (Commission 1978; Commission 1979). Faced with economic and industrial crisis, the Competition DG lacked the focus it would later assume. Not only was it without clear policy priorities, but it was also struggling against the practical problems associated with an ever rising tide of restrictive agreements, concentrations and protectionist national subsidies, all of which made a mockery of DGIV attempts to implement its policy effectively (Michelmann 1978).

By the mid 1970s, competition policy was judged to be ineffectual. Despite the procedural 'teeth' given it by Regulation 17, DG Competition had been unable to rise to the challenge of the economic crisis. No one can be faulted for failing to predict the massive changes that were to take place in the international political economy over the 1970s, and the proliferation of state aids that accompanied them. In view of its external environment, it could even be said that the very survival and adaptation of the policy was quite an achievement.

Just as the 1960s was dominated by restrictive practices concerns, the 1970s were characterized by growing alarm over abusive dominant practices. Attention turned, as a result, to the thorny issue of merger control. In the 1973 *Continental Can* judgment, the ECJ controversially confirmed Article 86 as a potential instrument of merger control (Hölzler 1990:10). This revived the policy line proposed by the Commission back in 1966 and acted as a catalyst for change. By emphasizing the uncertainty of the existing merger provisions, DGIV was able to persuade the member states to consider the possibility of a Council Regulation which might allow for the construction of a coherent and effective merger regime.

The objective was to be the 'introduction of an institutionalized system of preventative control' (Bernini 1983:349). However, failure to reach agreement in the Council reflected the general anti-supranational ethos of the time, and the desire of key member states to retain absolute control over their national industrial policies. This member state reluctance prevailed until the mid 1980s. The Commission therefore found itself reliant on provisions already agreed upon in the 1960s, and on the upholding of the

DGIV line in the ECJ. This marked a continuation of an earlier process of judicial policy-making. In selecting priority cases for Commission decisions, the DG was able to manipulate the appeals procedure to its own advantage so as to build up competition precedents and consolidate its legal base. Indeed, if it wanted to continue to expand the policy while remaining within the legal framework established by the Treaties, it had little choice in the matter. DGIV was also able to perfect and extend its quasi-legislative decision-making processes (van Gerven 1974). Increasing recourse to informal channels could allow less important cases to be dealt with speedily, and could also be used to establish policy guidelines without restricting the DG's freedom of manoeuvre. However, this failed to provide industrial or governmental actors with the legal certainty they desired. Legal certainty was essential if the competition system was ultimately to regulate itself. If firms and governments could second-guess the DGIV line, they could mould their agreements, their behaviour and their subsidies to fit the rules. If uncertainty reigned, however, firms and governments would have little opportunity to be law-abiding.

As far as DGIV was concerned, the positive face of legal uncertainty was discretionary flexibility. This too was not without controversy. A heated debate within the DG over the use of the competition rules as interventionist instruments was an obvious corollary to the post-1973 recession. It is not surprising that on the state aids side few procedures were initiated and very few negative decisions were taken. Until the Commission was able to develop an industrial strategy of its own, it was left to member state authorities to determine their own often market-fragmenting responses to industrial crisis. Although there was little real evidence of the use of state aid control as a positive tool of industrial policy at this stage, DGIV documentation did begin to talk of the policy as an instrument of structural change. It was as a result of a lack of decision-taking, rather than as a consequence of any concerted policy approach, that the original state aid objectives were undermined. It was clear that '[i]n the mid 1970s the Commission relaxed its position towards the grant of state aids in recognition of the need for national measures against unemployment and failing industries' (Merkin and Williams 1984:327). As a result, the aid rules tended to be ignored, and non-compliance was rife (Cownie 1986). Not surprisingly, the persistent undermining of the policy and the inherent inconsistencies in its application led to a series of unfortunate precedents and set an extremely bad example which would begin to be corrected only after the mid 1980s.

The crisis of ideology and morale, a consequence of the uncertainty provoked by mass avoidance and unclear policy objectives, culminated at the end of the 1970s in the rhetorical victory for those who rejected an overtly social interventionist role for European competition policy. The confusion that had reigned during the recessions of the 1970s had made DGIV susceptible to external pressures by actors who did not adhere to the market-oriented goals that underpinned its treaty-based functions. Between the end of the 1970s and the early 1980s, several elements emerged that would induce a policy change of a magnitude unseen in the earlier evolution of the policy.

However, while recessionary pressures dominated the policy's development after 1973, the incremental extension of case-law, in the form of an emerging body of legal precedents, had nevertheless continued unabated. In cases such as *Hoffman-La Roche*, *Belgian Wallpapers* and *BRT Sabem*, the frontiers of competition law were pushed forward and its detailed application was clarified. As a result, despite the weakness of policy enforcement at this stage, this period can still be characterized as a time of 'creeping legislation' (van Gerven 1974:40).

Towards a 'new' competition policy

By the end of the 1970s, criticism of European competition policy was widespread. The policy was condemned as overcentralized and overambitious, as possessing inadequate decision-making and enforcement procedures, as proving too readily susceptible to political pressures, and as failing to deliver what it promised (see for example Graupner 1973; Temple Lang 1977; Kon 1982). Not surprisingly, morale was at an all-time low in DGIV.

Incrementalism had become a liability. Although policy was being extended on a case-by-case basis, both the Commission and the ECJ had been unable to keep up with the flood of notifications, complaints and appeals that had continued to grow over the 1970s (Commission 1980). A reassessment of policy took place late in the decade which, though more subtle than a policy review, enabled DGIV to come to terms with new demands being placed upon it (Commission 1982). It allowed the officials to decide where the

balances in the policy ought to lie: the balance between transparency (or certainty) and flexibility (or discretion) on the one
hand; and between the policy's negative (neo-liberal) and positive
(interventionist) functions on the other.

The policy that emerged at the start of the 1980s encompassed a
recognition that incrementalism was not enough. Once again substantive change was to follow procedural change, with the initial
emphasis placed on increasing decision-making speed and making
the policy more transparent. Victories in specific cases before the
ECJ and successes in establishing block exemption regulations in
new fields helped to boost the confidence of the Competition officials. The settlement in the *IBM* case of August 1984, initially
deemed to fall under Article 82, was an important example of this
new-found confidence (ECJ 1984). In this case, the Commission
alleged that IBM, the largest computer manufacturer in the world,
held a dominant position in the supply of key products and
accused it of abusing that position. IBM challenged the validity of
the Commission, but its application to the ECJ was dismissed. This
led to discussions between DGIV and IBM on how the matter
should be remedied. IBM proposed that it would end the contentious aspects of its operation, which had, according to the
Commission, been discriminatory. This undertaking was subsequently accepted by DG Competition.

The 'window of opportunity'

What had been a largely reactive policy in the 1960s and 1970s,
became, over the course of the 1980s, much more activist, with an
increased rigour in its application visible as early as 1975. A
variety of external and internal factors explain the emergence of
this new policy approach. Wilks and McGowan point to three
factors which, alongside DG Competition's by now well-established procedural powers, account for the revitalization of policy at
the end of the 1980s: a new economic philosophy which was in
essence neo-liberal; dynamic political leadership; and '"socio-legal
maturation" – that is, the "maturing of both legal powers and staff
competence"' (Wilks and McGowan 1996:247–8). This latter
involved both the accumulated experience of Competition officials
and the body of case-law which went hand in hand with the incremental growth of policy over the previous three decades. This
accumulation of experience and precedence allowed DGIV (later

DG Competition) to move 'from a reactive, rather negative mode of administration to one that is proactive, more managerially aware, positive, and innovatory' (Wilks and McGowan 1996:247). On the state aid side, where there was little evidence of growth in case-law or, indeed, in staff experience, the equivalent rise in morale came more from a small number of landmark ECJ judgments, such as the *Philip Morris (Holland)* case, from legal recognition of the Commission's right to demand the recovery of illegal aid, and from the prioritization of the policy area as a whole, particularly under the leadership of Sir Leon Brittan, the Commissioner for Competition between 1989 and 1992.

Since the early 1980s, Competition Commissioners have acted openly as motors of change. The arrival of Frans Andriessen as Competition Commissioner in 1981 was perhaps the turning-point (Caspari 1987), as he was determined from the start to place competition at the top of the Commission agenda. His high-profile approach involved offering competition policy as a European-level response to the industrial malaise that had swept the region over the previous decade, and as such he focused attention on the need to create 'the conditions necessary for competition to work as a regenerative force in European industry' (Smellie 1985:270). The failure of the Commission to create a fully fledged industrial policy, and the apparent weakness of national (and interventionist) industrial solutions, meant that a pro-competition cure for recession was beginning to find favour within member state governments. Market remedies were seen increasingly as the means of resolving Europe's ills and ensuring its future prosperity. Competition policy was to be the keystone of this new approach. It is clear, therefore, that the later leadership roles played by Commissioners Peter Sutherland (1985–8) and Sir Leon Brittan (1989–93) merely consolidated and extended the policy approach and leadership style first adopted by Frans Andriessen.

Sutherland and Brittan, both barristers by training, provided DGIV with effective and visionary leadership. There was nothing technocratic about either of their leadership styles. Both men were effective, and both were committed to the market integration principles that provided the underlying justification for DG Competition's powers and functions. This ideological compatibility between political-executive head and administrative body was one of the reasons for the DG's success at the end of the 1980s. But it was also supported by the personal reputations of both

Commissioners for efficiency, decisiveness and conviction (Wilks and McGowan 1996:246).

The shift to market mechanisms was not just restricted to the Commission, of course. Although internal developments were essential in revitalizing the policy, the external environment in which DGIV was an actor also had a major part to play in facilitating policy change. The DG was able to latch on to and take advantage of the growing interest in and commitment to neoliberal economics that had begun to influence economic policy-makers in Western European at the end of the 1970s. The Chicago monetarists in particular were extremely visible at this time. Milton Friedman's Nobel prize for economics and his frequent visits to Europe popularized these ideas as an alternative to the neo-Keynesianism of the previous decade. Competition policy was central to the Chicago thesis, and although there was no adoption of the full theoretical baggage, the tide in favour of broadly pro-market or pro-competition solutions to industrial crisis began to place DGIV centre-stage within the Commission.

The effect of the single market project on the development of competition policy was unequivocal. Although supplementary to the 1992 programme, competition policy was always going to be a necessary condition of its success. Thus if conventional non-tariff barriers to trade (physical, technical, fiscal) are removed as part of efforts to complete the Single European Market, firms and governments are likely to be tempted to seek out alternative ways of restricting competition and protecting national industries. As the 1985 White Paper *Completing the Internal Market*, notes: '[a]s the Community moves to complete the Internal Market, it will be necessary to ensure that anti-competitive practices do not engender new forms of local protectionism which would only lead to a re-partitioning of the market' (Commission 1985a). Indeed, governments may collude in such activities. State aid control is important here, as governments may be tempted to grant subsidies to advantage their firms at the expense of their European competitors. Factors such as strong leadership, the activism of the Commission and the ECJ, the threat of competition from the US and the Far East, and the growing deregulatory consensus among national elites have been identified as motivating the creation of a Single European Market. They also served to create the conditions under which a revitalization of European competition policy could take place.

Widening the policy's scope

The late 1980s were a period during which two aspects of competition policy, namely state aid policy and merger policy, were ascendant. After lengthy delays, the speed with which these two policy areas appeared on the European competition policy agenda, assisted by a Single Market momentum, was remarkable.

Merger control became a focal point of policy activism towards the end of the 1980s. There were two reasons for a renewed impetus towards the creation of a fully fledged policy on mergers. First, from a political and economic standpoint, the single market provided a convincing rationale for European-level control. An intensification of cross-border merger activity revived old questions about legal and administrative barriers to what was seen as an essential element of the Single Market Programme. Without European-level regulation, there was certain to be confusion and possibly even a dampening down of merger activity, something that could only harm the Community's industrial prospects. Second, a more legal rationale came from the ECJ in the *Philip Morris/Rothmans* judgment in which the ECJ indicated that, under certain circumstances, it was acceptable to use Article 81 to control mergers. The legal implications of this judgment were labelled, with some justification, 'horrendous' (Korah and Lasok 1988). *Philip Morris* led the member states to realize that a comprehensive Council regulation which would avoid the pitfalls (that is, the uncertainty) of the combined use of Articles 85 and 86 (now 81 and 82) as tools for policing merger activity was now essential. The debates over the drafting of what became the 1989 Merger Control Regulation were heated and often acrimonious, however – though it is important to note that the arguments were largely about the form control should take, rather than about whether a regulation was necessary (see Chapter 6). The outcome was, not surprisingly, a political compromise. Yet the agreement signed at the end of 1989 was heralded as a major success by advocates of a strong European competition policy (Brittan 1990:357).

On the state aid side, the problem was not a legislative one, as the instruments necessary for effective enforcement already existed within the Treaty. But the weak application of the state aid rules before the mid 1980s had meant that the policy was almost non-existent. Under first Peter Sutherland and then Sir Leon Brittan, state aid control was given a new direction which rested upon more than just the strict enforcement of policy. The key to policy change was the outcome of an internal DGIV review of national subsidies which began in 1985. With the first set of results covering 1981–6, the statistics were put to good effect. Brittan initiated a policy review which in 1989 outlined the priorities and goals to be pursued in the following years. This involved scrutiny of all 'existing aid', that is, subsidies that had been approved by the DG in the past. As such, it became clear that the new state aid policy was to be based on an acknowledgement and rectification of past errors and inaction.

Alongside the revitalization of merger and state aid control, other new policy strands emerged in the 1980s. These, together with a restatement of the importance of policy effectiveness and continuity, were to form the basis of the 'new' competition policy of the 1990s. The Commission's policy towards restrictive agreements and monopolies continued to develop into a policy that was wide in scope. Satisfaction with an approach geared mainly to the manufacturing sector gave way gradually to a more wide-ranging emphasis which included the service sectors, with examples of new cases and policies in insurance, banking and broadcasting. At the same time, block exemption regulations continued to provide some legal certainty for industry, allowing the Commission to concentrate on more important cases while helping to guide firms on DGIV's definition of acceptable behaviour.

Public enterprises, utilities and regulated sectors also became a focus of the Commission's attention, as the confidence of officials dealing with cases traditionally outside their remit grew. The agreement of the Merger Control Regulation had much to do with this growing morale. Since 1985, Commissioners also extended the policy to cover the sensitive fields of air and sea transport. Even the Council seemed prepared to support DGIV in its attempts to apply the competition rules to almost all sectors of the economy, although in practice agreement was never easy. This most recent strand of the DG's new policy was perhaps the least understood, as it often relied on the use of Article 86, in conjunction with other treaty provisions, notably Articles 81, 82 and 87. Controversially, Article 86 allowed the Commission to issue directives without recourse to the Council. The first directive of this sort to apply to a particular industrial sector, telecommunications, was sanctioned by an ECJ judgment in March 1991. This was considered to be a further landmark in the evolution of DG Competition's competition control.

These changes went hand in hand with institutional changes that enhanced the status and prestige of DGIV both within the Commission and at national level. Yet, restrictive practices and monopolies policy continued to develop as before. Much of this development rested on efforts to apply more effectively the procedural tools at the Commission's disposal, tools that in the past the DG had been rather reluctant to use. This was particularly true of the Commission's use of fines and penalty payments. These reached record heights with the ECU48m fine in the 1990 Soda Ash case, followed by the large ECU75m fine imposed in 1991 on *Tetra-Pak*, and have continued to increase ever since. Fines have also been levied on non-EU firms.

Despite pressures from other Commission quarters, DGIV rejected the protectionist line that would place competitiveness above competition in the hierarchy of Commission objectives. Instead, DG officials continued to follow Sir Leon Brittan's often-quoted maxim that competition at home is the best training for competition abroad. The proactive and expansive role adopted by Sutherland and Brittan over this period led them to take a keen interest in the spread of competition policy first to the European Free Trade Association (EFTA) states, then to Central and Eastern Europe and Russia, and later to regimes even further afield.

National developments have also been crucial. Institutional overloading, together with a sensitivity to criticism about overcentralization, has led to the emergence of a policy of decentralization which, by the late 1980s, caused the Commission to state their intention to involve national courts more effectively in the enforcement of European competition law (Chapter 3). Both within the Community and outside it, DG Competition has been particularly keen to see the adoption of Article 81- and 82-type legislation in domestic arenas. This form of legislative export demonstrated the policy's new legal and institutional maturity and was a convincing sign that European competition policy had finally come of age (McGowan and Wilks 1995:151).

More recent trends and developments

Around the end of the 1990s the language of European competition policy changed with the reordering of the treaty provisions following the Amsterdam European Council, and the then new

Commission President, Romano Prodi, in 1999 deciding to drop the numbers by which Commission Directorates-General (DGs) had been known, in the rather vain hope of making the EU institutions seem less arcane to ordinary citizens. Thus, the cartel and monopoly provisions, which had been Articles 85 and 86, became Articles 81 and 82; and the state aid rules formerly found in Articles 92–94 now appeared in Articles 87–89. The Competition DG, known as DGIV, became DG Competition.

While these changes were cosmetic, both substantively and procedurally the policy also continued to evolve. Through the lens of four cross-cutting themes, first presented in Chapter 1, four trends are identifiable. This is not to say that these trends were not in evidence to some degree prior to the late 1990s; rather we use modernization, Europeanization, decentralization and liberalization as a way of drawing attention to more recent developments within the EU's competition regime so as to flag up some of the issues at this stage which we will revisit in the chapters that follow, and which will be picked up again in more detail in the Conclusions to this volume.

Since the end of the 1990s, modernization has become the watchword of European competition policy. The modernization agenda has been associated particularly with DG Competition's cartel reform which was introduced in 2003 and implemented thereafter. In terms of substantive policy, the Commission's modernization agenda in this policy field has become more of an overarching theme than a discrete one, encompassing under its umbrella decentralization, Europeanization and liberalization, in what was a package of initiatives contained within a new Regulation, conveniently known as Regulation 1/2004 (Council 2003). While more detail of the content of the Regulation and the agenda which justified it can be found in Chapter 4, it is worth emphasizing at this point that some have identified its introduction as a 'revolution' in European competition policy (Wilks 2005a for example) in that it swept away some of the fundamentals of cartel policy to date, including the notification requirement which had prior to 2003 been a key characteristic of the policy.

While modernization was associated mainly with cartel policy, there were also modernization agendas played out in other areas of competition policy, not least in the state aid domain – though reform was initiated only from 2005 (see Chapter 7). A key horizontal objective was to make economic analysis more central and robust in competition decision-making, reflected in the appointment for the first time of a Chief Economist. At the same time, DG Competition itself underwent a dramatic reorganization which took around two years to complete (from 2002 to 2004). This sought to undermine the segmented nature of European competition by structuring units around particular sectors and functions. So, for example, the state aid directorate of old was abandoned and many state aid case officials were integrated into directorates which also dealt with mergers and monopolies policy. One might see this as an attempt to respond to criticism that there was no one European competition policy, but several; though a separate directorate dealing exclusively with cartels was also formed in the process (see Chapter 3). Since the 1990s some evidence points to a Europeanization of competition policy. Europeanization in this context implies a process of convergence (often talked of as 'alignment' by competition lawyers). There are two obvious questions to ask, namely whether such a convergence has really taken place; and, if it has to some degree, then by what mechanisms this has occurred. One way of addressing the first question is to identify cases of countries where reforms have been initiated. One such case is the UK where new legislation was introduced in 2002 in the form of the Enterprise Act. However, the Enterprise Act was as much shaped by the UK's emulation of the US law (introducing criminal sanctions for the breach of competition law) as by the EU provisions. It is also ironic that the Commission's modernization agenda shifted the EU regulation away from the new UK law only a matter a months after the UK has sought convergence with the EU. Thus even where there are conscious attempts at convergence, the path of Europeanization is rarely linear.

Europeanization has not been just a matter for member states. It is at this point that it is important to consider a particularly important development for the competition regime since the late 1990s enlargement. The 2004 and 2007 enlargements, and the preparations for them, have preoccupied DG Competition since the 1990s, as the competition chapter of the negotiations was considered a core part of the European Union's *acquis*. Applicant states had an obligation to set up a legislative framework compatible with that of the EU regime, and to ensure that they had the administrative capacity necessary to enforce the policy. They had also to provide evidence that they had sustained a credible record of enforcement of the competition *acquis* prior to accession. While the Commission, in its annual progress reports, seemed unconcerned with the legal framework, which soon fell into line with EU norms (with legislation usually emulating Articles 81 and 82, and so on), it saw the application and enforcement of the law as the biggest challenge for prospective members. Although all the competition chapters were eventually closed, the Commission continues, even after accession, to keep a watchful eye on how the new member states apply European law in this field. The fact that enlargement occurred at the same time as policy enforcement was decentralized (see Chapter 3) suggested that problems of consistent application of the law might undermine the policy. As yet, it is unclear whether this is indeed what has happened.

Decentralization has been high up on DG Competition's agenda since the mid 1990s, forming a key component of the modernization agenda in the cartel field, though it can also be found in other competition policies. What is under consideration here is the decentralization of enforcement, however, not the decentralization of policy-making. The Commission's decentralization agenda has been driven by the huge weight of cases coming to the attention of DG Competition by the 1990s. One might go so far as to see DG Competition as a victim of its own success in this regard. Thus it was felt that some solution was necessary if EU competition policy was not to grind to a halt. The cure for competition gridlock was to push routine decision-making downwards to the national competition authorities and to the national courts. To a degree, the convergence process was a prerequisite for this new policy direction (albeit complicated by the enlargements of 2004 and 2007). It was only once there was a sense of a shared European (as opposed to EU) competition project in the national authorities responsible for competition cases that decentralization of this kind could be envisaged. And even then the Commission was careful to retain the power to claw back – or up – cases to the EU level. The setting up of a European Competition Network (ECN) reinforced this idea of a shared project, reflected in a quasi-federal (or perhaps neo-functionalist) structure for the management of the policy.

As in the 1980s and 1990s liberalization remains a key component for competition regulation. In the EU competition policy context, liberalization tends to mean liberalization of public undertakings, of utilities, formerly (and in some cases still) holding hard-to-challenge monopolistic positions in national markets, and what the EU institutions call 'services of a general economic interest', that is undertakings providing a service to the community which is deemed socially necessary but which would be uneconomical to provide on economic criteria alone. While some of the buzz has gone from the liberalization agenda since the late 1990s, the Commission (and not just DG Competition) continue to push back the boundaries of anti- or uncompetitive practices in areas still not subject to the full rigour of the market, in fields that are politically still extremely sensitive.

Yet it may be that the mainstream has shifted somewhat since the 1990s, not least as a consequence of the Lisbon Agenda. 'Lisbon' has become an umbrella under which new initiatives and modes of governance are introduced, and existing policies are subsumed. In the case of competition policy, DG Competition has tied its objectives to those of the Lisbon Agenda by emphasizing (as Lisbon does) the contribution made by the policy to growth and jobs. While the Lisbon Agenda's competitiveness goals are not necessarily incompatible with those of the EU's competition regime, the rhetoric of competition regulation (and possibly to some degree also its substance) has shifted somewhat to the extent that one might even view this as a move in the direction of a new form of interventionism, albeit one which stresses innovation and not the defence of national – or even European – champions. This is a question further considered in Chapter 9 below.

Conclusion

The evolution of European competition policy is the story of the cumulative expansion of a policy area, achieved incrementally through the widening and deepening of the policy's scope. From the initial emphasis on restrictive practices in the 1960s, to monopoly policy in the 1970s, and state aid and merger control in the 1980s and 1990s, competition policy has continued to expand into new industrial sectors using well-established legal and administrative instruments while at the same time continuing to consolidate and extend the competition *acquis* through the accumulation of case-law. The institutional context, the power and autonomy given DGIV by Regulation 17, the confirmed discretionary scope of the Commission, the activism of individual Commissioners, and the developing pro-competition culture of DGIV have together shaped the competition policy of the 1990s and beyond. Seidel

(2008) suggests that DGIV's culture dates from an earlier period, resulting from the establishment of the DG as an independent unit (which under an alternative schema would not have happened), under the leadership of a German Commissioner.

The story of the evolution of European competition policy juxtaposes the passive or reactive periods in the policy's history against its more activist and high-profile phases. After 1991, DGIV and later DG Competition once again entered a new phase. Since the early 1990s, there had been talk of decline, of a lowering of morale and of the emergence of a more cautious approach to policy enforcement. Despite the agreed success of the Merger Control Regulation, the failure of efforts to extend the scope of merger control in the early 1990s, alongside an acknowledgement that European competition enforcement can no longer remain exclusively in the hands of the Commission, seemed to infer a shift of emphasis within the policy. Yet, rumours of the demise of DGIV were grossly exaggerated. While it would be misleading to claim that the dizzy heights of competition policy activism under Commissioners Sutherland and Brittan have continued unabated, Karel van Miert, Competition Commissioner 1993–9, was far from being the intervention-loving protectionist some claimed he would be when he was first appointed. His watchword was, however, 'pragmatism', which suggests an acknowledgement of the inherently political character of European competition policy, though this has not meant that he has failed to take a tough line in controversial competition cases. However, he is remembered as a relatively weak Commissioner. It was his immediate successor Mario Monti (1999-2004) and Neelie Kroes who returned DG competition to its former glory (as discussed in Chapter 3).

Chapter 3

The Institutions of European Competition Governance

At the institutional heart of the supranational enforcement of competition policy sit the European Commission and the European Courts. The relationship between these institutions is pivotal both in day-to-day administration and for the broader evolution of policy. Yet while the interaction between the Commission and the Courts makes for a fascinating case study of European policy-making, it also poses important normative questions about the accountability of governance in the competition sphere. With both the EU Council and the European Parliament (EP) on the sidelines insofar as much of competition decision-making is concerned, the European-level bureaucratic and judicial politics of competition regulation has taken centre-stage and at times become extremely contentious. Since the mid 1990s, however, this top-down model of competition governance has been within a framework, which leans towards a more network-orientated approach to decision-making and enforcement. National Competition Authorities (NCAs) and domestic (national) courts perform an important role within this emergent network. While it may be too early yet to classify the Commission as a 'network organization' (Metcalfe 1996) or network manager, there has been a notable shift across the board in how competition decision-making operates.

This chapter begins however by focusing on the supranational institutions. First, it assesses briefly the limited role of the Council and the Parliament in competition enforcement. It then introduces the organization and functions of the main competition actor, the European Commission and, in particular, its Directorate-General for Competition (formerly known as DGIV). The chapter concentrates in particular on DG Competition's organizational and staffing characteristics and on its administrative culture as a way of moving beyond formal institutional attributes, to more ephemeral and less tangible elements of institutional life. The European Courts provide the focus of the second section of the chapter. Both the European Court of Justice (ECJ) and the Court of First Instance (CFI) come under scrutiny at this point. In examining the role of the Courts, the importance of case-law and the establishment of legal precedence in determining the procedural and substantive content of the European competition regime is acknowledged. The beginnings of a new phase of judicial activism in competition judgments, led by the CFI, are identified. Finally, the chapter uses the network concept to highlight recent changes in the governance of European competition policy, examining the roles performed by national competition authorities (NCAs) and national courts in the enforcement of the EU's competition regime.

The Parliament and the Council

Both the European Parliament (EP) and the EU Council have only a peripheral role in the regulation of European competition. With the instruments of decision-making almost exclusively in the hands of the Commission, both of the legislating bodies are clearly on the margins of competition policy-making, though both have been keen to see their participation and oversight of competition matters enhanced.

The EP and more specifically its Committee on Economic and Monetary Affairs has seen its involvement in competition policy develop incrementally as the regime has evolved, though it has always had some limited capacity to influence Commission policy. The Committee has a specific *rapporteur* now to deal exclusively with competition matters. Even before its direct election in 1979, the Assembly was putting pressure on DG Competition to open up its regulatory process to greater scrutiny; and it was the EP that persuaded the Commission to publish an annual competition report for the first time in 1972 (Goyder 1993:71).

There are two formal ways the EP is able to influence the Commission. Of most importance is undoubtedly its own initiative report on the Commission's annual competition report. This takes the form of a resolution, and is a response not only to the content of the report but also to broader developments in European competition enforcement. It is generally well informed and is taken extremely seriously by DG Competition. The Competition Commissioner addresses the EP annually to discuss both the Annual Report and its current activities. A second way for the EP to put pressure on the Commission is through what often appears to be a strategic use of written and oral questions. These are not only to be taken at face value by DG Competition, but are also judged to reflect general parliamentary concerns (Commission 2007a: point 78). The capacity to ask questions in this way gives parliamentarians the option to address detailed competition policy questions to the Commission in the gap between the delivery of annual reports.

Although the EP's relationship with DG Competition is usually judged to be constructive, there is little scope for systematic parliamentary control over competition enforcement. Over the years, the EP has been critical of the Commission on many counts, especially in cases where the Commission has not consulted fully with MEPs. However, relatively little has been done to improve the EP's position in this regard.

Surprisingly perhaps, the EU Council also has a relatively peripheral role in competition policy matters. All the Commission's annual report says on the matter is that the Commission cooperates closely, by informing it of major policy initiatives and participating in Council working groups (Commission 2007a:point 79). Although DG Competition's powers are those delegated to it through Council legislation, the regulatory framework for much of the competition regime's history was shaped back in the 1960s. With little need for new laws since then, the Council's legislative function had until recently been limited to occasional regulations exempting, en bloc, classes of agreements, now also in the field of state aid. The Council adopts these regulations by qualified majority voting (QMV) after consulting the EP. In the mergers field, the situation was different, and it was the Council that first prevented the emergence of a fully fledged policy from the 1960s to the 1980s; and the Council that were ultimately persuaded to legislate at the end of the 1980s, setting the framework for a new and very assertive European merger regime. More recently still, the Council has become involved in policy reform, with the agreement of new procedural regulations for both cartel policy and for state aid. Yet, in spite of all this activity, it is still appropriate to argue that the Council lacks direct involvement in the policy. This is because policy- or decision-making in the competition regime is very much about enforcement.

In this respect the absence of direct Council involvement is understandable. It is not the Council's function to involve itself in day-to-day managerial and executive tasks which, at least on the surface, are technocratic and administrative. Moreover, in the early years of the policy, when the legal framework was first established, the importance of competition policy – first for the Single Market and now for the Lisbon Agenda – would not have been so obvious. However, the realization that incremental decision-taking allowed the Commission to develop for itself a highly political policy-making function put the member states on their guard and has contributed to a more prominent role for the Council than existed prior to the late 1980s. Although there is no suggestion that the Commission's enforcement role ought to rest with the Council, the Commission has been willing to involve the Council in its policy deliberations. This demonstrates a perceived need on the part of the Commission to ensure member state approval, so as to pre-empt demands for drastic reform, demands which at one stage in the 1990s even led to specific proposals to set up a European Cartel Office.

Thus while the EP and the Council are not central actors in the regulation of European competition, it is clear that the Commission would be foolish to ignore the inter-institutional context within which all European policy is made. It should come as no surprise to find, therefore, that the Commission has often encouraged parliamentary and Council involvement where formally none was necessary, though this initiative has often rested on informal and ad-hoc practices, with an eye to ever-present demands for openness and transparency. The substantial change has come not in inter-institutional, Brussels-based relationships, but in a more federalizing direction, as will be explained later in this chapter.

The European Commission

Despite the introduction of a policy of decentralization, European competition policy remains a Commission policy. It is the Commission which determines what the policy is and how it is (or should be) implemented on the ground. It is the Commission which identifies the most important breaches of the rules, which undertakes the investigations that matter and which decides in such cases whether to take a formal decision. It is the Commission, too, which fines companies, and even establishes the level of the penalty.

However, these claims about the centrality of the Commission do not mean that decision-making power has not been dispersed downwards to some degree since the late 1990s.

Moreover, the Commission is not a monolithic or even a unitary body. It is made up of Directorates-General (DGs), each of which is responsible for a particular functional or sectoral policy and each of which is motivated by different goals and value systems. The potential for conflict across these Commission departments is therefore immense. This can make decision-making *within* the Commission a sensitive and highly political business, for in the Commission one often sees a microcosm of European Union politics as a whole, in which there exist national, ideological, functional, sectoral and many other cleavages underpinning familiar disputes over institutional resources, problem-solving, policy-making and policy substance.

Organization and functions

The European Commission performs a range of functions and roles across various policy domains. It is composed of executive and administrative wings. One Commissioner is given particular responsibility for the competition portfolio. Although some decisions are taken by that Commissioner alone under a delegated procedure, all potentially controversial and high-profile decisions must come before the College as a whole. Much of the impact of any DG within the Commission rests on the ability of its Commissioner to act as a voice for his or her policy and to create coalitions of support with other Commissioners. For Competition Commissioners, success on this score has varied, with some past Commissioners considered more successful than others. For example, Commissioner Sassen was considered to be rather cautious; Commissioner Vouel did not make much of an impact against Commissioner Davignon's more interventionist industry portfolio; while van der Groeben, Borchette and Andriessen were all very well respected. Two Commissioners, Peter Sutherland and Sir Leon Brittan are now viewed as authors of the revitalization of the policy at the end of the 1980s (Wilks and McGowan 1996: 247). Karel van Miert's style was very different and for many his term was something of a disappointment. By contrast, the DG's status increased once again under Mario Monti (as 'Super-Mario'), and then under the leadership of the first female competition Commissioner, Neelie Kroes (see Box 3.1).

With competition policy now seen as a prestige job, the calibre of the Commissioners appointed continues to be high. The previous holder of the competition portfolio, Karel van Miert, initially seemed different in style and approach from his two predecessors. He was criticized when first appointed for being too 'political': in other words, for being too ready to take a non-competition line when issuing competition decisions, and for being rather too susceptible to pressure from various sectional interests. However, his reputation as a tough competition policy actor grew during his term of office, culminating in 1997 with an important boost to his image in the *Boeing/McDonnell Douglas* merger case (see Chapter 6). He carried the label of 'liberal' within the ranks of the College of Commissioners and despite some criticism was a very active Commissioner, especially on the merger front.

Neelie Kroes, who took up the position of Competition Commissioner at the end of 2004, has a reputation for being rather formidable, and taking a hard line in competition cases. She has been nicknamed 'Nickel Neelie' and described as 'hard as nails' on occasions (Kawamoto 2003). The circumstances of her initial appointment were rather unfortunate, as when she came before the European Parliament, during the Commissioners' hearings, there was some disquiet about her extensive links to big business. This matter was cleared up fairly quickly, however, when the

---

BOX 3.1   The Competition Commissioners

Name	*County or origin*	*Term*
Hans van der Groeben (EEC)	Germany	1958–66
Emanuel Sassen	Netherlands	1966–70
Albert Borchette	Luxembourg	1970–76
Raymond Vouel	Luxembourg	1977–80
Frans Andriessen	Netherlands	1980–84
Peter Sutherland	Ireland	1984–89
Leon Brittan	United Kingdom	1989–93
Karel Van Miert	Belgium	1993–99
Mario Monti	Italy	1999–2004
Neelie Kroes	Netherlands	2004–(09)

Commissioner-elect agreed to step down over cases involving companies (some thirty or so) that she had been involved with (Mulvey 2007). Since then, she has sought to prove herself as an active and strong Commissioner, for example, in taking on the US anti-trust authorities over the conduct of Microsoft, even if at the time of writing it is too early to provide a full assessment of her term of office.

The potential for disputes within the College and among Commissioners is great, especially where matters of national or ideological interest are at stake. Indeed many of the most controversial disputes in the College have been over competition cases, especially those involving large-scale mergers and state aid (see Chapters 6 and 7). It is not unusual to see cleavages in the College emerge along liberal/interventionist lines. These have as much to do with national industrial policy preferences as with ideological beliefs. The log-rolling and package-dealing which is as much part of the College's day-to-day business as it is the EU Council's, means that such cleavages are not set in stone during a Commission's term of office. Deals are done, promises are made and debts are called in, and ultimately a competition decision or policy emerges from the College.

Each Commissioner is assisted by their personal staff or cabinet. Neelie Kroes has seven members in hers (not including the Hearing Officers and the Spokesman). The cabinet plays a crucial role as liaison between the executive and the administrative wings of the Commission. It filters information from the administrative services to the Commissioner; and it transmits the Commissioner's priorities and position down the Commission hierarchy to the officials responsible for specific aspects of competition enforcement. The function of the cabinet is, then, to assist the Commissioner in dealing with the daily business of the DG. Staff must also keep the Commissioner well briefed and maintain links between the Commission and national authorities. The cabinet acts as an aid to the Commissioner in the supervision of the DG, providing at one and the same time political reliability, technical expertise and administrative experience.

The administrative wing of the Commission is composed of directorates-general (DGs), such as DG Competition, and services. In the competition arena, the most important of these horizontal services are the Secretariat-General (SG) and the Legal Service (LS). The LS vets all Commission drafts to ensure their legal compatibility with the Treaty. It is the LS which has to defend the Commission should a legal challenge be made against it. The LS, not surprisingly perhaps, has a cautious reputation. Intra-Commission disputes may stem from the differing perspectives of the LS and the competition DG, with the LS trying to restrain Commission activism – though many of these disagreements are resolved through inter-service consultation (see below).

The Secretariat-General is another horizontal Commission service which is important in the regulation of competition. The SG is the Commission's coordination body, which acts as the formal point of liaison between the Commission and the other European institutions. It also coordinates activity within the Commission itself, resolving, where possible, inter-service disputes and ensuring consistency among the myriad Commission policies, a task which is not always easy. The SG is also the first port of call for formal external contacts made to the Commission. This allows for some centralized oversight of the policy, though in practice one should not overstate its importance. It does have a role to play, but this only impinges on the freedom of manoeuvre of the competition directorates-general in extreme cases.

The relationship between Commissioner and his or her staff on the one hand, and DG, led by a Director-General, on the other, is not always easy to fathom. The Commissioner and the *cabinet* may be viewed as the political-executive arm of the DG, throwing a more political perspective on the legal-economic investigations of the competition officials. Alternatively the Commissioner and *cabinet* may be more akin to a political *cap*, directing and controlling the work of the DG from the top of the hierarchy. However, executive and administrative functions can rarely be separated so easily. It would certainly be naïve to imagine that political/ideological questions do not enter into the decision-making of the DG. Likewise, although the Commissioner is clearly subject to external political (national, sectional and ideological) pressures, the need to ensure legal certainty, consistency and respect for the rules remains crucial at this stage in the decision-making process.

Disputes occur across DGs as well as at the level of the Commissioners and their *cabinets*. The bureaucratic politics of the Commission is now well documented (see, for example, Peters 1992), and nowhere are disputes more common than on competition matters. As a horizontal policy, competition policy cuts across the policy responsibilities of many DGs, and must be integrated into policies that are not primarily the responsibility of DG Competition. To complicate matters further, a number of other DGs have responsibility for competition enforcement, such as DG Energy and Transport.

Organization and staffing in DG Competition

DG Competition dominates the regulation of competition within the Commission. It has a distinctive departmental identity and a clearly defined set of policy responsibilities, though it continues to seek to extend its competence into sectors previously untouched by any competition ethos. At the head of the DG is the most senior official, the Director-General. The Director-General's function is to lead and represent the DG and to act as a top-level liaison between the DG and the Commissioner. The Director-General plays the role of sounding-board for the Commissioner and acts as a channel for DG contacts. This relationship is not without its tensions when the Commissioner and the Director-General are in disagreement, though the Commissioner will usually have the final say. However, Directors-General are important figures in their own right. For example, Alexander Schaub, appointed in May 1995, replacing another high-profile figure, Claus-Dieter Ehlermann, was, like his predecessor, a German appointee, supporting the impression that DG Competition was a 'German' DG. The subsequent Director-General, appointed in 2002, Philip Lowe, is British, however (see Box 3.2).

The structure of DG Competition reflects functional require-ments. However, its size is a source of constant consternation. As of 2006 there were approximately 750 staff to deal with all aspects of the policy from cartels and mergers to state aid and aspects of liberalization policy (see Box 3.3). Numbers have increased (from around 400 in the mid 1990s), but so too with enlargement has the number of member states. Inadequate staff resources clearly weaken the DG's capacity for enforcement and make leanness and streamlining something of an organizational obsession. Indeed, DG Competition has undergone a series of reorganizations over its history, in part as a way of taking on board new policy responsibil-ities, but also as a means of striving for greater policy effectiveness and efficiency. A restructuring exercise took place in October 1995, largely in order to create a specific directorate for merger control. A further reorganization took place between 2002 and

---

BOX 3.2　The Structure of DG Competition (2008)

Director-General
Deputy Director-General Operations
Deputy Director-General Mergers and Antitrust
Deputy Director-General State aids
Chief Economist

DIRECTORATE A
Policy and Strategic
1. Strategy
2. Antitrust and mergers: policy and scrutiny
3. State aid policy
4. Evaluation
5. European competition network
6. International relations

DIRECTORATE B
Markets and cases I : Energy and Environment
1. Energy, environment
2. State aids
3. Mergers

DIRECTORATE C
Markets and cases II: Information, Communication and Media
1. Antitrust: telecoms, liberalization directives, Article 86 cases
2. Antitrust: media
3. Antitrust: IT, internet and consumer electronics
4. State aids
5. Mergers

DIRECTORATE D
Markets and cases III: Financial services and Health-related markets
1. Antitrust: financial services
2. Antitrust: pharmaceuticals and other health-related markets
3. State aids
4. Mergers

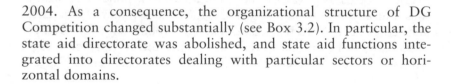

2004. As a consequence, the organizational structure of DG Competition changed substantially (see Box 3.2). In particular, the state aid directorate was abolished, and state aid functions integrated into directorates dealing with particular sectors or horizontal domains.

DIRECTORATE E
Markets and cases IV: Basic Industries, Manufacturing and Agriculture
1. Antitrust: consumer goods, agriculture and food
2. Antitrust: basic industries, chemicals and other manufacturing
3. State aids: industrial restructuring
4. Mergers

DIRECTORATE F
Markets and cases V: Transport, Post and other services
1. Antitrust: transport and post
2. Antitrust: other services
3. State aids:
4. Mergers

DIRECTORATE G Cartels
1. Cartels I
2. Cartels II
3. Cartels III
4. Cartels IV
5. Cartels V

DIRECTORATE H
State Aid: Cohesion, R&D&I and enforcement
1. Regional aid
2. R&D, innovation and risk capital
3. State aid network and transparency
4. Enforcement and procedural reform

DIRECTORATE R
Registry and Resources
1. Document management and procedures
2. Strategic planning and resources
3. Information technology

Source: DG Competition, http://ec.europa.eu.dgs/competition/index_en.htm © European
Communities 1995–2008

Thus, the characteristics of DG Competition in early 2008 were
as follows:

- At the head of the DG sits the Director-General, three Deputies
  (for operations, mergers and anti-trust, and state aids), and the

new post of Chief Economist (Box 3.3). This last position high-lights the importance that DG Competition now gives to pro-viding a rigorous economic analysis within decisions. At this level there are also other horizontal positions relating to ethics, security and procedures; to communications policy; and to con-sumer liaison.

- There are eight Directorates in total. Directorate A (Policy and Strategy) deals with overall policy matters, rather than with spe-cific cases. As well as dealing with strategy and scrutiny, it also has responsibility for evaluation, for the European Competition Network (ECN) and for international relations.
- Directorates B–H, seven directorates in total, have responsibility for markets and cases. Five of these directorates, B–F, are called 'Markets and Cases I–V'. Directorate B is responsible for energy and environment; Directorate C is responsible for information, communications and media; Directorate D is responsible for financial services and health-related markets (including pharma-ceuticals); Directorate E deals with basic industries, manufac-turing and agriculture; Directorate F deals with transport, post and other services.
- Directorate G deals exclusively with cartels, and is divided into five unnamed divisions.
- Directorate H, state aid: cohesion, R&D&I and enforcement; deals with residual state aid matters, not dealt with in other directorates above.
- Directorate R is the Registry and has responsibility for docu-ment management, strategic planning and resources and infor-mation technology within the DG.

What is interesting to note about DG Competition's organigram (particularly when compared to the structure of the DG prior to 2002) is that there is much more scope for a cross-fertilization of ideas about competition enforcement within the 'Markets and Cases' DGs, along sectoral or functional lines, than was the case before. State aid, for the first time, is integrated into mainstream DGs, as is merger control. This was clearly an effort to reinforce the coherence of the policy – as one policy, rather than as the sepa-rate policy domains of cartel policy, monopoly policy, mergers policy and state aid policy. Only in the case of cartel policy is there a discrete unit, dealing exclusively with cartel cases.

DG Competition staff are recruited through conventional

BOX 3.3   Human resources (staff numbers): DG Competition (2006)

Activity	Officials and temporary staff	Auxiliaries and contractual agents	Informal personnel	Seconded national experts	Other	Total
Anti-trust, mergers, liberalization, cartels	298	25	3	32	–	357
Control of state aid	160	19	–	9	–	188
International cooperation	10	–	–	–	–	10
Policy, strategy and coordination	98	7	1	2	–	108
Administrative support	67	7	–	–	13	87
Total	633	58	3	43	13	750

Source: Commission (2006a) © European Communities 1995–2008.

Commission channels, with the much-sought-after permanent posts allocated after a lengthy process of examination and interview (the *concours*). Once appointed, DG Competition officials have tended to stay in post for long periods. A detailed study undertaken back in 1982 found that 80 per cent of 'Λ' graded officials, those dealing with policy matters, had worked in the competition field for at least 10 years, while another 10 per cent had worked on competition matters for more than 5 years (House of Lords 1982). It is not clear whether a similar pattern is identifiable 25 years or more on from this date. Appointment as a *national expert*, often on secondment from national ministries or competition agencies, is a more flexible but temporary route into the DG. National experts perform a number of specific functions in DG Competition, which include contributing specialist national knowledge to the department and altering the balance between lawyers and economists (in favour of the economists).

Lawyers still dominate in DG Competition, though not as much as they once did. They make up no more than 50 per cent of personnel. Yet the legal/non-legal dichotomy which characterizes many European administrations still pigeonholes DG Competition as a legal DG, despite great efforts made to change this perception (and the substance behind it). Even though it is certainly not the only part of the Commission to employ a large number of lawyers, this external perception only heightens the sense of difference felt by many DG Competition officials. Staff from non-legal specialisms *are* present within DG Competition. As the economic effect on trade is arguably the most important effect, this emphasis on law-making and judicial interpretation at the expense of economic analysis has always seemed misguided, though it is only relatively recently that it has been addressed in anything more than a half-hearted manner. DG Competition is fully aware of the problems that the economic weakness of the DG has caused (not least in terms of criticism of inadequate economic reasoning in decisions and particularly by the European Courts). However, the pervasiveness of the legal ethos within the DG Competition is exemplified by the legal working practices which dominate the day-to-day administration of the policy. The emphasis is on case-work, as it is through dealing with individual cases that the policy is refined and extended.

The European Courts

The European legal system is the framework within which the supranational regulation of competition takes place. At the heart of the legal system sit the European Courts, the European Court of Justice (ECJ) and the Court of First Instance (CFI). Both institutions play a pivotal role in competition enforcement. They are responsible for the legal supervision of the competition rules, and have also had a crucial part to play in shaping the substantive and procedural characteristics of the European competition regime. With their judgments binding in all member states, and with the supremacy of European over national law, the Courts have been able to shape the environment within which Commission regulation has taken place. It has done this using both direct actions and preliminary rulings.

Direct actions in competition cases involve appeals to one of the European Courts. In making judgments in cases of this sort, the ECJ may establish a precedent which can be overturned only by Council/EP legislation (which is unlikely, if not impossible, in the competition policy field). Preliminary rulings, by contrast, involve the referral of a specific question to the ECJ by a national court during the course of national proceedings. The ECJ does not give a judgment in these cases, but provides a judicial interpretation which not only allows the national court to continue its case, but also clarifies for future reference some aspect of European law.

It is often claimed that these two functions performed by the ECJ allow for a process of policy-making, under the guise of judicial interpretation. The absence of Council and EP involvement certainly means that the Courts will often have the last word on Commission decisions, should that particular policy be appealed or referred to the Courts. One can see therefore why the Courts, alongside the Commission, are pivotal actors in the enforcement and evolution of European competition policy.

The European Court of Justice (ECJ) was founded in 1952 as the European Coal and Steel Community (ECSC) Court, and was enlarged in 1958 to cover all three European Communities after the European Economic Community (EEC) and Euratom Treaties of 1957. The visibility of the ECJ increased substantially with the 1986 Single European Act (SEA). As a consequence, the European legal system became subject to some criticism. This is not unrelated to the extended use of qualified majority voting in the EU Council. With governments losing their veto potential in an ever-growing number of policy areas, there is now a greater political sensitivity towards Court judgments and their consequences. The growing number of high-profile legal cases that have hit the headlines in recent years, such as those on football transfer rules, environment policy and employment laws, have also drawn public attention to the Court in policy areas previously immune from European controversy (Weiler 1993). This has clearly had an effect on competition enforcement.

The ECJ's impact on competition policy has been crucial. Ever since the Grundig case the Commission's windows of policy opportunity have come from the ECJ's willingness to interpret the European competition provisions in a broad and generous manner

(Goyder 1993:493). Such an approach was taken in the *Continental Can* judgment in 1973, allowing competition policy to develop in ways which gave the Commission a substantial freedom of manoeuvre. Arguably, the ECJ's most important contribution to competition enforcement has been its espousal of market integration as the determining principle in its competition judgments. Although this is now taken largely as a given, Goyder (1993:72) points out that other principles, such as efficiency or consumer protection, might quite easily have been prioritized at the expense of the single market. In placing market integration centre-stage, the ECJ identified competition policy as fundamental to the European integration process, giving the Commission scope to increase its competition competence.

However, the ECJ has been criticized for being too lenient with the Commission. These arguments claim not only that the ECJ has failed to act as a check on Commission expansionism, but also that it has done itself a disservice by frequently ignoring procedural irregularities in competition cases, and condoning the Commission's bad procedural habits. There have been times when the Commission has pushed the parameters of the ECJ's tolerance too far, however. This is what happened in the *Belgian Wallpapers* case, when the Commission was condemned by the ECJ for the inadequacy of its economic analysis. However

> the Court has often shown itself to be reluctant to interfere with the work of the Commission. In a number of cases, the Court, while recognising certain procedural irregularities, has refused to grant concrete relief to applicants and the offending decisions have remained in force. (Coppel 1992:144)

As Coppel goes on to say:

> Over the years, a significant number of Commission decisions in the area of competition law have been struck down by the ECJ, but the Court has been reluctant to lay down general principles, particularly principles based on individual rights . . . It is arguable that the ECJ has failed to see the wider issues in matters of competition law procedure. (Coppel 1992:144)

While the ECJ has been an ally to the Commission, allowing it to strengthen its competition policy hand, its relationship with DG

Competition may well have damaged its own standing as an independent institution. There is no doubt that without the assistance of the ECJ, European competition policy would not have developed either to the extent or in the form that it has.

Since the mid 1980s, the European Court system has been in flux. As a result, debates about the nature of the Union's 'judicial architecture' (Jacqué and Weiler 1990), the weaknesses inherent in the European legal system, and the potential for institutional reform have dominated legal discourse. Although these calls for reform continue, it is clear that the legal system within which competition enforcement occurs has altered substantially in recent years. This has been in part a direct result of the creation of a new European court, the Court of First Instance (CFI). The introduction of a two-tier court system was intended to challenge accusations that the large backlog and delays in the processing of cases were provoking a loss of confidence in the European rule of law. It was clear that something dramatic had to be done to reduce the burden on the ECJ.

The 1986 Single European Act (SEA) allowed the ECJ, supported by the Council, to spell out the type of reform necessary. The outcome was the creation of a European-level tribunal, the CFI, whose remit is to consider, in the first instance, 'certain classes of actions of proceedings' which take up a disproportionate amount of the ECJ's time. The new court is attached to the ECJ, although it has in practice developed an independent institutional existence.

Established formally in 1988, the CFI began its work in November 1989. Initially, it dealt with only three categories of case: staff cases, certain coal and steel cases under the European Coal and Steel Community (ECSC) Treaty, and competition actions (excluding state aid and anti-dumping). Seventy-three competition cases were thus transferred from the ECJ to the CFI at the end of 1989, and since then the CFI has been able to develop a certain expertise in dealing with anti-trust cases. The new court's role was extended in June 1993 when all cases, other than those involving anti-dumping, brought by individuals or groups (that is, not brought by governments or the European institutions) were transferred to the CFI. At this point, state aid appeals came under CFI scrutiny for the first time; and in March 1994 anti-dumping cases finally came under CFI jurisdiction.

Like the ECJ, the CFI has 27 judges. There are no advocates-general to assist the judges in their deliberations, though in difficult cases members of Court may be called upon to act in that capacity in competition cases. The CFI usually sits in chambers of 5 or 3 judges in competition cases. Decisions are reached in secret and by majority vote in a procedure similar though not identical to that of the ECJ (Weatherill and Beaumont 1995:184–90).

The CFI has been praised for the thoroughness of its decision-taking, and for its impact on the enforcement of the competition rules (House of Lords 1993). In realizing its ambition to scrutinize the fact-finding of the Commission, and in undertaking fact-finding of its own, it has forced DG Competition to respond and correct its deficiencies. However, in the *PVC* case, the CFI overturned the Commission's fine only to have the Commission appeal against the decision directly to the ECJ, with the latter upholding the initial fining decision. In the *Italian Flat Glass* case, however, the CFI introduced a number of innovations, both procedural and substantive. It stressed the importance of a thorough economic analysis in investigations and accused the Commission of doctoring its evidence (Pope 1993:172). In the *Woodpulp* case the Commission was once again criticized because of its failure to provide a firm, precise and consistent body of evidence (Jones 1993). The CFI's willingness to act in defence of individual rights in a number of controversial areas was broadly commended, as was the thoroughness of its preparation, the conduct of its hearings and the quality of its judgments:

> Not only does [the CFI] have the effect of assuring companies that any Commission decision will be subject to a full review, it also clarifies for the Commission the standards of proof that it must respect in order to adopt an infringement decision in a contested case. [T]his has led to an improvement in the standards applied by the Commission. (House of Lords 1993)

This apparent willingness of the CFI to act as a check on the Commission's reasoning suggested that the CFI's approach would differ substantially from that of the ECJ. This was particularly impressive if one considers the teething problems that new courts tend to face.

It is only fair to balance this rather rosy account of the CFI against some of the criticisms it has provoked, although these too have to be considered in the context of what is an extremely new jurisdiction. One of the fundamental objectives of the CFI was the reduction of the backlog of cases before the ECJ and the cutting of waiting times. Its success has been short-lived in these respects, largely because more cases are now being handled by the Courts. Delays are now what they were when the CFI was set up, with critics arguing that the length of time between the closing of proceedings and the oral hearing, and between the hearing and the judgment, is still unacceptable. Although the CFI succeeded in relieving the ECJ of a huge number of competition cases, the basic problem remains.

National actors and European networks

The institutions of European competition governance stretch beyond those based in Brussels, Luxembourg and Strasbourg. Particularly where anti-trust cases are concerned, the Commission has been engaged since the mid 1990s in a process of decentralization of enforcement to both national courts and national competition authorities (NCAs). More recently this policy of decentralization has been given a further boost by the dual drivers of enlargement and modernization. By the late 1990s it was becoming clear that DG Competition would be unable to cope with the accession of more than 10 new member states, while maintaining the level of scrutiny it desired. Even with only 15 member states, the Commission was under pressure to find new ways to make its policy more efficient. The solution, proposed as part of the Commission's modernization agenda, and implemented within the new procedural regulation of 2004, was to allow national authorities and courts a greater formal role in the application of the competition provisions – not just Articles 81(1) and 82, but also the exemptions to the restrictive practices rule under Article 81(3) (see Chapter 4). Yet to do this at a time when the EU was enlarging, and when a large number of countries with relatively little experience of European competition enforcement were just coming to terms with the policy, seemed risky. Although not a foolproof solution, a more structured network of competition agencies was initiated to reinforce the common threads in the policy.

This took the form of a European Competition Network (ECN). The ECN is composed of the Commission and the NCAs, and is intended to 'ensure the effective and constituent application' of the EU's competition rules (Commission 2007b) by pooling experience, sharing information and identifying best practice. There was also a more practical role for the ECN in the allocation of cases across the Network, where there was some doubt as to who the lead actor should be. Thus, members of the ECN agree to provide information to the Network when a case having a Community dimension is notified, and also just before a formal decision is to be taken (Commission 2007a:point 67).

The setting up of the ECN is a political understanding (Commission 2004a) if only by default, as the Network does not have a legal personality. Its ultimate objective seems to be the creation of a common culture of competition enforcement across Europe (Commission 2006a). To that end, a range of activities have been organized under the ECN's auspices. In 2006, there were four sets of activities: (1) an annual meeting of the Director-General of DG Competition with the Heads of the NCAs; (2) plenary meetings of the Commission and NCA officials; (3) 6 working groups examining specific issues or sectors; (4) 15 sectoral sub-groups (Commission 2007a:point 69). Moreover, the Commission offers the NCAs advice on ongoing cases, whether on a formal or on an informal basis. It did this on around 125 occasions in 2006 (Commission 2007a:point 68). To date, the Commission points to an example, that of the adoption of a national leniency model, as an example of how the ECN has already been promoting best practice across its members (Commission 2006a: point 208)

The decentralization agenda touches not only the national competition authorities, however, but also the member states' courts. While the ECN does not actively involve the domestic courts as participants – so as to avoid accusations that the independence of the judiciary is being tainted – these courts are expected to apply EU competition law provisions directly. To assist in this process, the Commission co-finances training. There were 15 training sessions of this sort arranged in 2006, covering all 25 member states. Moreover, the Commission can also play a more active role in national competition cases, where the EU rules are applied. In 2006, for example, it offered an opinion on request to two member states (the Dutch and the Belgians) (Commission 2007a:point 71). It also acted as an amicus curiae, presenting observations to the French Court of Appeal on its interpretation of the Motor Vehicles Block Exemption Regulation (Commission 2007a:point 72). In return, domestic courts have certain responsibilities vis-à-vis the Commission, most notably in forwarding their relevant judgments to the Commission for uploading (where appropriate) on the DG Competition website. Member state courts sent thirty such judgments to the Commission in 2006 (Commission 2007a:point 71).

Disagreements remain about the likely effectiveness of the establishment of an ECN. Doubts also exist over the role of domestic courts in competition enforcement. Moreover, there is no agreement on how these steps taken by the Commission ought to be interpreted. On the one hand, the most obvious way to interpret this development is that it constitutes a willing sharing of responsibility and control for competition enforcement by the Commission. Thus, the Commission, in recognizing that it does not have the resources to manage EU competition policy single-handedly, devolves certain aspects of control to domestic regimes, while compensating for this by establishing informal support mechanisms which – it is hoped – will help to sustain the system. The danger, as noted above, is that decentralization might lead ultimately to fragmentation, especially with an EU of twenty-seven (and many member states new to the EU regime).

An alternative interpretation, however, is that the Commission hopes to reinforce and strengthen its position as a kind of network manager in the process of decentralization. The Commission is not handing control over to the national regimes, but is creating the beginnings of a federalized system of enforcement. Its role is guaranteed at the head of that system, as it is the Commission which shapes the policy direction and retains ultimate control where disputes and disagreements arise. This is close to Wilks's (2005a) argument, which suggests that the Commission is centralizing control under the guise of decentralization.

Conclusion

This chapter has introduced the main competition policy institutions, the European Commission and the two European Courts. It has also discussed changes to the institutional context within which competition policy is made and enforced, focusing on the growing network characteristics of the regime. Yet it is still the function performed by the supranational institutions and the relationship between them that is at the heart of the EU's competition policy.

In order to understand the European competition regime, it is essential to have some understanding of the institutional context within which the policy operates, as it is the centrality of the

Commission and the Courts and the powers they wield which make European competition policy so unique and, indeed, so controversial. The Commission in particular plays a distinctive role, one in practice far removed from the purely executive or secretariat-like functions which are its formal function. However, this is not to say that the Commission acts independently when it acts as a European competition regulator. To say this would be to underestimate the importance of the Courts, and indeed the Council and Parliament (albeit informally) in determining the framework for Commission activism in the field of competition policy.

Chapter 4

Restrictive Practices Policy

Cartels and other forms of restrictive practice have long represented a standard feature of business activity. Today all forms of such collusive and secret agreements to undermine the competitive process are generally condemned, but this has not always been the case. Any assessment of national cartel laws in Europe need to be placed within two distinct time frames. Prior to 1945 cartels and restrictive practices were tolerated across Europe and even encouraged in the German-speaking states. In the period after 1945, however, a new anti-cartel ethos took hold, with the active support of the US Administration and further encouraged in the cartel provisions of the ECSC.

This chapter provides an overview of the European Commission's restrictive practices policy and focuses specifically on the pursuit, identification and termination of cartel arrangements. The Commission's strategies to unearth cartels have often been overshadowed by the seemingly more glamorous policy on mergers (Chapter 6) and the more politicized issue of state aids (Chapter 7). However, cartels have consumed most of the Commission's time, resources and efforts since the 1960s, and embody the area of EU competition policy that has been subject to almost constant revision since the end of the 1980s.

Yet cartels are an established feature of international business activity and pressure continues to intensify for action against them. According to Neelie Kroes, Competition Commissioner in the Barroso Commission (2004–): 'in the end, cartels make Europe less competitive and put the brakes on our future economic growth. Why invest, why innovate, when you can sit back and profit unfairly from an illegally engineered allocation of resources?' (Kroes 2007). From her arrival in office in 2004 Kroes has made cartel-busting her number-one priority. This focus on cartels within the EU competition regime reflects a variety of changes that include: amendments to the EU restrictive practices regime under Regulation 1/2003, operational since May 2004; the arrival of a new and determined Competition Commissioner in November

2004; the restructuring of DG Competition and the creation of a 'bespoke' anti-cartel unit; the revision of a highly effective leniency programme in 2002; and, significantly, a new and tougher Notice on fining infringements, introduced in October 2006.

It is now widely believed that cartels constitute the most pernicious form of anti-competitive behaviour. They arise when companies participate in 'deliberate, highly organized and covert collaborative' (Harding and Joshua 2003:1) practices that have been agreed by a number of independent firms from the same or from a similar sphere of economic activity. For firms, recourse to cartelization in the short term may indeed prove beneficial, but in the longer term what are deemed hard-core cartel arrangements are certain to have serious and detrimental repercussions. This is because in shielding their participants from competition they work to the detriment of the consumer (in terms of quality and price) and undermine overall competitiveness of the economy. These secret agreements take a wide variety of forms but most often comprise agreements that divide markets, fix prices and prevent newcomers from entering the market. These collusive agreements harm the competitive process. Condemnation of cartel agreements has become the norm today and their continuing existence has even been labelled as akin 'to cancers on the open market economy' (Monti 2000).

This chapter begins with an introduction to Article 81 of the EC Treaty, the provision dealing specifically with restrictive agreements. From this starting-point, a number of legal issues are explored, including the relevance of the distinction used in American anti-trust law between *per se* illegality and the 'rule of reason'. After outlining the scope of Article 81, we turn to consider the possibilities for exemption from the EU's restrictive practices rules, before outlining Commission policy towards horizontal and vertical restraints of trade, and joint ventures. The chapter then addresses changes in contemporary cartel policy, highlighting recent developments, trends and issues in the European-level regulation of restrictive practices, placing particular reference on the ever higher fines being imposed by the Commission on companies for violations of Article 81.

Article 81: regulating restrictive practices

Restrictive practices policy has always constituted the core activity of DG Competition's activities and such anti-competitive activities were the very first target identified in the competition policy chapter within the European Economic Community (EEC) Treaty of 1957. Article 81 (formerly 85) under the Treaty prohibits all agreements 'which may affect trade between Member States and which have as their object, the prevention, restriction or distortion of competition within the common market'.

The malignant threat posed by cartelization for both the European business environment and the European consumer was therefore signposted from the very beginning of the European integration process. Both historical experience and treaty objectives necessitated this emphasis. Hans von der Groeben, the very first competition Commissioner, sought to create nothing less than a European *Wettbewerbsordnung* or competition order. When he addressed the European Parliamentary Assembly he argued that:

> it is . . . beyond dispute . . . that it would be useless to bring down trade barriers between Member States if . . . private industry were to remain free . . . through cartel like restrictions on competition, virtually to undo the opening of their markets. (von der Groeben 1961)

Framed in very general terms, Article 81 comprises three paragraphs (see Box 4.1). It seeks to catch almost all agreements between firms, including anti-competitive agreements between direct competitors (horizontal restraints), and anti-competitive agreements between firms involved in different stages of the production/distribution/marketing process within a particular market (vertical restraints). The first paragraph clearly established the type and characteristics of anti-competitive activities that were not permissible. Where doubts existed over the legality of certain agreements it was possible for the relevant parties to notify the Commission and seek advice and hope for clearance.

Paragraph (1) of Article 81 prohibits agreements which affect trade between the member states, where they have as their objective or effect the prevention, restriction or distortion of competition within the common (or single) market. It identifies a number of agreements, decisions and concerted practices as incompatible with the common market, namely:

- Those that directly or indirectly fix purchase or selling prices or any other trading conditions.

- Those that limit or control production, markets, technical development or investment.
- Those that share out markets or sources of supply.
- Those that apply dissimilar conditions to equivalent transactions with other trading parties, thereby placing them at a competitive disadvantage.
- Those that make the conclusion of contracts subject to acceptance by the other parties of supplementary obligations which, by their nature or according to commercial usage, have no connection with the subject of such contracts.

Article 81(1) applies to both concerted practices which are agreed informally, where little documentary evidence exists to establish collusion, and to well-documented cases of concerted parallelism. Detection of such practices has never been straightforward, however, and case investigations not only have been drawn-out affairs, consuming DG Competition's efforts and energies, but also have on occasions been hampered and rendered unsuccessful on appeal to the Courts, owing to the lack of definitive proof. Many Commission decisions have been appealed to the European courts and in some cases this has proved disastrous for DG Competition (Whish 2003:474). Such difficulties were all readily apparent in the landmark *Polypropylene* case from 1986 for example, when the Commission's decision against fifteen petrochemicals firms who had simply engineered a market-rigging cartel through an oral agreement was largely confirmed, but when the fines were substantially reduced by the CFI and later upheld by the ECJ.

The second paragraph (Article 81(2)) declares that agreements or decisions that the Commission judges to run counter to Article 81(1) are prohibited and are thus automatically void, though there are legal issues over whether the entire agreement is void or whether it is only the offending part of the arrangement that is prohibited. At first sight this seems to be what the Americans call a per se rule. The concept of '*per se*' illegality derives from US anti-trust law as set out in the 1890 Sherman Act. In essence, the US model categorizes all named anti-competitive agreements as illegal, with no exceptions to the rule. This reflects the US regime's aversion to any concentration of economic power. In addition, arguments in favour of the introduction of a US-style rule-of-reason approach in the EU context arise from time to time. The rule of reason refers to a method used by the American courts to determine whether an

BOX 4.1   Article 81

1. The following shall be prohibited as incompatible with the common market: all agreements between undertakings, decisions by associations of undertakings and concerted practices which may affect trade between Member States and which have as their object or effect the prevention, restriction or distortion of competition within the common market, and in particular those which:
   a) directly or indirectly fix purchase or selling prices or any other trading conditions;
   b) limit or control production, markets, technical development or investment;
   c) share markets or sources of supply;
   d) apply dissimilar conditions to equivalent transactions with other trading parties thereby placing them at a competitive disadvantage
   e) make the conclusion of contracts subject to acceptance by the other parties of supplementary obligations which, by their nature or according to commercial usage, have no connection with the subject of such contracts.

2. Any agreements or decisions prohibited pursuant to this Article shall be automatically void.

3. The provisions of paragraph 1 may, however, be declared inapplicable in the case of:
   • any agreement or category of agreement between undertakings;
   • any decision or category of decisions by associations of undertaking;
   • any concerted practice or category of concerted practices;

   which contributes to improving the production or distribution of goods or to promoting technical or economic progress, while allowing consumers a fair share if the resulting benefit, and which does not:
   a) impose on the undertaking concerned restrictions which are not indispensable to the attainment of the objectives;
   b) afford such undertakings the possibility of eliminating competition in respect of a substantial part of the products in question.

agreement, which is not judged as illegal *per se*, does in fact result in a restraint of trade. This involves a detailed analysis by the courts of the pros and cons of the agreement. In the European context such an approach would require a more detailed economic investigation into agreements than is allowed for by the current analysis. DG Competition remains unconvinced that a rule-of-reason approach is necessary and claims that exemptions from the rule under Article 81(3), discussed below, provide enough of a safety valve for pro-competitive agreements, such as those involving research and development and intellectual property.

It is important to stress that the EU rules apply only in the first instance to agreements that threaten to have a detrimental impact on intra-European markets. In other words, agreements that are deemed to be of 'minor importance' and that fall under the so-called *de minimis* (or 'so minor as to merit disregard') rule are automatically cleared. The *de minimis* rule was established by the European Court of Justice (ECJ) in its *Völk v. Vervaecke* 1969 ruling, which stated that 'an agreement falls outside the prohibition in Article 81(1) where it has only an insignificant effect on the market, taking into account the weak position which the persons concerned have on the market of the product in question'. This ruling was extremely important as it meant that small-scale agreements would be excluded from the notification requirement. In a sense, the *de minimis* rule marks the dividing line between agreements that are to be dealt with at European level, that is, those likely to have an impact on the common market and those that remain the responsibility of national authorities. Guidelines in the form of a Commission Notice were produced on 3 September 1986 and have since been amended on several occasions. The latest Notice, published in 2001, served part of the Commission's modernization agenda (see Peeperkorn 2001) and aimed to reduce the compliance burden for smaller companies whose agreements, by the nature of their size and impact, did not restrict competition. This move also allowed DG Competition to focus its energies on the much more problematic agreements.

The amended Notice raised the *de minimis* to a 10 per cent market share for agreements between competitors and to 15 per cent for agreements between non-competitors. In short, agreements that fall below these new thresholds are judged not to possess even a minimum degree of market power and do not fall under Article 81. The Notice states that agreements between small and medium enterprises are rarely capable of affecting trade between the member states and do not fall under EU scrutiny. Agreements which exceed the thresholds do not always fall foul of the EU rules, however, as provisions exist for both individual exemption under Article 81(3) and group exemption through an existing block exemption.

The Article 81(3) exemption

Article 81(3) declares that Article 81(1) *may* be inapplicable where an agreement

> contributes to improving the production or distribution of goods or [promotes] technical or economic progress, whilst allowing consumers a fair share of the resulting benefit, and which does not (a) impose on the undertakings concerned restrictions which are not indispensable to the attainment of these objectives; [or] (b) afford such undertakings the possibility of eliminating competition in respect of a substantial part of the products in question.

Thus there are four conditions that an agreement must meet to qualify for exemption: the agreement must *benefit* the EU as a whole and its advantages must outweigh its disadvantages; it must produce a fair share of the benefits to consumers; any restriction to competition must be indispensable to attain the objectives sought; and there must be no substantial elimination of competition. In many ways contrasting the prohibitive rule in Article 81(1) against the exemption clauses in Article 81(3) demonstrates the flexibility of the EU's cartel provisions.

British Airways and Iberia/GB Airways applied for an 81(3) exemption in July 2002 to enable them to cooperate across their respective networks in terms of pricing, scheduling and pricing. Despite initial DG Competition concerns about consumer choice and price increases on certain shared routes where the airlines held between 50 and 100 per cent of the market (routes to and from London and Barcelona, and Madrid and Seville among others), the Commission approved the alliance, as its analysis illustrated the potential benefits to consumers travelling to non-EU destinations. For example, it was judged that the new alliance would provide Iberia's consumers with a wider range of routes to the Middle East and the Far East and GB's customers with greater choice if flying to Latin America. Approval was forthcoming, however, only when both companies agreed to free up some of their slots to other air-lines to and from the UK and Spain at selected airports (including London Gatwick and London Heathrow).

The Commission's freedom of manoeuvre within the framework provided by Article 81(3) often raises questions about whether restrictive practices policy might be used as an instrument of struc-tural policy. The Commission has in the past been sympathetic to the creation of 'crisis cartels', for example, where these have helped alleviate suffering in industries facing decline or recession, such as in the shipbuilding, coal and steel sectors. There are often time and other conditional limits on their sympathy, however. The under-lying assumption is that anti-competitive agreements may possess positive characteristics, which could compensate for their negative impact. As such, an element of judgment or discretion is required when undertaking this balance-sheet approach to assessing agree-ments, giving the Commission (that is, the responsible DG Competition officials) a flexibility which stretches far beyond the application of clearly established rules. Since the early 1960s, only the Commission has possessed the sole monopoly to grant exemp-tions under Article 81(3). Since 2004 there has been a major change in this aspect of cartel-busting.

Under the previous system, the Commission was swamped by a sea of notifications which produced an unmanageable workload for DG Competition, and more crucially prevented competition officials from being able to focus their energies on the most serious infringements. Regulation 1/2003 (Council 2003) was designed in part to assist the Commission in this respect. It abolished the noti-fication system and removed the Commission's exclusive right to exempt agreements. According to the Regulation, 'agreements, decisions and concerted practices caught by Article 81(1) of the Treaty which satisfy the conditions of Article 81(3) of the Treaty shall not be prohibited, no prior decision to that effect being required.' In other words agreements that meet the criteria set out in 81(3) are automatically exempt and no longer need be notified to the Commission. The undertakings concerned must be confident that their agreement and own 'self-assessment' would withstand investigation by either the Commission or a national competition authority.

The self-assessment exercise comprises two parts. In the first, parties to an agreement must determine whether their agreement has an anti-competitive objective or anti-competitive effects. If the answer is in the negative then the agreement is legal. If, however, the answer is positive then a second test follows. The second test establishes how far the anti-competitive effects of the agreement are outweighed by its pro-competitive effects. The Commission has published guidelines that are designed to allow companies to undertake their own 'self-assessment'. The balancing act between competitive and anti-competitive effects provides for a rule-of-reason approach and is moving DG Competition towards producing a more economics-based analysis on each of the four criteria outlined in 81(3) than it has in the past.

Block exemptions

A second route through to exemption following the Article 81(1) prohibition is the so-called block exemption. The block exemption originally emerged as a response by DG Competition to the huge number of cases that were notified to it following the introduction of the competition procedures under Regulation 17/62 (see Chapter 2). The task confronting DG Competition at this time was particularly problematic given its limited resources and a growing backlog of cases that had soared to 38,000 by the mid 1960s. The lengthy delays in dealing with the first round of notifications boded well neither for restrictive practices policy nor for DG Competition's reputation. The block exemption instrument offered a solution; it has since become a distinctive feature of European-level competition enforcement. Originally approved by the Council, responsibility has shifted to the Commission; DG Competition could allow its scarce resources to be devoted to the more important cases. These 'group' or 'block' exemptions allowed an agreement falling within its scope to be automatically exempt from Article 81(1). Where they applied, there would be no need for firms to obtain an individual Article 81(3) exemption.

Block exemptions provide some legal certainty for firms and have particularly benefited small and medium-medium enterprises (SMEs). There is even evidence that company lawyers now draft their agreements using the block exemption regulations as their starting-point in order to ensure that they fall within the Commission guidelines. As both policy statements and enforcement tools, they exclude the application of competition law for certain types of agreement (for example, liner agreements) and provide a dividing line between legal and illegal practice. Most block exemptions are adopted by the Commission but two current ones have been granted by the Council of Ministers on the areas of agreements in roads and inland waterways (Council 1968) and liner conferences in the maritime transport sector (Council 1986). The latter liner agreements or shipping conferences operate when a group of two or more vessel-operating carriers provide services on a particular route within specified geographical areas. Historically they have been granted some form of exemption or immunity from the competition rules in many jurisdictions. Practice within the EU has reflected this trend, though it should be noted that the Liner Conference Block Exemption is to be repealed from October 2008. There remain grey areas where the competition rules might apply, but the regulations also take these into consideration and make allowances for agreements that are not clear-cut. However, if there is any doubt, firms are wise to pursue the more conventional individual exemption route. This applies particularly when firms draft or alter their agreements to include provisions that are not covered by the block exemption.

A short examination of the history of the block exemption regulations reveals that they are frequently renewed and updated to take on board the latest data, and to build upon DG Competition's experience in specific areas. Updating may also be needed where there is new case-law. There are currently eight block exemption regulations in operation. These are listed in Box 4.2 and cover agreements on areas such as research and development, as well as specialization agreements.

Motor vehicles provide an interesting example of a block exemption in practice. Within this sector, restrictive supplier–dealer relationships have a direct impact on consumer choice in that they affect the maintenance and repair of motor vehicles. As a result, European consumer groups such as the European Bureau of Consumers' Unions (BEUC) have been putting pressure on the Commission to open up the market to enable motor vehicle dealers to sell cars and spare parts produced by a range of distributors. In the past, the supplier–dealer relationship has been a close one, with the dealers tied to one particular distributor and liable to penalties if that tie is broken. The latest block exemption regulations on vehicles (Commission 2002a) has gone some way towards responding to the concerns of the BEUC and other such organizations. They

BOX 4.2 Block exemptions regulations

Regulation 2790/1999	Vertical agreements: exclusive distribution
Regulation 2658/2000	Specialization agreements
Regulation 2659/2000	Research and development agreements
Regulation 1400/2002	Motor vehicles/distribution of cars
Regulation 358/2003	Insurance
Regulation 772/2004	Technology transfer
Regulation 1459/2006	Air transport

Source: http://ec.europa.eu/comm/competition/antitrust/legislation/entente3_en.html
European Communities, 1995–2008.

have allowed an injection of competition into the sector by permitting car dealers to sell the cars of rival manufacturers as long as this is done on different premises and as long as a distinct and separate legal entity is created for that purpose. Both regulations have also encouraged steps towards the opening up of the market for spare parts, and have enhanced the right of consumers to buy a car and have it repaired anywhere in the EU. However, they did nothing to address perhaps the longest-standing consumer complaint over persistent price differentials across the EU.

The application of the block exemption regulations has not been entirely problem-free, however. The relationship between national and European competition law is only one of the areas that have been problematic. For example, do national authorities have the right to override a block exemption if the agreement falls under the provisions of a national competition rule? As yet the Commission has failed to tackle this question, although it would be unwise for a national authority to intervene and apply its own stricter standards should such a case arise. So far it has been left to the ECJ and the

Court of First Instance (CFI) to address this question on a case-by-case basis.

There has also been criticism of the block exemption's lack of flexibility. The introduction of an 'opposition procedure' (borrowed from the German system) in some of the block exemption regulations has helped to dampen down criticism. The procedure introduces a special fast-track notification process in a number of grey areas. Where this applies and where the Commission does not respond to a notification within two months, an agreement is automatically approved.

In a major and much-welcomed development, at least from DG Competition's perspective, the Council opted to repeal its block exemption (Council 1986) for liner conferences on routes to and from the EU in September 2006. This decision followed an extensive three-year investigation into the shipping industry by DG Competition. Liner conferences have been an essential aspect of activity within shipping since the 1870s. However, they are no more than cartels by a different name, which determine issues such as prices and conditions of carriage. The repeal enters into force in October 2008 and promises to open up the shipping sector to greater competition and hopefully to lower transport costs. Both would be welcomed by consumers.

Policy practice

The active pursuit and condemnation of restrictive practices has formed the backbone of DG Competition's operations since its inception. Its activities on restraints of competition under Article 81 can be divided into three main areas: those that relate to horizontal agreements, those that relate to vertical agreements, and those that relate to joint ventures. There are a multitude of cases that have arisen under each of these headings (Goyder 2003; Whish 2003). Below we give some of the best-known examples that provide starting-points for further elaboration.

Horizontal agreements

Horizontal agreements are the product of arrangements between two or more firms at the same level of production. They involve firms that would be otherwise in direct competition with one another. In some ways horizontal restraints policy is the most straightforward of the Commission's competition policy responsibilities as, on the face of it, horizontal agreements have few redeeming features. They tend to divide up markets territorially and establish quotas or fix prices, with negative consequences both for the consumer and for market integration. Also frowned upon by the Commission under this heading are agreements dealing with terms and conditions, collusive tendering, and information and advertising. The prohibition of these sorts of agreement has become an Article 81 priority, as it is here that competition policy's pro-integration credentials are often proven. Horizontal restrictive practices continue to flourish within and outside the EU. On the one hand many prove short-lived and often fall apart before they are brought to the Commission's attention. On the other hand the most pernicious hard-core cartels are more persistent and problematic and tend to surface in key sectors that seem particularly prone to cartelization – most notably, steel, cement and pharmaceuticals.

The *Vitamins* case of 2001 provides an excellent example of such activity in the pharmaceuticals market. Until 2007 it held the somewhat dubious honour of constituting the highest fine (some €800m) in the history of EU cartel policy. As vitamins are used in a wide variety of products including cereals, biscuits, drinks and animal feed, this particular agreement had major financial benefits for consumers and the companies concerned. The decision followed a lengthy investigation of 8 companies (with Hoffmann-La Roche in the leadership role) that had sought to eliminate competition in 12 different vitamins markets. This global cartel operated from 1989 until its detection in 1999. It is interesting to note that the Commission dealt with several infringements involving the same companies in this one decision and treated them as a single conspiracy. It examined each company's importance in each of the vitamin markets in question and their world-wide annual turnover. The huge levy on one firm, Hoffmann-La Roche (€462m), reflected not only its role as the cartel instigator but also its accumulation of fines for each of the vitamins markets and was also a means of deterring, if possible, any repetition in the future. Some of the fines were later reduced on appeal to the courts.

More recently the European Commission fined four firms €345m for fixing prices and operating a cartel in the sale of acrylic glass products in the *Methacrylates* decision in May 2006. This case is illustrative of another characteristic of cartel-busting, namely the identification of repeat offenders. This raises questions about whether the severity of the fine can act as a deterrent. In this case the French group, a serial offender, was Arkema, which alongside the British firms ICI and Lucite, and the Irish business Quinn Barlo, was charged with fixing prices and exchanging sensitive market information between 1997 and 2002.

It would be misleading, however, to claim that all horizontal agreements are anti-competitive. Writing in 1988, Whish stated that '[e]ven restrictions on competition which appear to be detrimental to consumer welfare may have compensating advantages of which account should be taken' (Whish 1989:399). Certain categories of agreement clearly have the potential to be pro-competitive, or at the very least have redeeming features that justify exemption. On the whole, these types of agreement are covered by the block exemption regulations which establish the parameters within which cooperation among firms is permitted. Research and development, specialization and standardization agreements are perhaps the most obvious areas covered. The Commission favours agreements of this sort within certain clearly defined boundaries.

Vertical agreements

The Commission's policy on vertical restraints has always been much more contentious than its policy on horizontal agreements. While a balance is required in determining the pros and cons of all restrictive agreements, an assessment of vertical restraints is complicated by the fact that these arrangements often have pro- rather than anti-competitive effects. A vertical restraint involves an agreement between firms at different levels in a market: for example between supplier and distributor, or franchiser and franchisee. It may involve an exclusive distribution or purchasing deal, or regulate the operation of franchising arrangements. It tends to affect the conditions under which firms sell, buy or resell goods and services, with the large majority of agreements dealing with matters of distribution. Such agreements are often important to firms seeking to enter new markets or to expand within existing markets. They may also help to promote more efficient distribution networks and encourage inter-brand competition, which can have positive knock-on effects for the consumer. However, the positive, pro-competitive elements do not appear in all vertical restraints. In some cases, firms use this type of agreement to protect their markets from competition in a number of different ways: by limiting third-party access, by restricting access to distribution networks or even by encouraging restrictive practices between distributors. Where distribution is organized along national lines, vertical agreements may also fragment the single market and inhibit market integration. In such cases, deciding whether a vertical agreement restricts or promotes competition really depends on specific circumstances such as the nature of the commodity in question and the extent to which competition already exists in the market.

Volkswagen and Nintendo serve as two fairly recent instances of high-profile companies that had created artificial markets through recourse to vertical restraints. Car sales and especially price differentials within the EU market have always proven problematic and have been the subject of numerous complaints to DG Competition. In 1998 the Commission fined Volkswagen for prohibiting its Italian dealerships from supplying potential customers in Austria and Germany with lower-priced cars. This decision was duly appealed to (and confirmed by) the Court of First Instance, though it reduced the level of the fine from €102m to €90m. As a step towards providing greater transparency of prices and to ameliorate the situation, the Commission now publishes a six-monthly review of pre-tax car prices in each of the member states.

The Nintendo case in 2003 identified an anti-competitive agreement between the Japanese giant electronics company and seven of its official distributors in Europe. This deliberately sought to maintain high prices for games consoles and cartridges such as 'Game Boy' across the EU. The arrangement, which operated from 1991 until its detection in 1998, compelled each distributor to prevent exports (a form of parallel trade) from one territory (EU member state) to any other territory (EU member state) through unofficial distribution channels. Distributors who were party to this agreement and who ignored the provisions risked being boycotted by Nintendo or being supplied with smaller consignments. Ultimately Nintendo and its distributors were fined €168m. This case from October 2002 is noteworthy because the fine on Nintendo of €149m was at the time the highest on record for a vertical infringement.

Commission policy in this area has relied on the wide application of Article 81(1). This applies automatically to cases of resale price maintenance where agreements limit the freedom of distributors to set resale prices, and when agreements involve absolute territorial protection. Where this is the case, there is unlikely to be any scope for an Article 81(3) exemption. With all other vertical restraints, except those covered by the de minimis rule, a case-by-case approach is taken to see if Article 81(1) applies. However, given that many vertical agreements are in fact beneficial to competition, block exemption regulations perform an important function in the policy, setting out the categories of agreement that are automatically exempt.

Critics of the Commission's vertical restraints policy have pointed to a divergence between the analysis undertaken by DG Competition and the approach taken by the ECJ and the CFI in their judgments. The Commission has tended to play down the context within which an agreement is formed (most notably the impact on the market), focusing heavily on the analysis of clauses within the agreement. As one critic comments: 'the approach is formalistic in that it tends to abstract from the actual consequences of the restriction in its economic context' (Lugard 1996:167). The Courts and the CFI in particular, on the other hand, look consistently both at the object of the agreement and at the effects that it might have on competition. However, it is acknowledged that the Commission does not always take such a hard line. Even so, its apparently ad hoc approach to analysis is far from conducive to an atmosphere of legal certainty.

There has been criticism of the Commission's vertical restraints policy on a number of fronts. The breadth of Article 81(1) has been one bone of contention. This is not surprising given that even the Commission agrees that vertical agreements can have a positive impact. Many would argue that these agreements should not need an exemption as they should not in fact fall under Article 81(1) in the first place. Second, while block exemption regulations have been helpful in weeding out agreements that are clearly exempt under Article 81, they themselves have been labelled as overly formalistic and rigid. In addition, the fact that they fail to cover the full range of pro-competitive agreements has proven problematic. It implies that ostensibly beneficial agreements must be notified to the Commission individually and must face the delays that are now an inevitable part of the notification process.

Responding to a wave of seemingly constant criticisms, the Commission published its *Green Paper on Vertical Restraints* in January 1997 (Commission 1997a) and called for reactions to a list of options for possible reform. The approach in the Green Paper marked a sea-change in the Commission's line on this aspect of restrictive practices policy, and suggested a growing acceptance that the policy had indeed been too legalistic in the past, that it lacked flexibility and that a 'one-stop shop' for vertical agreements was necessary. This was the start of a real turnaround in the Commission's vertical restraints policy, potentially opening the door to a more liberal regime. More economic analysis on the relevant market, that is, on the context within which the agreement is formed (rather than on the nature of the agreement itself), was always likely to be the actual consequence, although the Commission was certainly keener to stress that the role of economic analysis will always be limited. As the Green Paper states:

> [i]t is clear that economic theory can not be the only factor in the design of policy. Firstly it is only one source of policy. Secondly a full evaluation of every individual case would be too costly in resource terms and may lead to legal insecurity. Its use is therefore primarily to help develop basic policy and rules. (Commission 1997a)

The challenge for the Commission was to reform the policy while at the same time keeping a firm hold on enforcement. Control, however, represented only one aim. Other, now familiar ones included greater legal certainty for firms, a speedier decision-making process, a consideration of the anti-competitive effects of the agreement and a convergence of Commission and Court thinking on policy (Lugard 1996:175). The four options suggested in the Green Paper – maintaining the current system, wider block exemptions, more focused block exemptions, and reduced scope of Article 81(1) – were all designed as ways to these ends. The Green Paper suggested that the reform of the block exemption instrument lay at the heart of the Commission's new approach to vertical restraints.

A follow-up document appeared and paved the way for the Commission's adoption of a new Verticals Regulation (Regulation 2790/1999; and see [1999] OJ L336/21) in December 1999 (Whish 2000) that sought a more flexible approach to the handling of vertical agreements. This new regulation entered into force on 1 January 2000 and replaced the earlier block exemptions on exclusive distribution, exclusive purchasing and franchising agreements. Effectively this new arrangement provided safety or a presumption of legality for all those agreements that centred on distribution where a market threshold of 30 per cent was not exceeded. Indeed, it was to be left to the firms involved to determine whether they met the criteria for an overall 81(3) exemption. In operation the new regulation should be regarded as a clear enhancement from the older block exemptions on vertical restraints but it would be foolish to ignore some of the continuing problems for firms, for example, when they try, as Jones and Sufrin argue, to construct agreements that contain both territorial and price constraints that impact directly on intra-brand competition (Jones and Sufrin 2008). No more significant movement in the area of vertical restraints is likely before the expiry of the current regulation in 2010.

Joint ventures

The term 'joint venture' applies to any commercial arrangement between two or more companies to describe an arrangement whereby the firms concerned (that is, the parent companies) agree to integrate their operations to secure a certain economic goal. Such alliances between two or more firms are constructed within a particular sector and are generally intended as a way to facilitate joint research and development, or the setting up of a joint distribution service. As such, they may exist as either horizontal or vertical agreements. Article 81 concerns itself with so-called 'cooperative' joint ventures, agreements that lead to the creation of a firm which is auxiliary to its parents. This type of agreement, it must be stressed, is distinct from a 'concentrative' joint venture, or a merger-style agreement that is treated in the same way as concentrations, and as such falls within the merger rules (see Chapter 6). DG Competition's task is, first of all, to determine the type of joint venture and then to assess the extent to which this form of cooperation is likely to affect competition within the EU.

Increasingly, European firms are turning to transnational joint ventures as a way of establishing collaborative projects and forging strategic alliances, especially where markets are judged to be global. There has been strong evidence over the last decade of increased joint venture activity in the information technology sectors, in telecommunications and in the transport industries. Cooperation of this sort does not necessarily infringe the Commission's competition rules. Indeed DG Competition has been keen to reassess the stringency of its rules on joint ventures where international competitiveness may be enhanced. As such it takes a positive view of cooperative joint ventures which it sees as a potential source of efficiency and technological innovation, ultimately benefiting the consumer. Where this is judged to be the case the joint venture is likely to be approved.

In the telecommunications sector from the mid 1990s there were a number of agreements of note, such as between British Telecommunications and the US-based MCI Corporation to establish a joint venture called Concert; and between France Télécom and Deutsche Telekom, two of Europe's telecommunications giants, to establish the Atlas Phoenix venture. The rationale for these joint ventures rested on the potential benefits of cooperation in the telecommunications sector and the contribution that might be made to the quality and availability of advanced technology. Ten years later the potential for this rapidly changing and competitive sector to engineer joint ventures had not diminished. For example, in 2003 the Commission concluded that an agreement between T-Mobile and MMO2 (and now known as Telefonica O2 Europe) on site-sharing and national roaming did not contravene Article 81 because it did not concern the basic network infrastructure. In this instance the Commission was convinced that this agreement allowed both parties to differentiate their services, and thereby to compete. In the same year the Commission also gave the green light to an agreement between Teleno Broadband, Canal+ and Canal Digital which related to pay television channels.

It is not only within the telecoms industry that the Commission has taken a positive line on joint ventures. It has also been supportive of attempts to establish joint research programmes and facilitate production techniques in a number of other sectors. In March 2006 the Commission approved a joint venture between SONY and NEC that specifically sought to develop, design and market an optical data storage disk drive that incorporates both rewritable CDs and DVDs. Such cooperation promises technological advances and does not severely restrict competition given the other players in this market (and these include Hitachi, Panasonic, Pioneer, Samsung and Toshiba).

In the end every cooperative joint venture that comes before the Commission is different and its assessment will turn on the actual facts relating to the case. The central part of any case centres on an economic analysis of whether the agreement actually restricts competition. It is realistic to conclude that the abolition of the notification system under Regulation 1/2003 and the new 'self-assessment' approach must place a considerable burden on any firms interested in pursuing a joint venture.

Assessing restrictive practices policy

Any exploration of the EU's restrictive practices policy uncovers four distinct temporal phases of historical development. The first, which occurs during the late 1960s and 1970s, was largely exploratory in nature as the Commission sought to develop its procedural practices and train its staff, appreciate its powers and gain experience, especially vis-à-vis its relationship with the Court of Justice. Attention focused at this time frame on vertical restraints, but gave way to a more confident second phase in the 1980s that led to a growing number of substantive DG Competition investigations. The most notable development in this decade was a growing determination on the part of DG Competition to really start to levy harsher fines on companies breaching the restrictive practices rules, especially those engaging in horizontal agreements. Regulation 17/62 provided for the imposition of fines for breaches of Article 81. There was, however, little in the way of any detailed provision on a fining regime and it was certainly not made clear whether the fines were supposed to punish or to act as a deterrent, but fines could be imposed for as much as up to 10 per cent of the previous year's annual turnover. By the standards of 2008 the initial fines appear somewhat modest but their significance should not be underplayed and in themselves marked a decisive moment in the development of EU competition policy.

The very first case occurred in 1969 when the Commission imposed a fine of some 500,000 units of account in the *Quinine* case. Fines remained relatively modest over the next fifteen years (for example, an ECU1,250,000 fine was imposed in the *Cast Iron and Steel Works* case in 1983. In retrospect, the beginnings of a decisive shift in fining policy and a move to steeper fines in an effort to penalize companies can be found in the Commission's XIIIth Report on Competition Policy (Commission 1983:62). From the mid 1980s it is possible to detect an upward trend in the imposition of fines. The sea-change was illustrated with the ECU58m and ECU23.1m fines in the *Polypropylene* and *PVC* cases in 1986 and 1989 respectively and has seen the fourteen highest fines in the history of EU cartel policy levied after 2000 (see Table 4.1).

Table 4.1   Selected fines under Article 81, 1994–2004

Decision	Date	Size of fine
HOV SVZ/MCN	1994	ECU11m
Euro beam producers	1994	ECU104m
Cartonboard	1994	ECU132m
Ciment	1994	ECU248m
Far Eastern Freight Conference	1994	ECU10,000
Tretorn and others	1994	ECU640,000
PVC	1995	ECU25m
BASF/Accinato	1995	ECU2.7m
Adalat	1996	ECU3m
Ferry Operators	1996	ECU645,000
Novalliance	1996	ECU100,000
VW Audi	1998	ECU102m
British Sugar/Tate & Lyle	1998	ECU50.2m
Preinsulated Pipes	1998	ECU92.21m
Stainless Steel Flat Producers	1998	ECU27.3m
Greek Ferry Operators	1998	ECU9.12m
Vitamins	2001	€855m
BASF	2001	€296m
Arjo Wiggins (paper)	2001	€184m
Plasterboard	2002	€478m
Nintendo	2002	€149m
Aventis Pharma	2002	€2.85m
Nucleotides	2002	€20.56m
Speciality Graphites	2002	€60.6m
Concrete	2002	€85m
Yamaha	2002	€2.86m
Sorbates (chemicals)	2003	€134.4m
Beer	2003	€90m

DG Competition's determination intensified as its metamorphosis into a fully fledged and powerful competition regulator took place in the late 1980s and 1990s and fines grew in size (see Table 4.2) as anticipated after the publication of the Commission's XXIst annual competition policy report (Commission 1992:para. 139) and is illustrated by DG Competition's determination to get nearer to the 10 per cent annual turnover mark. This third stage also saw significant legal challenges and overrules of Commission decisions by the European Courts. Part of the problem, of course, was the absence of specific rules, and the Commission's wide degree of discretion throughout the investigative and decision-making processes convinced some that the Commission made up its cartel policy as it went along. Such criticisms and doubts led the Commission to publish its first Guidelines on its fining policy. This notice, other inventive tools and a new Council regulation have enabled the Commission to intensify its pursuit of cartels after 2000, in the fourth phase of activity, as discussed below.

DG Competition's record of cartel-busting activities, particularly since the early 1990s, has been impressive. Horizontal price-fixing and market-sharing agreements have been attacked robustly and vociferously. Action has also been taken against common sales syndicates where price-fixing has formed an important part of the agreement, against deals which by their very nature have meant restrictions to competition through the application of quotas and output rates, and against pacts in favour of territorial market-sharing. DG Competition has obstructed the abuse of intellectual property rights, opposed export bans and discriminatory distribution agreements and various other exclusive distribution and licensing arrangements.

The Commission clearly enjoys a formidable regulatory role in the competition policy arena and considerable discretion in the imposition of fines. It has turned cartel policy into a success story and along the way has revealed degrees of ingenuity to facilitate its work. Specifically the Commission has used its authority and powers to create norm-interpreting administrative rules which take the form of guidelines, communications, notices and letters (see Hofmann 2006). Together these have allowed DG Competition to develop and deploy a simultaneous carrot-and-stick approach to uncover and combat cartelization and tackle the backlog of outstanding cases. This chapter can only provide an overview of what is a fascinating case-study on EU policy.

The stick is best illustrated in more repressive measures to penalize and therefore deter the attractiveness of cartel arrangements through resort to higher fines. The Commission revised its guidelines on the method of setting fines in June 2006. The latest guidelines updated the original 1998 Notice and effectively now define more clearly the methodology the Commission uses when it sets fines. The latest Guidelines seek to overcome some of the perceived shortcomings, to reflect the Commission's latest approaches

Table 4.2   The fourteen largest fines

Case name	Year fine imposed	Amount of fine (€)
Elevators and Escalators	2007	992.3m
Vitamins	2001	790.5m
Gas Insulated Switchgear	2007	750.7m
Synthetic Rubber	2006	519m
Flat Glass	2007	486.9m
Plasterboard	2002	478.3m
Hydrogen peroxide	2006	388.1m
Methacrylates (Glass)	2006	345m
Hard Haberdashery/Fasteners	2007	328.6m
Fittings	2006	314.7m
Carbonless Paper	2001	313.6m
Industrial Bags	2005	290.7m
Dutch Brewers	2007	273.7m
Bitumen	2006	266.6m

Source: http://ec.europa.eu/comm/competition/cartels/statistics/statistics.pdf (accessed 4 February 2008).

and to incorporate judgments from the European courts. In short, they not only have been designed as a means to provide both greater transparency for the business community but also have afforded the Commission the opportunity to steer policy along more 'draconian' lines (Jones and Sufrin 2008:1228). The revised 2006 guidelines state that fines will now be calculated on a proportion of the value of sales (and not as before on the seriousness categorization of the actual activity; see McGowan 2000). Under these new rules companies are automatically fined a so-called 'entry fee' and this amounts to something in the region of 15–25 per cent of their specific annual turnover from the infringement in question while repeat offenders can expect even tougher financial levies, as Shell experienced in *Bitumen* in 2006. In *Bitumen* the highest individual fine fell on Shell (€80m) and the decision reflected the Commission's determination to punish habitual cartel offenders (given Shell's earlier involvement in the *PVC* and *Polypropylene* cases). The fact that many companies will re-engage in cartel activity aptly illustrates the value and the financial advantages of a cartel arrangement. Fines need to bite harder but just how much harder remains open to debate.

An alternative and more imaginative option for removing and destabilizing cartels has seen the Commission introduce 'sweeteners'. The Commission's 1996 Leniency Notice or 'Whistleblowers Notice', which was further revised in 2002 and more recently in 2006, is the best illustration of this approach as it sought to reduce DG Competition's backlog by encouraging cartel members to inform on their colleagues in the expectation of substantially reduced fines and even total immunity. Interestingly, the original Notice had referred only to the possibility of a 75 per cent reduction from the final fine and simply overlooked the issue of total immunity. Complete immunity has been added in the later notices but is available only for the first informant who provides sufficient information for the Commission to launch an inspection of premises and only if they provide sufficient information and continue to cooperate throughout the investigation. For example, in 2003 a Japanese firm, Chrisso Corporation, was granted complete immunity when it brought to the Commission's attention a price-fixing and market-allocating cartel in the sorbates market. (Sorbates are a chemical preservative used to prevent the emergence of moulds and bacteria in foods and beverages.) This infringement had been in operation from 1978 to 1996. Following an investigation, the Commission fined four companies €138.4m. The German giant Hoechst suffered the bulk of this fine (some €99m).

Immunity for only one company often increases the incentive to provide evidence before one of the other cartel members does and further enhances cartel instability. Companies which do not meet the criteria for complete immunity can also hope to benefit from a reduction in the fine they receive if they can contribute to the DG Competition's investigation. Whereas experience of the first programme occasioned reluctance towards this Commission initiative (Reynolds and Anderson 2006) and concerns about potential subjective evaluation on the part of the Commission, the policy has proved very effective and in most case where cartels are now being discovered and unravelled by the Commission this follows the receipt of insider evidence. Indeed, whereas the Commission received 80 applications (both for total immunity and a reduction in fines) in the period from 1996 to 2002, it is interesting to note that following the introduction of the 2002 Notice such requests rose to 186 and 79 for a reduction in fines (between 2002 and 2006). It is interestingly to note that total immunity was provided for the main whistleblower in every one of the Commission's cartel decisions in 2006. For example, in *Bitumen* BP's role as a whistleblower ensured total immunity from a Commission fine for cartel activity among oil producers.

The publication of the most recent Leniency Notice in December 2006 reinforced the fundamental shift in attitude by the business community towards the leniency initiative. This revised *Notice on Immunity from Fines and Reduction of Fines in Cartel Cases* represented another significant step in both the detection and the termination of hard-core cartel activity. It clarified the information the Commission demands if an undertaking is to benefit from immunity, as well as providing greater guidance on how to obtain a reduction in fines. The Notice even provides for a discretionary 'marker system' whereby an applicant is allowed to reserve its place at the front of the informant queue and can supply further information later.

Thus far, the leniency strategy has been a success. Nevertheless, DG Competition has still found itself incapable of dealing with all suspected cartels on account of its relatively scarce resources. Groups such as the European Round Table of Industrialists (ERT) have long argued that insufficient staffing is a major problem for the EU competition regime. This reality can simply not be denied, but the lack of staff continuously propels DG Competition to come up with ever new means to allow it to prioritize cases and eliminate the backlog.

The origins of the 2004 reforms should be viewed as part of this agenda and form part of an ongoing comprehensive review process to modernize, simplify and improve the administrative machinery to help tackle cartelization. The first of the two main factors pushing the reform was recognition that the existing practices that had been in place for over forty years were becoming problematic as the EU competition authorities were always struggling to clear the accumulating backlog of cases. Alongside block exemptions the granting of comfort letters from the 1960s onwards had been designed as a mechanism to free much-needed DG Competition resources, but these were only a partial solution. The receipt of a comfort letter effectively signalled the Commission's approval of a particular agreement, which was not deemed to breach the competition rules and was therefore legal. They were much sought after by companies. Was there a better means to focus DG Competition's more limited resources on the most pressing cases? The second factor centred on the prospects of an increasing caseload after further EU waves of enlargement. The reform sought to provide a more efficient protection of competition by refocusing Commission action on enforcement, the creation of a more level playing-field and a greater degree of predictability for the business community, while reducing the more bureaucratic characteristics of the regime.

The 'old' framework placed responsibility on the Commission for administering and enforcing the competition rules. This may have made sense when the competition regime was first set up, but the requirement that all agreements that potentially violated Article 81 had to be notified, especially if an exemption was sought, proved extremely time-consuming. This centralized system pushed DG Competition into reactive mode, leaving it to process notifications while hard-core cartels went unpunished. Block exemptions and *de minimis* thresholds may have been used to lessen DG Competition's workload, but they did not come close to eradicating the backlog of cases, which stood at more than 1,000 for most of the 1990s. EU enlargement to 25 and now 27 may not have meant paralysis but it certainly threatened to undermine the effectiveness of the EU competition regime: hence pressure built up for a reform of administrative and procedural practices, the product of which was Regulation 1/2003.

This Regulation can be summarized neatly under three key headings: the abolition of the notification system; the decentralization and sharing of enforcement power with the member states to ensure uniformity in the application of rules; and lastly, enhanced powers for the Commission. Taking these reforms together, this new Regulation marked a substantial shift in the administration of the policy. Firms who wish to abide by the rules now need to familiarize themselves with the new regime as all 'agreements, decisions and concerted practices caught by Article 81(1) of the Treaty which do not satisfy the conditions of Article 81(3) of the Treaty shall be prohibited, no prior decision to that effect being necessary' (Article 1, Regulation 1/2003). In marked contrast, firms involved in cartel activity need to realize that the odds of being detected have increased considerably.

The reforms established a system of parallel competences and a flexible mechanism for case allocation between the national and supranational levels. Thus, at its heart, the new Regulation sought to enable the national competition authorities to apply Article 81 directly to any agreement which may affect trade between states. Consequently, as Goyder (2003:551) remarked, 'the long running uncertainty about the rights of such national authorities to apply national law that is stricter than Community law has been removed since it is no longer allowed'. Put another way, the Regulation means that the status and authority of the national competition bodies have been transformed into something very akin to anti-cartel agencies of the European Commission. Thus this Regulation represents a seismic change in the interactions between the EU actors and the national competition authorities (NCAs) while illustrating the extent to which EU restrictive practices policy has become Europeanized (see Chapter 8); but does it work?

The age of aggressive enforcement: the situation after 2004

Cartel policy has moved centre stage over the last decade. There is, of course, nothing particularly new in this anti-cartel drive, but current opportunity structures and internal developments suggest that the focus on cartel policy is here to stay for the time being. DG Competition's almost missionary zeal, its commitment and its harsh stance on cartels have nurtured a pro-competition bias among all its officials. In terms of management, DG Competition has undergone a number of regular administrative changes that have been designed to improve its administrative efficiency by enabling it primarily to become more proactively engaged in detecting and dissolving cartels. One of the most significant developments in recent years was the creation of a new dedicated Cartels Directorate to combat hard-core cartels in 2005. This new directorate commenced operations in June 2005 and is staffed by some 60 personnel of whom two-thirds are case-handlers. It is tasked with streamlining and accelerating the number of investigations and plays a leading role in liaising with the Directorate for Policy and Strategic Support in developing cartel policy.

Regulation 1/2003 can be portrayed as a means of modernizing the EU's restrictive practices regime; but in another major landmark it also entails the decentralization of anti-trust that both allows and enables the national competition authorities (NCAs) to be involved directly with decision-making. For decentralization to

---

BOX 4.3   The lifts and escalators cartel

In February 2007 the Commission imposed its highest fine to date of €990m on bid-rigging cartels that had deliberately been created to deal with the installation and maintenance of lifts and escalators in hospitals, railway stations and shopping centres throughout Belgium, Germany, Luxembourg and the Netherlands. The lifts and escalators cartel comprised 17 subsidiaries of the Otis, KONE, Schindler and ThyssenKrupp companies and had been in operation between 1995 and 2004. It had also included the active involvement of Mitsubishi Elevator Europe in the Dutch market. This particular cartel had angered DG Competition, not only on account of both the wide geographical market that its instigators had covered (given the limited number of lift manufacturers) and the maintenance contracts which would keep the firms active for years to come but also because this cartel arrangement had even fitted out the refurbishments to the Berlaymont building and the European courts in Luxembourg. DG Competition's investigation of this suspected cartel began with a number of 'dawn raids' on the premises of the companies in question in January 2004. These inspections confirmed suspicions of cartel activity. In response the companies immediately filed for immunity or at least a reduction in fines for providing information on the cartel.

This particular Article 81 violation epitomizes the archetypal and classic form of a cartel as its members had rigged the bids for procurement markets, fixed prices, allocated projects to each other and not only shared markets but exchanged both commercial and confidential information (on bidding practices and prices). The seriousness of the infringement was never going to be in question. The Competition Commissioner, Neelie Kroes, stated that   ➡

---

work, consistency of both purpose and rules across all 27 NCAs had to be ensured and this meant not only the adoption of the EU rules in all member states but also more contact between the NCAs and the Commission. The new relationship between the Commission and national authorities centres on the European Competition Network (ECN) and foresees an improvement in horizontal and vertical exchanges of information, consultation and interaction across all member states both over policy in general and over individual cases. It can be read as an ingenious mechanism to foster and develop a consistent competition culture across the EU.

it is outrageous that the construction and maintenance costs of buildings, including hospitals, have been artificially bloated by these cartels. The national management of these companies knew what they were doing was wrong, but they tried to conceal their action and went ahead anyway.

This was a serious accusation for the managers of each of the companies if true and DG Competition collected evidence that many of the meetings relating to the cartel's operations were taken in bars and restaurants and that the managers even used prepaid mobile phone cards to avoid detection and tracking.

The cartel represented one of the worst infringements of Article 81 in the EU's anti-trust history and the amount of the overall fine reflected the size of the market, the duration of the agreement and the weight of the firms involved. It is significant to note that they even tried to share their involvement within the Commission's leniency programme. The KONE subsidiaries were granted full immunity from the fines in respect of the cartels' operations relating specifically to Belgium and Luxembourg while Otis received the same outcome for providing the first information on the activities of the cartel's activities in the Netherlands. ThysssenKrupp were far less fortunate and given their role as a repeat offender had their fines increased by some 50 per cent and faced a final bill of €480m. It should be noted that the cartel's impact extends far beyond the dissolution of the agreement in question, as many of the purchasers of these lifts and escalators are already tied to these companies for regular maintenance and repairs for the foreseeable future.

Individual case allocation under Article 81 is determined following discussions within the Network, and in most instances this does not prove too problematic as it is clear which authority is best placed to handle the case. All information forwarded to DG Competition prior to the start of any investigation is also transmitted as a matter of course to all members of the Network. This is particularly useful as it avoids parallel proceedings and reinforces the one-stop-shop principle. In operation the ECN is expected to strengthen information symmetry and reduce conflict. The significant point here is that the ECN aims to strengthen the emerging 'federal' relationship.

Table 4.3   Commission cartel decisions, 2003–07

Year	Number
2003	5
2004	7
2005	5
2006	7
2007	8
2008 (to February)	1
Total	33

Source: European Commission at: http://ec.europa.eu/comm/competition/cartels/ statistics/statistics.pdf (accessed on 4. February 2008)

However, the Commission is empowered to investigate any case of its choosing involving intra-state trade, and when it does so the national competition authorities will cease (see Article 11(6)) any investigation already underway. Such intervention from DG Competition, however, is expected only in exceptional circumstances. Nevertheless, this point raises interesting questions about where power actually resides. This issue will require greater exploration as cases come forward in case potential tensions between the Commission and member state authorities arise.

Referrals to the national level have been problematic in the past in relation to EU merger control, but it is still too early to provide an assessment of how the policy is working in practice. According to the Commission, the ECN is already proving effective as a forum for consultation and information exchange. One of the first positive outcomes of such dialogue is the readiness of national competition authorities to alert the Commission and other ECN members to potential cartel infringements, and thereafter to embark on joint cooperation at the very early stages of investigations. The *Italian Flat Glass* case which culminated in the Commission assuming responsibility for the case is a prime example of this. In 2005 the Commission was notified of 180 new case investigations by the NCAs. The potential risk of conflict between the national and supranational competition authorities did not materialize initially and the first year passed without any contentious issues arising. Indeed, very few individual cases have changed

Table 4.4　Cartel fines (not corrected by Court judgments) 2003–08

Year	Amount (€)
2003	404.8m
2004	390.2m
2005	683m
2006	1,846m
2007	3.334m
2008 (until February)	34.230m
Total	6, 682m

Source: http://ec.europa.eu/comm/competition/cartels/statistics/statistics.pdf (accessed 4 February 2008) © European Communities 1995–2008.

hands. A closer examination of the settled formal cases in 2005 illustrates some success in the fight against cartels and the further development of case-law.

The Commission's determination to hunt cartels has intensified after 2004, and its efforts represent what amount to some of the most notable years in DG Competition's entire history of cartel-busting. The figures in Table 4.4 demonstrate the Commission's heightened activity. Eight cartels involving some 45 companies were unearthed and fined in 2007. The highest fine ever was imposed recently in the lifts and escalators cartel in March 2007 (see Box 4.3) and helped to push the overall total size of the fines for that year past the €3.3m mark.

Once again chemicals and pharmaceutical cartels featured in DG Competition's investigations, and seven companies were fined a total of €388m for operating a cartel that exchanged commercially important and confidential information, limited output and allocated both market share and customers. The firms involved were the Belgian Solvay, the Dutch Akzo Nobel, Finland's Kemira, France's Arkema, Snia and Edison from Italy, and Spain's FMC Foret.

Such cases reflect the Commission's determination to prosecute EU-wide cartels but they are also designed as a means of deterring the creation of many more. The leniency programme continues to play a crucial role in DG Competition's detection efforts, enticing 'whistle-blowers' to come forward. Interestingly, the fortunes for the companies concerned are mixed. For example, in the *Mono-*

chlororacetic Acid (MCAA) case, Clariant cooperated with the Commission under the terms of the 1996 Leniency Programme and obtained total immunity. However, in the very first decision stemming from the 2002 Notice in *Raw Tobacco Italy* the original whistleblower's hope of conditional immunity was dashed when it was discovered that it (Deltafina) had actually pre-alerted its competitors/cartel members to the pending Commission investigation. Nevertheless, Deltafina was deemed to have provided sufficient information to warrant a 50 per cent reduction in the level of the fine. The *Plastic Industrial Bags* case began likewise with information from a cartel member (British Polythene Industries) and in the final Commission judgment it saw an additional increase in the level of fine for one of the companies involved, Bischof & Klein, which was caught trying to destroy a document during the investigation.

The future of successful cartel-busting is very much dependent on the new interactions within the decentralized network that is the ECN. There is some concern that the ECN merely represents a second-best solution (Maher 2006). Granting more powers to the Commission might have made better sense in terms of overall efficiency and consistency, but this option was not politically possible as the member states were set on some form of decentralization. As such it may still be too early to provide an assessment, but it appears to be working well (ABA 2005). Still, federalizing competition policy within a system of federal courts was a radical idea, though doubts have been raised about the challenge that the fragmentation of enforcement poses for legal predictability and consistency in a multilevel governance system like the EU, especially given the enlargements of 2004 and 2007. It is one thing to enact competition legislation and another to implement it. In order to prevent any inconsistency in approach the Commission has already financed two training programmes to the value of €600,000 in 2005, for example to train and retrain national judges on the latest developments in competition law. These should help foster and reinforce a new transregional competition culture.

Relationship with the Courts

One of the most important relationships in EU cartel policy has been the symbiotic relationship between the Commission and the Court of Justice (and since 1989 also the Court of First Instance). Particularly important is how the Courts have interpreted

Commission decisions. A degree of harmony existed almost undisturbed between these two supranational institutions in the promotion of market integration until the CFI was set up with its altogether more independent and critical approach to the Commission's analysis and argument. This was reflected in decisions in rather infamous cases such as *Solvay/CFK/Soda Ash* in 1991. The Commission issued its second decision on those cases in 2000. This is interesting because it is essentially the same decision as the one it had reached originally in 1990. However, this earlier decision had been annulled after an appeal to the CFI in 1995, only for this decision itself to be appealed to the final arbiter, the ECJ, which ruled in the Commission's favour in 2000.

Relations between the Commission and the Courts were fraught during the 1990s when the CFI overturned a number of Commission decisions on the grounds of a supposedly flawed analysis which often rested on the absence of clear proof and documentary evidence that cartels were actually in existence. It may have been correct, but such Court pronouncements have been perceived as unhelpful within DG Competition because cartels have deliberately sought to conceal their anti-competitive activities and in order to do so have met outside the EU, opting to conceal and even not to keep records about the structure of the infringement. In more recent times evidence suggests (and very much in contrast to developments in EC merger cases) that the Courts have come to appreciate the intricacies of cartels and supported more or less all Commission decisions which have further enhanced the credibility of the Commission. In 2005, for example, the European Courts reviewed eight cartel decisions (comparing with some four in 2004) and, significantly, backed the Commission's stance in each case. In January 2007 the Commission welcomed the ECJ's dismissal of an appeal from four seamless steel tubes producers against its (the Commission's) 1999 Decision. To this extent the supranational competition regime is working more effectively than at any time in its history. The Courts have had an impact and compelled DG Competition to provide careful and rigorous analyses of individual cases.

It is important to emphasize that pressure for reform of the EU's restrictive practices regime has been the product of extensive consultations and deliberations, not only between DG Competition and the national competition authorities, but also with the wider competition policy community. This has involved peak associations such as the European Employers Confederation (Unice/

BusinessEurope), the European Round Table of Industrialists (ERT), national business organizations, such as for example the Confederation of British Industry (CBI), the EU branch of the American Chamber of Commerce (Amcham-EU) and the legal community at both national and European levels. All have been consulted and are fully active in expressing their views on the evolution of EU competition policy.

These organizations meet on a regular basis to discuss and comment on EU policy and have long sought the establishment of a level playing-field for business so as to improve the consistency of policy enforcement across the EU. Such aspirations are not restricted to the EU, however, since the globalization of trade and the growing prevalence of international cartels has meant calls for action at the international level. The Commission has been arguing the case for an international agreement on competition policy since the mid 1990s but all moves towards it have proven difficult, the more so once the attempt to include competition policy as part of the Doha Trade Round agenda failed at Cancun in 2003. In the absence of any international accord the EU regime has signed up to a number of bilateral enforcement agreements (Holmes and Sydorak 2006) as a way of forging new networks at the international level (Maher 2002). The International Competition Network (ICN) is the best known and serves as a forum for international cooperation and the voluntary exchange of information and ideas about competition policy and its implementation.

Conclusion

EU restrictive practices policy provides for a fascinating study of supranational activity. Cartel policy has matured, and

> it is interesting to note how a more adversarial and combative system of enforcement (in some senses a quasi-criminal law model) was gradually created and grafted over time onto a seemingly 'softer' more administrative culture of regulation. (Harding and Joshua 2003:3)

The Commission has consistently displayed imagination and drive in its efforts to combat cartels and there can be little doubt that its growing resolve to uncover, penalize and end cartel infringements wherever they exist is serious and reveals a genuine degree and continuity of purpose.

One of the latest incentives to aid the Commission's drive can be found in its December 2005 Green Paper and in a Commission staff working paper on damages and actions for breach of the EU anti-trust rules. The Green Paper (see Pheasant 2006) sets out a number of possible options which would help to facilitate private damages actions where loss has been suffered as a result of an infringement of the EU's rules. It is an ingenious move and, if approved by the Council, would amount to a radical step-change in the development of the policy (Kroes 2006). Although the European Court has argued that the right to damages is necessary to ensure the useful effect of the EU competition rules, there has been little movement towards enabling consumers to exercise this right. In practice, however, there are also risks involved, as this initiative marks an attempt to begin a new era in competition culture, one that derives largely from US experience of private litigation. The Commission supports this approach, not least as it is an entirely cost-free exercise from the Commission's perspective.

DG Competition also has built-in mechanisms (such as the ECN) which allow it to secure greater cooperation and consistency with the national competition authorities to aid detection. Both the revised guidelines on fines and the recent review of the Leniency Programme represent important steps in the Commission's pursuit of cartels, and both are to be complemented in 2008 by a new Notice on a settlement procedure for cartels, which would allow the Commission to levy a lower fine on parties who approached the competition regulator. Moreover, the recent modernization process has enabled DG Competition to prioritize the most important harmful types of agreements, such as some horizontal agreements.

However, just as DG Competition's resolve and abilities increase so do those of many companies involved in cartel agreements to conceal their anti-competitive activities – and by all means possible. It is highly unrealistic to expect DG Competition or, for that matter, any of the domestic competition agencies to eradicate cartelization completely or, indeed, to get anywhere near to this objective. History and experience both indicate that although the objective that underpins cartel-busting is laudable it remains an arduous challenge for the regulators. As such international cooperation can only be expected to intensify.

Chapter 5

Monopoly Policy

EU monopoly policy or, more accurately, the pursuit of undertakings who abuse their dominant position in the marketplace, has constituted the weakest link in the Commission's competition policy chain. Although the regulation of exploitative and abusive monopolies has much in common with the control of restrictive practices, there has been a marked difference in the evolution of these two policies. Whereas the Article 81 regime developed rapidly in the early years of the Community, monopoly policy, as laid down in Article 82 of the Treaty, lagged very much behind. Considerably fewer cases were pursued. In practice, the Commission found the application of Article 82 more problematic than Article 81. The difficulties in implementing the policy centred on identifying and defining the characteristics of both abusive behaviour and dominance. The Commission's handling of the application of Article 82 has given rise to considerable controversy.

Still, Article 82 remains an integral component of the EU's competition regime. It deals with a vital aspect of abusive market power and holds the greatest potential among the EU competition treaty provision for incremental expansion. In the late 1990s the Commission initiated a much more proactive approach towards Article 82 and its latest plans seek to make Article 82's aims easier to assess. This has brought the Commission into direct confrontation with many of the world's leading companies, attracting substantial media interest. In fact, EU monopoly policy has led to many of the Commission's most controversial competition decisions and provides a fascinating field of study, if a rather complex one. This is because monopolies concern economic power and raise important questions about the compatibility of significant dominant economic power with democracy. This, in turn, raises the further question of whether all monopolies are by their very existence problematic or whether it is simply how a monopoly acts that can cause problems.

This chapter sets Article 82 in context. Space constraints allow for only a general overview of this most neglected aspect of EU competition policy. From a political science point of view, the chapter therefore presents a short overview of Article 82 and how it has operated since its inception. Most of this chapter deals with the way the Commission assesses its monopoly cases: first, in terms of the principle of *dominance*; and subsequently through its analysis of abuse. As neither term had been specifically defined in the EEC Treaty it was left to the Commission to add flesh to the bones of the policy. To this end the Commission's task has been facilitated through powers conferred upon it by Regulation 17/62 and more recently by Regulation 1/2003. This chapter identifies some of the groundbreaking cases in this area and provides an assessment of the policy, identifying the criticisms that have been levelled at the Article 82 regime. The final section explains the current transformation of EU monopoly policy by means of both the Modernization Regulation (Regulation 1/2003) and the Commission's Discussion Paper on the Application of Article 82 of the Treaty to exclusionary abuses of December 2005 and, subsequently, comments on the emerging consensus that it is consumer welfare and the efficient allocation of resources that should be the real criteria for judging monopoly abuse.

Article 82 in context

With fears of weakening industrial competitiveness dominating national political agendas in the 1950s and 1960s, it is hardly surprising that a concentration of economic power was deemed necessary for West European economic recovery and was thereby encouraged as a counterbalance to the American industrial challenge. As only large European-scale firms would be able to compete against the huge multinationals that were investing large amounts of money in Western Europe, it fell in part to the Commission to find an appropriate way of facilitating the growth of transnational European firms and for DG Competition in particular to determine how far dominance harmed the competitive process. In short, European monopoly policy was shaped by an acceptance of the necessity of large firms in the marketplace. In contrast, the US anti-trust system was very much predicated upon the desire to prevent dominant firms from emerging in the first place. Such different points of departure lead us to question the nature and objective of the monopolist and to consider whether all monopolies are in themselves dangerous.

Classical economic theory deems monopolies particularly problematic for three reasons that relate to the setting of prices, issues of innovation and product quality, and the distribution of wealth. The first issue is the most serious charge laid against monopolists who as the sole suppliers of a particular product or service are in a position to affect market price. If the maximization of profits is their primary goal, a monopolist can simply limit supply and charge a higher price. Such a move, however, creates what is known as allocative inefficiency, as it leaves consumers with no option other than to spend their money on goods that they may not have wanted to purchase. Under such a scenario the market is performing below its true potential and the 'social welfare cost of monopoly' (Whish 2003:5) whereby the consumer suffers directly from the affects of a lack of any alternative source of competition. In the longer term even the monopolist may be harmed by his or her own activity because monopolies can also lead to productive inefficiencies. These occur in the absence of direct competition from rival companies. Product quality can suffer as there is little incentive to invest in new technology and research. Moreover there is a real danger that monopolies will not only become less efficient over time, but will come to rely on outdated processes, especially if led by a carefree management team who spend more time on the golf course, say, than in the boardroom. In short, monopolists can affect price for their own ends and abuse their dominant position in the marketplace, but do all monopolists operate in this way, and how should states and in this instance the EU respond to monopoly power?

For DG Competition, monopolies and restrictive practices have similar effects: on consumer welfare, on competition and on market integration. However, it is one thing to denounce monopoly and the holding of a 'dominant position' within a market, and quite another to condemn the abuse of a dominant position. Monopolies may not be inherently bad, becoming problematic only when they seek to abuse their dominant position. It is the abusive conduct or behaviour of the firm within a market that is the target of EU monopoly policy, as opposed to agreements between undertakings under Article 81. This is the approach found in Article 82, which states: 'Any abuse by one or more undertakings of a dominant position within the common market *or in a substantial part of it* [our emphasis] shall be prohibited as incompatible with the common market in so far as it may affect trade between Member States.' It goes on to highlight the four types of abuse the Commission are likely to prohibit:

- Directly or indirectly imposing unfair purchase or selling prices or other unfair trading conditions (Article 82a).
- Limiting production, markets or technical development to the prejudice of consumers (Article 82b).
- Applying dissimilar conditions to equivalent transactions with other trading partners, thereby placing them at a competitive disadvantage (Article 82c).
- Making the conclusion of contracts subject to acceptance by the other parties of supplementary obligations which, by their nature or according to commercial usage, have no connection with the subject of such contracts (Article 82d).

These abuses are illustrative only and do not provide an exhaustive list (Jones and Sufrin 2008:255). It is also important to stress that in contrast to Article 81, under Article 82 there is neither provision for an exemption nor any *de minimis* thresholds. However, Whish points out that 'the requirement that market power should exist over a substantial part of the common market is in a sense the equivalent of the *de minimis* doctrine' in practice (Whish 2003:191).

Article 82 identifies four essential conditions that must be met before DG Competition can challenge an abusive monopoly. A firm (or 'undertaking' in Article 82-speak) must be dominant; its actions must have an effect on the common market or a substantial part of it; the dominant firm must be abusing its position in the market; and finally, the abuse must have an effect on trade between member states. These four conditions may seem fairly straightforward in that they identify the two central principles, namely *dominance* and *abuse*, which shape the Commission's analysis. In reality, however, it is often extremely difficult to ascertain the degree to which these criteria have been satisfied. How is a dominant position to be determined and what constitutes abuse? In theory at least, the Commission's investigative procedure involves a two-stage process, in which the existence of a dominant market position has to be demonstrated first, before an assessment of abusive conduct can be undertaken. Critics have argued that DG Competition first decides whether there is an abuse and then rigs the analysis of dominance to get the result it wants. Not surprisingly, DG Competition has vehemently rejected this accusation.

Before proceeding it should be clarified that monopolies can sometimes be orchestrated by more than just one undertaking, as Article 82 itself indicates. The concept of collective dominance has proven to be one of the most contentious issues arising under Article 82 and has been confirmed and dismissed in a series of court judgments. A substantial and expanding legal (and economic) literature (Temple-Lang 1979; Korah 1980; Temple-Lang and O'Donoghue 2002; O'Donoghue and Padilla 2006; Vickers 2006) now covers the evolution of the Courts' interpretations on this issue from *Continental Can* where it was accepted and *Hoffmann-La Roche* where it was rejected to *Italian Flat Glass* where once again the principle was accepted. The concept of collective dominance was given greater clarity in *Compagnie Maritime Belge Transports* and is said to occur when two or more legal entities 'present themselves or act together on a particular market as a collective entity' (Whish 2003:525). What constitutes dominance?

The Commission's analysis: demonstrating and establishing 'dominance'

In the absence of dominance, Article 82 simply does not apply. As a result, the onus rests with the Commission to prove the existence of a dominant position where it sees behaviour which is likely to have a detrimental effect on competition, on consumer welfare or on market integration. By contrast, firms facing a Commission investigation will seek to demonstrate that they do not hold a position of dominance. With the burden of proof resting with the Commission, the analysis is a difficult one and is exacerbated by the fact there is no statutory definition of market dominance. This omission made DG Competition's regulation of monopolies problematic from the outset. Yet it is quite understandable when we realize that many economists accept that economic theory offers little in the way of guidance as to what is meant by a dominant position of a kind which could be of substantial help in framing a legal definition. Dominance is far from being a rigid concept, although two elements within the Commission's assessment of dominance shed further light on the concept. The first, the 'relevant market', establishes the parameters (or context) within which the Commission makes a judgment about a firm's dominance. The second, 'market power', establishes the position of the firm in both quantitative and qualitative terms in that relevant market, allowing the Commission to decide whether a firm does or does not hold a dominant position. Both are considered below.

The relevant market

Before it can determine dominance, DG Competition has to define the relevant market. It is important to bear in mind that the notion of dominance does not exist in an economic vacuum. Its point of reference is the market within which the firm is an actor, and the firm's status and relationships within it (Fitzpatrick 1995:56). Indeed, a firm identified as having a dominant position in a narrowly defined market may become just one of many competitors when the market is defined more broadly. Significantly, the ECJ emphasized the necessity of providing a definition of the relevant market in its *Continental Can* judgment. It has not only come to expect such a definition in all the cases that it handles but has also displayed a readiness to overturn any Commission decision that fails to do so. However, defining the relevant market is not a simple task. The complexities that are part-and-parcel of this assessment have meant that the Commission's analysis has become subject to a great deal of criticism from the business community who claim that markets are consistently defined too broadly. To aid definition the Commission helpfully published its *Notice on the Definition of the Relevant Market for the Purpose of Community Competition Law* in 1997.

According to the 1997 Notice 'the definition of the relevant market in both its product and geographic dimensions allows the identification of the suppliers and the consumers/customers active on that market'. Alongside these two dimensions attention is also placed on the *temporal* market. In practice DG Competition has placed most emphasis on the first of these, although the European Courts may require all three to be investigated. Analysis of the product market involves an investigation into a *class* of products. The market is defined in terms of the 'interchangeability' or 'substitutability' of the product. To put it another way, the 'key criterion is the extent to which the market for the product in question is differentiated from other markets' (Fitzpatrick 1995:57). This judgment has proven extremely difficult to make. Although the legal exercise of defining the relevant product market is important, in practice markets often overlap: hence the scope for challenges to the Commission's analysis. It is clearly in the interest of companies under investigation to have the market defined as widely as possible, as a wide market makes it more difficult for the Commission to establish dominance. In *United Brands,* for example, the Commission (and later the Courts) had to define the relevant product market for bananas. The decision centred on whether bananas represented a distinct fruit in their own banana market or whether bananas were part of the wider fruit market, as the company maintained. The Commission rejected the company's argument, deciding that the bananas were not interchangeable with other fruits and as such comprised a market in itself, a market in which United Brands was the dominant force. Without this distinction United Brands' market share would have been considerably lower and dominance would have been more difficult (and perhaps impossible) to prove.

The difficulties involved in providing an adequate definition of the product market were highlighted in the *Hoffmann–La Roche* case of 1976. DG Competition maintained that the firm held a dominant position in the manufacture of certain vitamins and as such controlled competition in a large part of the vitamins market. The Commission's decision to challenge Hoffmann–La Roche's position in the market, vitamin by vitamin, frustrated the arguments advanced by the company, making its dominance in the individual vitamins markets highly transparent. Hoffmann–La Roche appealed to the ECJ which not only approved the Commission's analysis but also used the occasion to draft its most comprehensive definition of dominance to date (see also Jones and Sufrin 2008:397–9).

Even the Courts have not escaped criticism. The initial reluctance of the ECJ in the 1960s and 1970s to become involved in economic analyses, leaving this aspect of decision-taking to the Commission alone, often led to frustration among firms keen to challenge the Commission's assessment. Appeals to the Court on the basis of an inaccurate analysis of the product market, for example (usually arguing that the Commission had drawn the market too narrowly), were rarely successful. This was in spite of the fact that the Commission's discussion of product markets in its decisions was often very brief (Whish 1989:279). However, with experience the Commission rapidly came to appreciate the necessity of defining the relevant market after the ECJ in 1972 had opted to quash the Commission's analysis in *Continental Can* on the grounds that DG Competition had failed to demarcate the relevant product market.

The product market is not the only relevant market, however. The Commission must also identify the relevant geographical market, a territory in which the conditions of competition are homogeneous (Fitzpatrick 1995:57). This is a less contentious area of analysis. Just because a single market might exist for a product, there can be no assumption that the relevant geographical market will be the EU. Other factors must also be taken into account. Once again, the narrower the market the more likely it is that dominance will be proven, as was demonstrated in the *Stena Sealink* case in 1992. It has to be said, however, that in some instances the geographical market is fairly obvious, as was clear in the *British Telecommunications* case, where BT was shown (in 1982) to be holding an absolute monopoly in telecommunications services in the UK. However, for the majority of cases falling under DG Competition's scrutiny, defining the relevant geographical market has generally proven more problematic. The Commission's analysis usually involves a search for barriers to export and an investigation into where those barriers might lie. In many of the cases dealt with by the Commission, the capacity for the product to be transported has been an important consideration in judging the territorial extent of the market. In other cases, legal and technical barriers have limited the geographical market.

Finally, the Commission may also consider the temporal dimension of the market, and changes in the character of a market over time. This can also be a difficult area to deal with, although the analysis undertaken here tends to be the least contentious of the three. This particular dimension is often downplayed by the Commission as few markets lend themselves to such an analysis. However, some markets do prove highly volatile over the course of time, as a consequence of all sorts of changes, from weather conditions to consumer habits. Indeed, a firm facing cut-throat competition one year may find itself without any major competitors a year later. The temporal market issue was raised, for example, in the United Brands case in the mid 1970s when the company argued that the character of the market for bananas changed according to the season.

Market power

Only after a particular market has been defined can an assessment begin on the degree of power an undertaking has on that market and the extent to which its position can be judged to be dominant. The actual analysis can be a complex one, but the essential question is whether the company in question is in a position to behave independently of its competitors and customers, and to exercise economic power unfettered by the constraints usually operating in markets subject to effective competition. There are a number of ways the Commission reaches its conclusions.

The percentage of the market controlled by the firm (market share) is an important indicator of dominance, though it is not always conclusive. As Whish comments (Whish 2003:180), 'as far as Article 82 is concerned, it is obvious that the larger the market share, the more likely the finding of dominance. A market share of 100% is rare ... although not unheard of'. The Commission has determined very high market shares in some cases, for example *Tetra-Pak* and *BPB Industries plc*. In the former Tetra-Pak possessed a 92 per cent market share for machines capable of filling cartons by an aseptic process while BPB held a market share of over 96 per cent in the United Kingdom for the manufacture of plasterboard.

Such market shares are unusual and have led to claims of super-dominance. It is important to stress that neither the Commission nor the European Courts have openly used this term, but it is useful to stress here that the risks for such firms, if abusing their dominant position, are greater where market shares are unusually high. There can be little doubt that companies who hold a quasi-monopoly are deemed to have special responsibilities as to the state of competition. For example, in *Compagnie Maritime Belge* the ECJ indicated in 2000 that a dominant firm with only one smaller competitor would be more likely to be deemed to have abused its dominant position than in the case of where a dominant player held a lesser degree of market power.

However, a state of dominance can also be proven with considerably reduced percentages. For example, the ECJ maintained in 1978 in *Hoffmann–La Roche* that a 50 per cent share could in exceptional circumstances be deemed to constitute dominance. From the Commission's perspective dominance is likely to exist where a company controls over 40 per cent of a particular market. However, where market share rests in the region of between 25 per cent and 40 per cent dominance may still exist, although this will be dependent on the specific characteristics of the market. For example the *Virgin/British Airways* case from 2000 provided the first example of the concept of dominance being applied to a company with just less than 40 per cent (some 39.7 per cent) share of the market. The initial complaint had come from Virgin against BA's practice of giving commission to travel agents who sold BA tickets to customers. The Commission was swift to recognize the rivalry between the two airlines and condemned BA for abusing its dominant position. The case was appealed to the CFI where the Court supported the Commission's interpretation in 2003.

In *United Brands*, a market share of between 40 and 45 per cent was deemed to constitute a dominant position. It was argued that the firm's prominent position in the supply of bananas in certain member states, under the tradename Chiquita, was strengthened by its involvement at both the production and distribution stages. Refrigeration facilities regulated the ripening process, allowing the firm to control the circulation of goods in the market. The firm ran its own ships, and huge investments in its plantations also contributed to its control of the supply of bananas. According to the Commission, United Brands had a strategic advantage over all its competitors, gained by reaping the benefits of substantial economies of scale and considerable investment. Indeed, its nearest competitor controlled only 9 per cent of the market. On appeal, the ECJ clarified the law in 1978 by ruling that dominance by a firm or undertaking

> relates to a position of economic strength enjoyed by an undertaking which enables it to prevent effective competition being maintained on the relevant market by giving it the power to behave in an appreciable extent independently of its competitors, customers and ultimately, of its consumers.

The ruling thus confirmed the criteria mentioned above. Thus, it seems that the market share criterion is something of a moveable feast. Firms have rough guidelines as to what could be defined as dominance in this respect, but they offer little legal certainty. Many other factors have also to be taken on board.

In the majority of cases, however, market share alone will not determine market power. Other factors have to be taken into consideration, requiring an economic analysis of the constraints upon the firm and on the extent to which that firm's behaviour may influence conditions within the market. The Commission must look into the structure and operation of the relevant markets and also takes into account the availability of capital. In a number of Article 82 cases, the performance of the firm and its conduct, restrictions imposed by national legal systems and the existence of economies of scale have also been taken as evidence of market power.

The final stage in determining dominance involves an assessment of the firm's position within the common market. This relates explicitly to the wording of Article 82 which states that an abuse of a dominant position is prohibited 'within the common market or in a substantial part of it'. While there is little disagreement over what is meant by the 'common market', disputes have arisen over the meaning of 'substantial' in this context. Thanks to an increasing number of Court rulings, it has now become much clearer that the word 'substantial' is not just defined in terms of the territory covered, but can also refer, for example, to the volume of the firm's production, as in *Suiker Unie* from 1975. Although this particular case was concerned primarily with a sugar cartel and was targeted under Article 81, the Commission found the rebate scheme of one of the sugar producers to be a clear example of abusive dominance, which also ran contrary to 82. The scheme was designed to reward, by means of an annual quantity rebate, those customers who bought their annual requirements from just one producer.

A substantial part of the common market could also be viewed as one member state, as in the *1998 Football World Cup Finals* decision, or even a part of a member state. Whish comments that the Football World Cup decision from 2000 'epitomises the possibility of very narrow market definitions' (Whish 2003:193). In this case the Commission condemned the French organizers of the tournament for abusing their dominant position by selling 574,300 so-called blind tickets (an unknown ticket to any of the games) only to customers who had a postal address in France. A strangely minimal fine of €1000, however, seems hardly significant for an act that had openly discriminated in favour of French nationals.

With no scope for exemption under Article 82 much rests on the Commission's interpretation of an abuse. The economic assessment is a complex one. For example, it must take on board the contestability of the relevant market, in other words, the ease with which potential competitors are able to enter the market, thus providing an injection of competition. Where the Commission determines that an abusive monopoly has affected competition it is empowered under Article 23 of Regulation 1/2003 to levy fines and to compel the dominant firm(s) to cease and desist from the problematic conduct. The Commission is also able to order the complete divestiture of a firm's assets, or even to break up an undertaking if it will result in the end of the infringement. Formal Commission decisions in Article 82 cases now tend to be taken only when there is a likelihood of a fine being imposed, or when, perhaps as a result of some novel point of law or policy, the abuse is deemed to be of particular importance.

In most Article 82 cases the Commission reaches a negotiated settlement with the company concerned. Such informal decisions are a useful means for both the Commission and the firm in question and enable the latter to escape a fine or anything worse in exchange for agreeing to the Commission's suggested remedy. Arguably the Commission may attain more from pursuing the informal route than from opting for a formal decision which can then be appealed to the Courts. In more contentious cases of abuse and dominance, as in Microsoft (see Box 5.1), the formal route is usually the only and preferred option.

BOX 5.1   DG Competition v. Microsoft

Arguably the most infamous of all cases in the history of Article 82 is the long-drawn-out dispute between DG Competition and the US computer software giant Microsoft. It also represents the biggest investigation of its kind that the Commission had ever carried out (with assistance from the US competition authorities). It was temporarily resolved in 2004 after five years and following an intense battle between the two giants. The two sides had been locked in negotiations since the early 1990s. However, a more recent case had begun in 1999 after complaints from rival makers of audio-visual software that Microsoft was protecting its own media player brand and as such was effectively squeezing out other rival manufacturers. This particular charge was far from new in the software market. Indeed, the Commission had reached an accommodation as far back as 1984 with IBM after DG Competition had accused the computer giant of abusing its dominant position by tying various products together. In this instance IBM refused to admit any wrongdoing but agreed to open up its systems.

➡

Such an outcome seemed more unlikely in the Microsoft case as both sides found little room for agreement. Both realized that the outcome of the case would have huge implications for the future of the software industry. The question posed by the Commission was whether Microsoft had deliberately used its market power to try to force its rivals out of business. Microsoft certainly held a dominant position as it supplied the Windows software package which operates in 90 per cent of the world's PCs. But had it abused its position? The Commission was severely critical of Microsoft's activities and deemed the company to have withheld information which rival server software companies required to align their products with Windows-based computers. Microsoft was also condemned for making the purchase of Windows conditional on the simultaneous acquisition of the Windows media player product. In other words by ensuring that Microsoft's media player was already installed in its own machines Microsoft had effectively distorted competition from other firms at one stroke, by removing the need for consumers to buy other media player products. The Commission argued that Microsoft was effectively putting the brakes on innovation and freezing out its rivals.

The Commission's 2004 decision to impose a fine of €497m on Microsoft, for abusing its dominant market position between 1998 and 2004, reflected its concerns. It was also the largest fine to date for a breach of Article 82. Moreover conditions were attached to the decision. Microsoft was told to provide rival firms with more information about its software, in order to enable them to write programs that could run more smoothly on Microsoft's widely used Windows operating system. The judgment also called for Microsoft to unbundle its Windows Media Player from its Windows operating system. By setting limits on Microsoft's practice of bundling software and services with its Windows operating system, the Commission had struck a blow against a key part of the software firm's commercial strategy.

Microsoft immediately went onto the offensive and launched an appeal against the ruling. Stakes were certainly high, because if Microsoft lost it was likely to face further legal assaults from the Commission. However, if it ultimately won the argument then the prestige of the regulator was going to be severely tarnished. Relations between the Commission and Microsoft proved particularly tense and fraught, and further deteriorated in July 2006 when the European Commission imposed a penalty payment of €280.5

(£194m) million on Microsoft for its continued non-compliance with some of its obligations under the Commission's March 2004 decision. Disagreements over interpretation remain as strong as ever. Kroes stated:

> Microsoft has agreed that the main basis for pricing should be whether its protocols are innovative. The Commission's current view is that there is no significant innovation in these protocols. I am therefore again obliged to take formal measures to ensure that Microsoft complies with its obligations. (Kroes 2007)

Accordingly, in March 2007 the Commission sent Microsoft a further Statement of Objections for the company's failure to comply with the obligations set out in 2004 and rejected Microsoft's 'unreasonable' pricing policy', and threatened to impose a daily penalty for continued failure to comply. Finally, the company seemed to submit to the inevitable when it withdrew its appeals at the European Court of First Instance in September 2007. In doing so it opted to comply with its obligations under the Commission's 2004 ruling that required Microsoft to open up access to its Windows operating system. The deal seemed to mark the end of this long-running saga. However, it was not the end, and the European Commission fined Microsoft some €899m euros in February 2008 for failing to comply with the 2004 ruling. Microsoft now holds the unenviable record of becoming the first company in the history of EU competition policy that has been fined for failing to comply with a final decision. In January 2008 DG Competition also opened two new investigations against Microsoft over its dominance of the internet market and the continued incompatibility with rival manufacturers. Microsoft has just launched an appeal (May 2008). The story continues.

The Commission's assessment of 'abuse'

As the list of abuses identified in Article 82 is far from exhaustive, both the Commission and the Courts have sought to clarify in policy statements and in legally enforceable decisions and judgments the types of conduct likely to be in conflict with the Treaty. The Commission and the Courts have dealt with different types of abusive activity which can be loosely categorized as unfair pricing practices (excessive and predatory pricing); rebates (which have attracted considerable attention); discrimination; various forms of refusal to deal; and examples of non-price-related tying and exclusivity deals. Although these categories do not constitute an exhaustive list, they do help to emphasize the range of activity under Article 82 which preoccupies DG Competition and enables us to provide below four concrete types of abusive activity that fall within the meaning of Article 82.

The Commission undertakes its case analysis on an ad-hoc basis. The scope for legal certainty and indeed for the emergence of a coherent and comprehensive policy has therefore been somewhat limited. What is clear, however, is that the concept of an abuse has been broadly interpreted. The firm does not even have to intend to act anti-competitively for Article 82 to apply. The Commission has argued that

> [a] dominant company . . . has a special obligation not to do anything that would cause further deterioration to the already fragile structure of competition or to unfairly prevent the emergence or growth of new or existing competitors who might challenge this dominance and bring about the establishment of effective competition. (Commission 1994:114–21)

The Commission is concerned primarily with conduct that excludes competitors from the market place. A large percentage of DG Competition's workload under Article 82 relates to the pricing policies of dominant firms. Abuse can clearly arise when undertakings in a position of undisputed market power can adopt excessive or predatory pricing policies, but abuse can also emerge where any firm opts to pursue discriminatory pricing (and usually in the form of discount and rebate schemes). It should also be added that abusive pricing policies cannot really be divorced from a range of other forms of abusive behaviour that include tying policies and exclusive contracts. The following section provides brief details of the main forms of such abusive conduct. The reader should be aware that there can be a degree of overlap between these specific examples (see Jones and Sufrin 2008:432–612).

Discriminatory pricing

The ability to be able to charge persistently different prices is a clear example of market power. Price discrimination (see Phlips 1983) occurs when, first, different customers or users are charged different prices for the same product for no good reason (that is, first price discrimination), as in *United Brands*; and, second, when different prices are charged in different markets (that is, third-degree price discrimination, as in *Tetra-Pak*). The second type provides more work for DG Competition. Such practices might be tolerable for firms with a limited share of the market but they are deemed objectionable when the company in question holds a dominant position and where the customer has no alternative source of supply. More recently, such conduct is deemed worse when a vertically integrated player which holds a dominant position intentionally discriminates in favour of its own subsidiary and especially against the competitors of that subsidiary. Those that do are attracting greater Commission scrutiny.

The activities of the German national railway in the *HOV-SVZ/MCN* case best illustrate this type of exclusionary activity. After receiving a complaint in 1994, the Commission discovered that Deutsche Bundesbahn's charges to firms using German ports were lower than those for firms operating from either the Netherlands or from Belgium, regardless of the additional distances involved. In 1994 the Commission concluded that as Deutsche Bundesbahn held a monopoly within Germany, the company had abused its dominant position by operating a discriminatory policy. A fine of ECU11m was imposed on Deutsche Bundesbahn for infringing Article 82.

Unfair pricing practices: exploitative and exclusionary

The issue of unfair pricing forms an integral aspect of DG Competition's Article 82 activities. Unfair pricing encapsulates both excessive and predatory pricing arrangements. The concept of excessive prices is alien to the American anti-trust system and it is an area that is fraught with problems of determining when prices can actually be deemed to be excessive, that is, when they bear little or no resemblance to the economic value of the product in question. In practice the Commission has displayed a general reluctance to pursue such cases over the years and has certainly not wanted to transform itself into a price regulator. In any case it is difficult to measure excessive pricing and to identify remedies. Consequently *United Brands* remains one of the few leading cases in this area where the Commission has focused on price.

Where firms hold a dominant position in a market and charge a price far beyond the real economic value of the product, as in the

General Motors case from 1975, the Commission is likely to identify the existence of an abuse. This particular case saw the Commission's first decision against excessive pricing and it came with a fine, although the ECJ later quashed the Commission's verdict on the grounds of inconclusive evidence. However, it should be noted that unfair pricing does not necessarily equate with higher prices, as it can also apply to the setting of low prices which form part of a strategy to force rival competitors out of the marketplace.

Predatory pricing occurs when an undertaking deliberately sets out to charge low prices for a particular product with the sole intention of driving a minor rival from the market altogether. Predatory pricing may actually appear to benefit the consumer but any such gains will be short-lived because once the competition has been eliminated prices will once again rise, and often will rise enough to cover the losses incurred. Of course, one of the greatest challenges confronting DG Competition and all competition policy regulators centres on determining where robust price competition ends and where predatory pricing begins. Predatory pricing clearly exists but how can it be identified? The answer has been provided by a definite series of economic tests and measurements that focus on different types of costs that extend from variable costs and total costs to marginal costs and long-run average incremental costs. These have produced an economic minefield that this chapter does not have the space to traverse.

Two economists (Areeda and Turner 1975) also sought to provide an answer of what exactly constitutes predatory pricing in the 1970s, sparking off an intense debate and stirring up some controversy on the subject (Brodley and Hay 1981). From the Commission's perspective, however, predatory pricing normally occurs when prices are set below marginal cost and are part of a deliberate strategy to undermine competition. In the US, the possible recoupment of losses is an essential asset of the predation test. Companies will of course be able to pursue such a strategy only if they are economically strong and able to sustain short-term losses. Thus examples of predatory pricing are rather rare. There have only been four recorded cases to date in the EU, all of which have attracted considerable media attention. The first two cases from the early 1990s, relating to *AKZO* and *Tetra-Pak* (see Box 5.2) respectively, set new precedents. In both decisions the Commission was able to identify a breach of Article 82 and penalize illegal behaviour by imposing hefty fines.

The Commission's stance has toughened since and has been reinforced in the *DP AG (Parcels)* and the *Wanadoo Interactive* cases in 2001 and 2003 respectively. The latter case provides another excellent illustration of predatory pricing in operation. The Commission uncovered evidence during its investigations and in company records of Wanadoo Interactive's intention to eliminate its rivals from the market. Its decision against this company also signalled that mere inhibition (as opposed to the total exclusion of rivals) was sufficient to be deemed predation under EU competition law. A third and final form of unfair pricing relates to a so-called price squeeze where a dominant firm (usually vertically integrated) sells its goods to a smaller competitor (and thereby enables the rival player to remain in the marketplace) but at a higher price than that at which it sells the same goods to other consumers. Again, few examples exist and only two can be deemed to represent examples of price-squeezing, namely *Napier Brown/British Sugar* from 1988 and *Deutsche Telekom* in 2003. In the former case, British Sugar enjoyed a dominant position in the sugarbeet and sugar markets and had sought to eliminate its smaller rival Napier Brown by reducing the price of retail sugar. The Commission found British Sugar guilty of having deliberately sought to abuse its dominant position and fined the company €3m. The CFI later upheld the Commission's judgment following an appeal against the original decision by the British company.

Tying agreements and exclusive dealing arrangements

Tying is an activity that is identified clearly as an abuse under Article 82(d). It involves the practice where an undertaking supplies something on condition that the customers obtain something else from the supplier as well. Such tying agreements are an issue of real concern for competition authorities and especially when the supplier holds a dominant position in the marketplace because they are then in a strong position to 'extract two monopoly prices, one from the tying and one from the tied product' (Jones and Sufrin 2008:514). In short, tying agreements not only restrict competition but also thwart the treaty goal of market integration. As with exclusive dealing arrangements, tying agreements can, for example, require customers to purchase products or services for a specified time period exclusively from one producer. Such contracts may bring benefits and efficiency gains (for example, to

BOX 5.2   The AKZO and Tetra-Pak Cases

The *AKZO* case first came to light in 1979 and involved a small British plastics firm, ECS, and AKZO Chemie, a subsidiary of the Dutch international company AKZO. Both companies were producers of benzoyl peroxide, which was used for both plastics production and flour-milling. The British firm had traditionally focused on the latter within the UK market while AKZO Chemie had concentrated on the continental plastics market. The conflict between both companies arose when ECS opted to move into the German plastics market. AKZO Chemie responded by threatening to enter the UK flour market and undercut ECS through a series of selective price cuts. ECS lodged a complaint with DG Competition about AKZO's abusive behaviour and cited a flagrant breach of Article 82. The Commission determined that AKZO had sought to eliminate its smaller rival even before it was able to gain a foothold in the German market and was guilty of abusing its dominant position. AKZO was duly fined some €10m. On appeal in 1991, the CFI upheld the Commission's decision but reduced the size of the financial penalty to €7.5m and developed a more structured case for such predatory pricing. In so doing it rejected AKZO's arguments, including its definition of the relevant market. The principles underlying the AKZO judgment resurfaced almost immediately in *Tetra-Pak II*.

Tetra-Pak represented the second, and most infamous, high-profile case of the early 1990s. This case first came to DG Competition's attention following a complaint by Tetra-Pak's major competitor, Elopak. Originally a Swedish firm, though now based in Switzerland, Tetra-Pak was the largest supplier of liquid foods packaging (mainly for milk and fruit juices) in Western Europe. In one particular area, aseptic packaging for long-life products, it controlled 95 per cent of the market. Elopak argued that Tetra-Pak's dominance was so great in this market that profits from this sector

➡

stimulate greater investment in the company) and there may be good commercial reasons to engage in tying, but such arrangements can have anti-competitive repercussions and severely restrict customer choice. Indeed, they often represent a vertical form of dominance which restricts competition by limiting the freedom of distributors to choose the providers of essential services or facilities. This has become an issue of note since the *Kodak* judgment (Shapiro 2006), a US Supreme Court judgment (in 1993) which were able offset losses in others, and thus accused Tetra-Pak of predatory pricing. In many cases the start of an investigation into abusive behaviour is enough to persuade firms to alter their behaviour. However, although cooperation is encouraged, this cannot protect the accused firm from fines covering the period before cooperation began. Tetra-Pak acted speedily to alter its conduct but always refuted DG Competition's assertions of abusive conduct. Tetra-Pak's defence rested on its definition of the relevant market, with the firm claiming that its market position could be understood only if one took account of the entire liquid food packaging market. The history of this case aptly demonstrates the difficulties of defining the relevant market. Tetra-Pak claimed that with substitutes including cans, and plastic and glass bottles, the company controlled only 15 per cent of the market.

Tetra Pak's interpretation failed to convince DG Competition. The Commission decided that Tetra-Pak had knowingly abused its dominant position by engaging in a series of practices designed to eradicate competition between 1982 and 1986. These practices had included discriminatory and predatory pricing; requiring purchasers of the company's machines to use only Tetra-Pak-manufactured cartons; excessively long leasing contracts; and restrictions on resale of machines. Accordingly, in 1991, the Commission fined Tetra-Pak €75m. Although this was the largest fine ever imposed by the Commission on an individual firm at the time, it still fell well short of the maximum penalty. While the Commission was empowered to impose fines of up to 10 per cent of turnover, the €75m represented only 2 per cent of the group's 1990 turnover. Tetra-Pak challenged the Commission's decision. The story was far from over. Tetra-Pak lodged its first appeal against the Commission decision to the Court of First Instance (CFI) in 1991. When unsuccessful the company lodged a further appeal to the ECJ claiming that the CFI's analysis was flawed. The ECJ, however, confirmed the CFI's judgment.

has been used by the Commission as a form of guidance. In the *Plasterboard* case, BPB Industries was fined €3m and its subsidiary, British Gypsum, €150,000 for engaging in practices which restricted French and Spanish imports into the UK. The Commission's decision rested on the argument that the conduct of the firms ran contrary to Article 82 on the grounds that a system of loyalty payments existed for individually selected merchants if they bought plasterboard from BPB. In addition, a scheme existed whereby customers who did not handle imported plasterboard had access to suppliers of plaster. In the landmark Microsoft decision from 2004 the Commission explicitly stated that tying agreements fell foul of Article 82 (Pardolesi and Renda 2004) when the tying and the tied goods are two separate products; when the undertaking concerned was dominant tin the tying market; and when the firm concerned did not give customers any choice to secure the tying product without the tied product and when competition was restricted.

Refusal to supply

The refusal to supply customers has been a core element within the rubric of Article 82 over the last two decades and one that has consumed much of DG Competition's time and resources. The notion of a refusal to supply is by its very nature controversial, as it conflicts with long held notions of freedom of contract and the right for undertakings to choose who they do business with and when. However, the refusal to supply can operate as a form of a abuse and a means to restrict competition under Article 82. The Commission has adopted a much more interventionist position in this area than its US counterpart. The European courts have never articulated a view that all dominant firms have a duty to supply all those who request to be supplied, but both the Commission and the Courts have developed their own notions and concepts of when and why such fundamental business freedoms should be limited to protect competition. It should be noted that any refusal to supply that is based just on grounds of nationality is held automatically to infringe Article 82.

According to existing case-law the refusal to supply manifests itself in different guises and any exploration of this abuse may be divided into a number of subheadings. These include: a refusal to supply in order to exclude competitors; a refusal to supply in response to an attack on the dominant undertaking's commercial interests; a refusal to supply spare parts; a refusal to supply and the essential facilities concept; and a refusal to supply intellectual property rights (Jones and Sufrin 2008:529–85).

A number of illustrative examples of such abusive behaviour give some flavour of the types of abuse that occur under the refusal to supply category. The very first case to arise under the refusal to supply category occurred in 1974 in *Commercial Solvents*. It centred on a pharmaceutical company (Zoja) that had opted to cease purchasing a particular raw material (aminobutanol) from its supplier (Commercial Solvents/Instituto) in the hope of finding a cheaper source. However, Zoja was not only dismayed not to find one, but found in the meantime that the original supplier had opted to expand its activities into the same area and refused to supply Zoja with aminobutanol as before. Zoja lodged a complaint with the Commission, which found Commercial Solvents guilty of having abused its dominant position. Commercial Solvents appealed to the ECJ but the judges upheld the Commission's findings of dominance and abuse.

Under the refusal to supply and the essential facilities concept category we site the *Sealink/B&I Holyhead* case which arose following a complaint made to the Commission in April 1993 by the ferry company Sea Containers. Trying to define exactly what is meant by 'essential facilities' is particularly problematic but it is deemed to refer to something that is owned or controlled by a dominant undertaking and something to which others need access to provide services. The expression arose for the very first time in *Sealink/B&I Holyhead*, although the idea had emerged in earlier cases such as *British-Midland/Aer Lingus*. Sea Containers challenged the practices of Stena Sealink, its rival on the Holyhead (Wales) to Dun Laoghaire (Ireland) route. Sea Containers maintained that Stena Sealink, which was also the port authority at Holyhead, was preventing it from launching a high-speed catamaran ferry service to Ireland by denying it access to the port. In its Statement of Objections, the Commission agreed that Stena was violating Article 82 in refusing its rival access to Holyhead harbour. This was enough to encourage Stena to conclude a new agreement with Sea Containers, allowing its competitor to offer a high-speed service from Holyhead to Ireland starting in the summer of 1994.

Having traced the key components that arise under Article 82 the chapter now examines the Commission's handling of monopoly policy.

Assessing monopoly policy

Compared with the Commission's pursuit of restrictive practices, European monopoly policy was slow to evolve. The Commission did not make its first formal decision under Article 82 until 1971 (in *GEMA*). Indeed, even by the end of the 1980s, when European competition policy was fast developing on all fronts, there seemed little policy momentum to focus on monopolies. The statistics tell a story. Between 1958 and June 2006 (van Damme *et al.* 2006) there have been only 53 relevant Commission decisions under Article 82. Just over half (27) were brought before the European courts for judicial review, with some 9 Commission decisions being over-turned and 3 judgments still pending. We should be careful not be too dismissive here because in more recent times the Commission's interest in monopoly policy has been awakened.

Interestingly, a closer inspection indicates that 22 of the Commission's decisions have been taken since 1997, reflecting DG Competition's more recent endeavours and growing determination to do more with Article 82. The Commission's efforts to bolster its activity in this area have also been furthered by the more frequent imposition of fines for anti-abusive behaviour (to complement its activities under Article 81). However, with a few notable excep-tions, such as Microsoft, the size of such penalties is noticeably smaller than those that have been imposed for Article 81 viola-tions. For example, in May 2003 *Deutsche Telekom* (DT) was only fined €12.6m for an abusive activity, while a more substantial levy of €40m was imposed on *Astra Zeneca* in June 2005 for abusing its dominant position within the EEA in the market for anti-ulcer medicines (and especially Lobec). Astra-Zeneca has since appealed this decision citing the Commission's legally and factually flawed argument. In March 2006 the Commission fined *Prokent/Tomra* €24m for abusing its dominant position in the vending machine market. This fine amounted to 7 per cent of the firm's total turnover for 2005 and marks the largest fine the Commission has ever imposed under Article 86 in terms of share of revenue. Tomra rejected the Commission's accusation that it had abused its domi-nant position in the Austrian, Dutch, German, Norwegian and Swedish markets between 1998 and 2002 by deploying a range of rebates and discounts to deliberately undermine competition.

Despite greater use of Article 82 since the end of the 1990s, monopoly policy has still remained the poorer relation of the com-petition family. Why? The pursuit of abusive monopolies has been far from easy and this goes some way towards explaining the Commission's hesitancy. Article 82 represents one of the most dif-ficult parts of the EU competition policy regime to fathom and navigate. Decisions are based on economic modelling and complex legal interpretations. In the 1980s and 1990s a number of important legal challenges were initiated against Commission decisions. Many of these argued a faulty and/or incorrect analysis on the part of the Commission. Given the scope and nature of this particular article, challenges to Commission decisions should come as no real surprise.

In some cases there proved to be a clear weakness in the Commission's reasoning. In many of its decisions certain factors were identified as being indicative of dominance, even though there was little to explain why *these* factors were important and others not. In the past, the ECJ's reluctance to involve itself in economic assessments prior to their judgments proved to be another bone of contention for DG Competition, as non-economics-based judgments clearly conflicted with DG Competition's assessment. Indeed, left to its own devices, the Commission's effect on competition might in fact be at odds with its actual intentions. There is a serious point to be made here because if the Commission's analysis is flawed, and firms shape their behaviour in line with what they perceive to be Commission policy, then the detrimental effect on European competition could be staggering. It is extremely difficult to translate economic realities into legal principles and frameworks. In the Commission's monopoly policy this often proved more problematic than in any other part of DG Competition's competition regime.

It is important to recall that EU monopoly policy was initiated at a time when the existence of larger companies was assumed to guarantee greater competitiveness. From this perspective encouraging transnational business actors was in line with the Commission's pro-integration mandate. However, global industrial competitiveness often comes at a price: the loss of competition within national and European markets. The closer the EU moved to the creation of a truly single market, the more relevant this argument became. Paradoxically, however, the Treaty stated categorically that the preservation and indeed the promotion of competition *within* the Community was a priority. As such, the Commission's early approach to industrial concentration seemed to work against the very principles on which the Community was constructed; hence the ambivalence. This same ambivalent approach to monopolies has also had an effect on the policy's development.

In practice, the Commission has pursued a policy of balance between potentially conflicting objectives. This has been achieved on a case-by-case basis and has involved a weighing up of the pros and cons of the monopoly. The main priority of Article 82 has certainly been to control market power but there are a number of other potential goals that have influenced policy. These include ensuring fairness in the market by protecting small and medium companies and facilitating the liberalization of the public utility sectors from the late 1980s onwards. The Commission enjoyed much more room for manoeuvre under Article 82 than any of the other competition articles and began in the early 1990s to use this provision in conjunction with Article 86 to push liberalization into the public utility sectors. So, what is the state of play in 2008?

The Commission's application of this particular article has give rise to considerable controversy that has often centred (see Jones and Sufrin 2008:294) on questionable definitions of dominance; an over-reliance on the behaviour of the undertaking in question rather than looking at its the effects; the continuing absence of a coherent and consistent approach; a failure to identify and specify actual policy objectives; and often a readiness to reach decisions that are designed to strengthen the single-market objective.

Consequently, much of the current law under Article 82 has been described by leading competition practitioners as a 'patchwork quilt of distinctions which are unclear and difficult to justify, and which can lead to heavy fines for companies whose commercial behaviour towards the competition is considered abusive' (Sher 2004:243). Such critics point to various problems such as the lack of internal consistency of application, the inconsistency between the application of Article 82 and the application of the other competition rules. Some question the coherent policy basis for applying this article at all.

In theory Article 82 should certainly be about combating abusive market power, but its pursuit in practice has often led to other issues being considered. The story of Article 82's development, as set out above, has to a large extent been compartmentalized. The Commission has developed a series of headings categorizing the abuses it has sought to tackle, but questions remain over the degrees of coherency and variance in day-to-day decision-making. Sher cites the example of the 'refusal to deal' category where rules change depending whether you are an existing or a new customer or when differential treatment is given to different customers.

There have also been cases, for example, where the Commission appears to be driven more by ensuring the protection of smaller competitors than by seeking to protect the competitive process (Jones and Sufrin 2004:243). There is also a fundamental issue regarding the connection between dominance and abuse – and especially the degree to which seemingly abusive monopolies provide benefits for their customers, as in the case of Microsoft. Why should dominant firms with some 45 per cent of a market share be treated in the same way as those with 95 per cent?

Together these present problems for business. Particularly noteworthy and problematic are a number of internal inconsistencies which arise when the Commission stretches its wording (that is, different rules for different actors in terms of refusal to deal) and, most critically of all, the absence of any clear distinction between dominance and abuse. When does dominance lead to abuse and must it always? On top of these concerns there arise a number of external inconsistencies. Foremost are the different perspectives held by the Courts and the Commission. These inconsistencies create more than just analytical problems: they pose substantive consequences for the application and successful implementation of Article 82.

The degree of uncertainty left the door open for challenges and posed a problem for the Commission. To deter such moves the Commission has been compelled to tighten its approach and definitions and also to seek informal deals where possible. It is interesting to note that many decisions in the Article 82 field are reached informally between the Commission and the undertaking in question. This course of action has suited the Commission as it has prevented interference from the courts and the likelihood that DG Competition might face embarrassing defeats, but has not solved the problems surrounding the interpretation of Article 82. This realization fed directly into discussions on the reform of Article 82.

The modernization of Article 82

Article 82 has been subject recently to a spate of reforms. In addition to the changes brought about under Regulation 1/2003 for the institutional handling of cases (discussed in Chapter 4), ongoing doubts about and criticism of the EU monopoly regime led DG Competition to begin an internal review of Article 82 in terms of assessing monopolies in 2003. The latter culminated in the 2005

Discussion Paper which provided the basis for an extensive public consultation on the future trajectory of Article 82 (which ended in June 2006) and new Guidelines (originally planned for 2006) are now expected in early 2008. Most commentators and practitioners greeted the Commission's revisiting of Article 82 with enthusiasm. Commentators suggested how the regime ought to be revised. Sher (2004:245–6) argued that the Commission should keep the notion of market power very much at the centre of its deliberations and provided a series of observations on how a fully modernized Article 82 would look. In short he maintained that a reformed monopoly provision should conform to the same policy goals that apply to every other aspect of EU competition policy. This means the introduction of a more integrated approach to the competition regime as a whole, with fewer incentives built into the system for allowing other policy goals to cloud the decision-making process in this area. More specifically he advocated greater use of economic criteria when undertaking case investigations and argued that consumer welfare should also inform decisions. If met, these suggestions would certainly transform Article 82 and inject it with greater clarity and coherence. Majority opinion seems to suggest that the sensible road ahead appears to be one which involves the Commission drawing up a far more economics-orientated approach rather than trying to codify what is and is not allowed under Article 82.

The 2005 Discussion Paper on the application of Article 82 to exclusionary abuses (Commission 2005) was drawn up by two economists and two lawyers within DG Competition. It was designed as a means to re-evaluate existing policy and to consider how policy could be made more effective and more transparent. To this end it has considered how monopolies are dealt with in other jurisdictions and sought to establish an analytical economic framework for dealing with the thorny issue of abusive monopolies even though no such guidelines exist, for example, in the American system. The Paper concerned itself neither with exploitative nor with discriminatory abuses. Two main factors explain the Commission's approach. First, the review process was an attempt to modernize Article 82. The second and related factor was the need to establish a clear and consistent approach in the period following the introduction of Regulation 1/2003 which allowed national competition authorities to apply Article 82 for the first time.

The Commission's attempts to summarize its review of Article 82 in the form of a single document have been warmly received. There was widespread support for the Commission's signalling of a broader, effects-based approach on the longer-term impact of any Commission decision and how it affects the state of competition. There has been a tendency in the past to view certain types of behaviour as abusive irrespective of their impact on competition. The goal of this latest initiative if approved, will be to combine both an economics-based and an effects-based analysis that together facilitate predictability and certainty. The task in each individual case will be to determine the effects of, for example, price-based or tying contracts upon competition. To this end the Paper revisits the concept of dominance and argues that market shares remain an effective means to calculate this in most cases. Indeed, firms can be found to be dominant with market shares below 40 per cent and even as low as 25 per cent, but such instances will be rare. It is interesting to note that the Paper proposes to remove the dominance presumption that the courts have created for a firm with a 50 per cent market share.It is important to remember that the Commission's monopoly policy is not crafted in isolation and to acknowledge the pressure from the business community for greater guidance on the rules to increase certainty over which aspects of their activity might be deemed abusive. Kroes remains determined to 'enforce the Treaty's prohibition on abusive conduct. Dominant companies should be allowed to compete effectively' (Kroes 2005). Interested parties were invited to submit comments on the Paper before the end of March 2006 and to participate in a public consultation in June 2006 before the Commission started its deliberations on the revamping of Article 82. It was expected that new draft Guidelines would have been issued by the end of 2006 but none have been issued at the time of writing in early 2008. The Commission may still be reflecting carefully on the comments it has received from the public and on the issues at stake to determine the best way to move forward with the review. It seems, however, that DG Competition is moving towards a more reliable framework that that is more firmly rooted in sound economic analysis:

> First it is competition, and not competitors, that is to be protected. Second, ultimately the aim is to avoid harm to consumers. I like aggressive competition – including by dominant

companies – and I don't care if it may hurt competitors, as long as it ultimately benefits consumers. (Kroes 2005)

Conclusion

Monopoly policy has developed in a somewhat piecemeal fashion. It is clear, first and foremost, that the practice of monopoly control proved much more difficult in practice than the theory (and the law) may have at first suggested. While restrictive-practices control evolved in leaps and bounds, monopoly policy developed much more slowly. The vagueness of definitions and the need for complex economic and legal analyses forced the Commission to undertake complex and time-consuming investigations which have proven extremely contentious. One commentator has likened the entire EU monopoly regime to 'the last of the steam powered trains' (Sher 2004:243) within the regime. Yet this situation does appear to be changing and monopoly policy may be coming of age. If we retain the analogy above, moves are already far advanced to re-lay the tracks and to provide new and more reliable diesel engines. The new emphasis on consumer welfare and efficiency provides a pivot around which the 'new' policy evolves, with DG Competition's intention being the adoption of a more favoured 'effects-based' route to replace the older practice of prohibiting behaviour simply because of the monopoly's form. It is hoped that the latest changes will provide greater efficiency and security. Many firms will look forward to travelling on a potentially new and revamped anti-monopoly express train after 2008.

Chapter 6

Merger Policy

Merger policy is arguably the most dynamic and most high-profile aspect of EU competition policy. Merger control as a weapon in DG Competition's policy armoury is a recent development that dates only to 1990. The European Community Merger Regulation (ECMR) applies to 'concentrations' of economic power where two or more formally independent companies combine to create a single entity or where there is a change in control of one undertaking by another. The purpose of merger control is to enable competition authorities to regulate market structure. They do this by determining whether mergers should be allowed to take place. Mergers judged to have an adverse affect on competition will be prohibited. The pursuit of mergers involving household names such as *Time Warner/EMI*, *PriceWaterhouse/Coopers & Lybrand*, *Boeing/McDonnell Douglas* and *General Electric/Honeywell* attract huge media attention and frenzied political lobbying, ending up as quasi-theatrical events of almost Shakespearean power and intensity (Wilks 2005b:120). Mergers are as much about politics (see Zweifel 2003) as they are about economics and EU merger policy often involves heated interchanges between national governments and the Commission and open confrontation between the EU and the United States. The Commission's merger policy is perhaps the most potent weapon at DG Competition's disposal.

In line with the focus of the book our central concern is with issues of politics and governance rather than with legal analysis (Navarro et al. 2005) or with economic theories (Morgan 2001; Motta 2004). The chapter begins by explaining merger control's late arrival on the European competition policy scene. It unpacks the rationale for and the procedures involved in the regulation of merger activity, the powers of the Commission and the interplay of other actors involved, before looking briefly at the impact the policy has had since it was established. It considers some of the criticisms and the recent blows inflicted by the European courts on the EU's merger regime before accounting for later amendments both to the Merger Regulation in 1997 and to the recast Merger Control Regulation approved on 20 January 2004.

127

The origins of European merger control

While a system of merger control which could declare mergers unlawful was included in the European Coal and Steel Community (ECSC) Treaty of 1951, there were no such provisions among the European Economic Community (EEC) rules drafted six years later. There were two reasons for merger control exclusion at this point. First, the EEC and ECSC Treaties were radically different documents: 'whereas the ECSC is a *traité-loi* which specifies the regulatory content, the Treaty of Rome in contrast represents a *traité-cadre* that established a framework of action but which compels further legislation to apply the principles' (Bulmer 1994:423–4). Indeed, it was much easier to agree on the rules governing a specific industrial sector than it was to establish a more general regulation. The ECSC Treaty was intended to secure Franco-German reconciliation through the creation of supranational institutions which would prevent any revival of German revanchist ambitions. Given the political (and military) significance of the coal, iron and steel industries in any such revival, merger control was deemed a necessity. The second reason why merger control was absent from the EEC Treaty was that there was a generally held view in the 1950s that economic expansion (identified in Article 2 of the EEC Treaty) would necessitate large concentrations of economic power. Economic concentration was not regarded as particularly problematic at this time and mergers were not seen as a threat to competition. Economies of scale were held to benefit industrial competitiveness, create national or European champions, bring about greater efficiencies and even provide an escape route for companies otherwise facing closure, with the inevitable job losses that would entail. This thinking was also reflected in the newly evolving domestic competition regimes which also failed to take on board the potentially anti-competitive impact of concentration.

Attitudes changed rapidly over the course of the 1960s as the more damaging effects of concentration on market structure, whether they resulted from horizontal, vertical or conglomerate mergers, were realized. Concerns grew over the economic power of big business. As the political leaders increasingly acknowledged the dangers of market dominance, so action was taken to fill in gaps in the law. This led to the incorporation of merger control into UK competition law in 1965; and to West Germany becoming the first

Community member state to adopt a merger policy in 1973. At the European level, however, progress was much slower. With the Council of Ministers reluctant to give new powers to the Commission, DG Competition had little choice but to look to existing regulatory instruments as potential tools of merger control. Thus, in its 1966 *Memorandum on the Concentration of Enterprises in the Common Market* (Commission 1966) the Commission asserted that Article 82 might be used to regulate concentrations. The uncertainty caused by this assertion lasted only until 1973 and the European Court of Justice's (ECJ) *Continental Can* case. For not only did the ECJ's ruling support the Commission's decision, but it also applied a rather liberal interpretation of the Treaty in this area, establishing that under certain circumstances a firm holding a dominant position could be regarded as abusing its position when taking over or merging with a competitor.

Although the judgment was welcomed by DG Competition as a clarification of the rules, it did little to compensate for the absence of a real merger instrument. In practice, Article 82 had an extremely limited use, as it could be used to deal only with mergers where a pre-existing dominant position was strengthened. In other words, DG Competition could investigate a concentration only where there was a clear 'abuse of a dominant position'. In theory at least, this left DG Competition with the highly complex task of unscrambling mergers that had already occurred. In addition

> this ruling left a serious anomaly in EEC law: a merger involving at least one firm in a dominant position might be prohibited under article 82; a merger between a small number of equal size firms would contravene no law even if it created a 100 per cent impregnable monopoly. (Fishwick 1993:115)

Recognizing the limitations of Article 82 used in this context, the Commission issued a draft regulation in 1973. But this came up against stiff opposition from certain member states, and most notably from the UK, France and West Germany. From the outset it had little chance of becoming law given the sensitivity of the issue in the national capitals. While the Commission continued to press for legislation throughout the 1970s and into the 1980s, a decline in merger activity during this period meant that this issue did not feature high on the European political agenda. Indeed, three further attempts at merger legislation, in 1982, 1984 and 1986, also failed to find favour with the Council.

National attitudes changed quickly, however. There were dramatic changes to the economic and business environment in Europe in the 1980s. With the prospect of a European single market in view, the Council finally began to understand why merger control had to be a priority. Although the Commission's 1985 White Paper *Completing the Internal Market* (Commission 1985a) included no mention of merger control, business restructuring was to prove a natural corollary to the '1992' programme. Mergers tend to come in waves of activity and the second half of the 1980s was characterized by a rapidly growing number of mergers, acquisitions and joint ventures. According to Commission data, there were 115 mergers in 1982–3, 208 in 1984–5, 492 in 1988–9 and 622 in 1989–90 (Tsoukalis 1993:103). It was against this backdrop that industry demands for the creation of a 'level playing-field' and a 'one-stop shop' for merger control became more vehement. The Commission's efforts to incorporate merger control into its competition armoury was aided by the ECJ's 1987 *BAT* [British American Tobacco] and *Reynolds* v. *Commission* judgment which stated that under certain circumstances Article 81 (as well as Article 82) might be used to regulate mergers.

The *BAT and Reynolds* case had begun with complaints to the Commission by two tobacco companies, BAT Industries and RJ Reynolds, about an agreement between two of their competitors, Philip Morris and Rembrandt. This agreement not only gave Philip Morris control over one of Rembrandt's subsidiaries, Rothmans International, but also provided the company with first refusal on any future sale of Rothmans shares. Following an investigation, DG Competition insisted that the agreement be altered. In Philip Morris's appeal, not only was the Commission decision upheld, but the ECJ also commented on Article 81's applicability to mergers. Article 81, it was stated, could be used in such circumstances if a concentration occurred as a result of agreements entered into between two or more companies. In other words, the ECJ affirmed that an agreed share transaction could be classed as a restrictive agreement under Article 81, thus giving the Commission the right to intercede in so-called 'friendly' mergers. The Commission subsequently exerted its new-found powers in 1988 by forcing British Airways to surrender some of its routes to its main competitors after it had taken over British Caledonian.

Although the ruling pleased the Commission and enhanced DG Competition's prestige, it again failed to compensate for the lack of an effective merger regime, and served only to intensify the level of insecurity and confusion felt by the business community. Industry complained to national governments about the confusion, putting pressure on the member states to deal with the issue as a matter of urgency. It was no coincidence that less than two weeks after the judgment, issued on 17 November 1987, the Council gave the Commission the green light to draft a new merger regulation. The Commission seized this opportunity with enthusiasm.

Towards a coherent merger regime: procedure and practice

The Commission's fifth draft merger regulation reached the Council of Ministers in March 1988. Although it was agreed that the legislation was necessary, the negotiations were no less controversial than previous efforts at merger control. For some, the biggest sticking-point was the transfer of control from the national to the supranational level. For others, specific substantive and procedural issues were the major stumbling-blocks. It was not clear, for example, just how much discretion the Commission would have in merger cases, where the thresholds for European-level jurisdiction would lie, what the relationship between the national and the European authorities should be, and what criteria would be used to assess concentrations. This last point proved particularly contentious, provoking a debate about whether or not merger policy should be used to promote an industrial policy and the fostering of European 'champions' through active state intervention, the oft favoured approach of the French, Italian and Spanish governments (see Brittan 1994).

After protracted and often passionate negotiations, a radically altered version of the Commission's original draft Regulation was agreed on 21 December 1989. The European Merger Control Regulation (EUMR), effective as of 21 September 1990, laid the foundations for the first coherent European-level merger regime. It is important to emphasize that although the Merger Control Regulation sought to prevent a new entity abusing its dominant market position, its primary concern was with the maintenance of a competitive market structure producing benefits for consumers.

But what exactly is a merger and when does one occur? A merger is normally deemed to take place when two separate undertakings form an entirely new entity, as occurred for example with the fusion of the two pharmaceutical companies Glaxo Wellcome and SmithKlein Beecham to form GlaxoSmithKlein in 2000. However, it should be stressed that the concept of a merger, as used by competition lawyers, incorporates a far broader range of corporate transactions that also includes the acquisition of a minority shareholding in a company or the establishment of a joint venture company. Understanding why companies resort to mergers may be important in assessing their likely market impact. Their motives can be accounted for in a number of variables that impact to a greater or lesser degree on the public interest. It may be that economies of scale and other efficiency gains, the creation of a national champion or greater corporate control that is, merging to prevent any detrimental moves by another rival company in buying shares from disgruntled shareholders. Mergers may even be driven by greed and the drive to enhance market power.

The fundamental premise underpinning EU merger control can be found in Article 2(3) which states that 'a concentration which creates or strengthens a dominant position as a result of which effective competition would be significantly impeded in the common market shall be declared as incompatible with the common market'. The Merger Regulation established an architecture with distinct and 'separate jurisdictional zones' (Davidson 2005), first at the EU level and second at the national level. Under Article 1 all proposed mergers (or 'concentrations' as they are referred to in the Merger Regulation) that had a community dimension (CD) fell under the competence of the European Commission. This was the only logical way to proceed if cross-border mergers were to be tackled efficiently. The CD was triggered when the firms involved had an aggregate worldwide annual turnover of more than €5bn or where each of at least two firms had an aggregate EU-wide annual turnover of more than €250m. (The exception to this, under the two-thirds rule, was where each of the merging parties earned more than two-thirds of their aggregate EU-wide annual turnover within one and the same member state.) Essentially, all mergers with a CD had to be notified to the Commission. It was the Commission that possessed the sole authority to approve mergers, to sanction them with conditions, or to prohibit them completely.

Significantly, there is no formal involvement either from the Council or from the Parliament in the decision-making processes. Both were, and remain, as is the case in other areas of competition policy, marginal actors who are little more than observers in the day-to-day case investigation and decision-making process. That said, the European Parliament can debate competition issues and can ask the Commission to explain certain decisions. In fact the Competition Commissioner briefs the EP about policy activities and current objectives on an annual basis. Competition policy issues are discussed within the Internal Market and Consumer Protection committee and some of the EP party groups have developed particular interest in the area. For example, and in relation to merger policy, the Alliance for Liberals and Democrats for Europe (ALDE) drew up its own report in 2006 on mergers (ALDE 2006).

Viewed from the perspective of 1989, questions immediately arose about this new form of European governance. Could the Commission deliver? Did it have the expertise? And did it have sufficient staff to deal with the merger cases that would come before it? Time and experience would answer such questions. The final deal, it must be stressed, had been based on a compromise among all the parties, which meant that the higher thresholds originally proposed by the Commission had been lowered to reduce DG Competition's involvement. With fewer cases falling within the scope of the Regulation and a smaller jurisdiction for the Commission, this allowed national competition agencies to retain some control over large mergers within their jurisdiction. This proved, in hindsight, to be a blessing for the Commission, as the smaller number of cases gave DG Competition more time to organize itself, to recruit appropriate staff and to get to grips with its new rules.

While the creation of a 'one-stop shop' for large-scale mergers met with the approval of the business community, there was a steep learning curve for all involved, both with the Commission and outside. To assist understanding of both procedural issues and aspects of practice, the Commission has published a number of Notices and Guidelines summarizing its policy approach on a range of issues on, for example, the concept of concentration or simplified procedures for assessing mergers and, more recently, on jurisdiction (Commission 2007a; see also Goyder 2003; Whish 2003; Jones and Sufrin 2008).

Perhaps the most difficult aspect of the negotiations which led to this Regulation was the relationship between the European- and national-level authorities, centring on two referral mechanisms. The threshold issue was a part of this, but there were also other dimensions that would affect the two levels of merger regulation. The first concerned the possible repatriation of cases from the EU to the national level, in instances where the Commission would normally have competence. The German government had been keen to ensure that national authorities were given the right to deal with cases that were likely to have a major impact on their national markets. In a last-minute concession, the so-called 'German clause' (Article 9) was agreed, which allowed national authorities to request that a case be repatriated under certain circumstances. The second issue was somewhat less contentious. Article 23(3), known as the 'Dutch clause', allowed member states to invite the Commission to undertake a merger investigation on their behalf, where a merger does not fall within the member state's jurisdiction. This was useful in cases where national laws were weaker than those at European level. According to the Merger Regulation, all mergers exceeding the aforementioned thresholds had to be notified to the Commission. There was one exception to this basic rule: member states retain jurisdictional competence to examine any merger that may affect national security and defence (Article 296 EC Treaty).

Initially, responsibility for merger investigations within the Commission had been allocated to the Merger Task Force (MTF) or Directorate B within DG Competition. However, a reorganization in 2003 broke up the MTF into seven separate units. Three horizontal units dealing with coordination and remedies were retained in the merger policy unit Directorate A and within each of the four sectoral directorates of the DG (B-E) (see Chapter 2). From 2003, all staff dealing with concentrations are now recognized as belonging to the Merger Network.

A special form, Form CO, was drafted by DG Competition, which when completed by the proposed merging parties would bring together all the details it required to undertake its assessment (Navarro et al. 2005:356–60). This form is divided into eleven sections and seeks substantial information about company accounts, about the proposed merger, about the relevant market, about shares held by the companies, about the ownership and control of the firms involved and about any relevant links between them. One hard copy plus five photocopies and a further 30 copies in DVD format are required by DG Competition. In order to secure both accuracy and greater honesty, the Commission was empowered to levy fines of between ECU1000 and ECU50,000 where incorrect or misleading information was supplied at this stage in the procedure.

Compared with Articles 81 and 82 cases, the investigation of a merger is fairly straightforward. It begins with a case analysis, during which three fundamental questions are addressed: 'whether the notified concentration falls within scope of the Regulation . . . its compatibility with the common market . . . [and] whether or not it creates or strengthens a dominant position in the common market' (Commission 1993:130). The Commission's analysis was to be based on an examination of the likely effects on competition, though it could also take into account other factors such as economic progress and technological developments. It was only able to prohibit a concentration 'where it clearly believes that there will exist a lasting period of dominance which cannot be defeated by existing potential competitors and therefore will lead to substantial impediment to effective competition' (Downes and McDougall 1994:301).

Critics of the policy argued that any competition-orientated analysis that took place within DG Competition could be overridden easily once the decision fell into the hands of the more political College of Commissioners, the body that takes the final decision. The active participation of Commissioners in the final merger decision opens the doors to extensive lobbying not only on behalf of the firms concerned but also, on occasions, by member state governments, as was clearly evident in *Aerospatiale/Alenia/ de Havilland*, and this case is discussed below.

Even where political factors enter into play the Commission's decision must stand up in the European Courts if appealed against. Much depends on the Courts' interpretation of what constitutes 'the development of technical and economic progress', which was the only real clause in the Merger Regulation which provided scope for a more industrial-policy approach within a decision.

The Merger Regulation included an explicit timetabling mechanism that reflected the Commission's interest in speeding up decision-making and making the process more transparent. A speedier response would reduce the negative effect on share prices and minimized the likelihood of rival and hostile takeover bids. The Regulation envisaged two time frames, simply entitled Phases I and II. Phase I involved the preliminary analysis. Mergers had to be notified to the Commission before they took place. When the MTF had received a notification and the formal procedure had begun, the responsible officials began to extract the necessary information from the parties involved. Phase I proceedings were limited strictly to a period of four weeks, during which time the national authorities kept in close contact with the MTF.

Negotiations were intense and complex. After hearing from all the interested parties, the MTF drew up a preliminary draft report in all official EU working languages which was submitted to the Advisory Committee on Concentrations. Established by the Merger Regulation, the Advisory Committee in many ways mirrors its Article 81/82 counterpart, the Advisory Committee on Restrictive Practices and Monopolies. It is again a consultative forum which enables the member states to have a direct input into the decision-making process. Meetings of the Advisory Committee all take place in private and do not involve the interested parties. Although its decisions are published in the EU's *Official Journal* (OJ), how the member states voted is never made public. In terms of procedure, once the Committee has made its views known, and its decisions do not bind the Commission, a draft decision is prepared and sent to the College of Commissioners for approval or rejection.

In fact there were three avenues open to the Commission at this stage:

- It could proclaim the merger to be beyond the scope of the EU's jurisdiction.
- It could approve the merger on the grounds that it did not have any substantial effects on competition within the common market.
- It could determine that the proposed concentration raised some serious questions as to its compatibility with the common market. As such, it could decide that the case warranted closer scrutiny. If so, proceedings were opened for a more complex and lengthy second-stage (Phase II) investigation.

In the first decade of its operation over 96 per cent of mergers were settled during the Phase I proceedings. These were not deemed problematic and as such Phase I decisions were not published in the EU's *Official Journal* but were, and still are, listed on DG Competition's website. Article 8 of the Merger Regulation empowered the Commission to conduct a further four-month investigation when dealing with trickier cases. At the end of that process, the Commission was empowered to accept a merger, accept it with conditions, or prohibit it. A mechanism was built into the Regulation enabling all such prohibitions to become subject to judicial review by the European courts at the request of the companies concerned.

The original Merger Regulation had anticipated a review of the thresholds, and indeed a lowering of them, by the end of 1993. Severe opposition from certain states and most noticeably Germany and the UK, had dissuaded Karel van Miert from postponing any move in this direction until the Commission was more prepared to present its case in the light of a longer analysis of the Merger Regulation in operation. As a consequence the Commission did not bring forward its Green Paper on Community Merger Control (Commission 1996), which re examined the operation, the successes and the failures of the Regulation until 1996. Designed to inject greater clarity and efficiency into merger decision-taking, this Paper argued that concentrations just below the existing thresholds that were likely nonetheless to have a substantial impact on interstate trade should henceforth be covered by the Regulation. In so doing, the proposal would clearly have enhanced DG Competition's authority.

While the economic rationale for a reduction in the merger thresholds was advanced forcefully in the Green Paper, the political case against a transfer of cases to the European level also remained strong. While seven member states supported the Commission's line, there was still opposition from the British, French and Germans, who were supported cautiously by another five 'doubters' (Commission 1996). The Germans, and the *Bundeskartellamt* in particular, notoriously distrustful of the Commission's motives, were vehemently against any change in the rules, because they feared the EU competition regime was more open to politicized decision-making than was its German counterpart (discussed below). Nevertheless, the Council settled on an agreement in June 1997 on more modest amendments to the 1989 Merger Regulation (Council 1997).

The amendments introduced a second set of criteria. Under these, a concentration had a CD when the combined, aggregate, worldwide turnover of all the undertakings concerned exceeded ECU2bn and an EU turnover of ECU100m. These lower thresholds, which came into effect on 1 March 1998, were designed to capture those concentrations that were of a particular interest to the Commission, but had not previously come under the original CD test. In retrospect, however, and according to the Commission itself, the new CD test did not make much noticeable difference.

Another frenetic wave of merger activity occurred at the turn of the new millennium. As Whish (1993:781) illustrates, some 292 merger notifications were received by the Commission in 1999, an increase of 24 per cent from the previous year and 70 per cent more than in 1997. Ironically, as more and more cases came before its increasingly overstretched officials, and as the number of notified mergers continued its upward climb from 212 in 2003, to 244 in 2004, to 313 in 2005, some doubts were raised over the rigour of the Commission's case analyses. One of the striking characteristics of this wave of merger activity was the size of the mergers and the global ambitions of the companies involved, covering a range of economic sectors that extended from car manufacturing to entertainment and news broadcasting. SmithKleinBeecham, for example, emerged as the largest pharmaceutical company on the planet in 2000. This merger between Glaxo Wellcome and SmithKleinBeecham represents the latest merger in a sector that has seen ever greater concentration since the end of the 1980s. This new company has a worldwide workforce of over 56,000 people and an annual turnover of over some £8bn. Similarly, the Commission gave the green light to Exxon's link-up with Mobil to establish the world's largest oil company in 1999.

For over a decade it seemed to many observers that the MTF ayatollahs were practically invincible. This perception was transformed completely in 2002 when the Court of First Instance (CFI) overturned three previous Commission merger decisions in *Airtours/First Choice*, *Schneider/Legrande* and *Tetra/Laval* respectively. The overturning of prohibition orders had been extremely rare until this point in time. Indeed, only one of the 15 prohibitions between 1990 and 2001 had been annulled. The rejection of all three rulings in 2002, in the Commission's own *annus horribilis*, reflected the Court's concerns about DG Competition's decision-making process, and in particular about the lack or selected use of evidence and the questionable application of economic analysis. This seriously damaged the Commission's credibility.

Ultimately, it was judged that poor economic analysis lay at the heart of the Commission's problems. Time constraints were often to blame. For example, in the case of Tetra Laval, the MTF officials had only forty-eight hours to read over thirty opinions from interested parties as well as assessing the concessions made by Tetra Laval itself to secure a clearance. The language used by the Courts in all three cases was scathing. For example, in *Schneider/ Legrande*, the Court referred to the Commission's analysis as strewn with errors, omissions and inconsistencies. In this particular case, which concerned two French electrical manufacturers, the Commission did come to admit that a lack of resources had prevented them from undertaking a detailed economic analysis to support their view that the agreement was anti-competitive in nature. Of course, judicial review cannot revive a merger, but it does provide the parties involved with some hope of an approval subject to certain conditions. For both sides the final outcome is hugely significant. For business, conditional clearances are preferred to outright prohibitions. For the Commission, any rejection of its own analysis by the CFI not only proves damaging to its credibility but also provides the opportunity for parties behind a Commission-prohibited merger to seek damages against it – as occurred in both the Airtours and Schneider cases.

Each of the three rulings (on *Airtours/First Choice, Schneider/ Legrande* and *Tetra/Laval*) identified deficiencies with the way mergers are investigated and assessed and led DG Competition to initiate a complete shake-up of its operations, under the guidance of the then Commissioner, Mario Monti. This entailed a review of DG Competition's procedures and working arrangements, and a re-evaluation of merger policy itself, with particular regard to the need for greater economic analysis that would stand up to external and judicial scrutiny. As part of the re-evaluation it was decided to restructure DG Competition and specifically to disband the MTF as a separate entity and to spread its staff throughout all parts of DG Competition.

In practice, the transfer of former MTF officials into other directorates can be viewed as an attempt to 'export' the MTF's best practices to the other directorates and thereby share experiences with the other areas of the EU competition policy regime. Specifically, it was hoped that staff working on mergers would not only be able to assist with cartel cases and vice versa (Maudhuit and Soames 2005:144) but also be able to facilitate faster decision-making. This latter objective was simply too ambitious an objective, as DG Competition's investigations in other areas of competition policy generally take longer given their nature and the evidence that has to be collected. At the same time as the internal reform was getting under way, more significant changes that were to affect DG Competition's relations with the business community and with the national competition authorities were contained within the most recent revisions to the Merger Regulation that came into effect in May 2004.

The recast 2004 European Merger Regulation

The origins of the 2004 version can be traced back to Article 1(6) of the Merger Regulation, which called for the Commission to report to the Council on the working of merger control and the thresholds before July 2000 (Commission 2000). The Commission duly did this and made use of the opportunity to press for a much more in-depth analysis of the EU's merger system. The Council's agreement paved the way for the Commission's consultative Green Paper on the Review of Council Regulation 4064/89 in November 2001 (Commission 2001a) and the publication of a draft notice proposal in December 2002. This draft proposal explored a number of jurisdictional and procedural issues, such as for example the two referral mechanisms, the role of the Advisory Committee and the issue of fines. This fed into discussions with the wider policy community consisting of peak business organizations, legal practitioners and national government representatives. It culminated in an agreement in the Competitiveness Council on 27 November 2003 on a recast EU merger regime, incorporating the two earlier Regulations and supported by a number of other Commission Notices (see Box 6.1). How should this revised Regulation be interpreted? Does it reinforce the one-stop-shop principle and continue to provide legal certainty for the business community?

The 2004 reform package certainly reinforced existing EU norms and values. However, it also included a number of new and welcome innovations. Mergers (or 'concentrations') occur when one or more undertakings merge their businesses or where there is a change in control of an undertaking and it also applies to full-function joint ventures. The repackaging of EU merger policy can best be judged by summarizing its contents in terms of jurisdictional, procedural and substantive reforms (Parisi 2005).

BOX 6.1 Notices in force to assist understanding of the principles and aims of the Merger Regulation

Notice on the concept of a concentration
Notice on the concept of undertakings concerned
Notice on the calculation of turnover
Notice on the concept of full-function joint ventures
Notice on simplified procedure for certain concentrations
Notice on remedies
Notice on restrictions directly related and necessary to
  concentrations
Notice on appraisal of horizontal mergers
Notice on vertical and conglomerate mergers

The issue of who has jurisdiction over which mergers where two or more independent companies come together within the EU has been one of the most controversial aspects of the European regime. The 2004 Regulation has reaffirmed the jurisdictional boundaries between the national and supranational competition regimes. Put simply, merger policy remains a core EU competence, where the Commission maintains its triple role as investigator, prosecutor and decision-maker. Member state authorities are not permitted to deal with mergers that have a CD. The CD thresholds have not been altered, but the revised Regulation incorporated several refinements to make the administrative processes more effective.

Jurisdiction should be reattributed to another competition authority only where the latter is better suited to deal with a particular merger. Interestingly, for the first time, firms are entitled to trigger the referral process themselves. From May 2004 concentrations which would not otherwise have a Community Dimension, but which are capable of being reviewed under the national competition laws of 'at least three Member States', can be dealt with by the Commission at the request of the merging parties (Article 4(5)) so long as all merging parties are in agreement. Alternatively, at the pre-notification stage and according to Article 4(4), the merging parties may, in a so-called 'reasoned submission', request the Commission to refer the concentration to a particular member state, 'where the concentration may significantly affect competition in a market within a Member State which presents all the characteristics of a distinct market' (Jones and Sufrin 2008:997). In both instances the companies will continue to benefit from a 'one-stop-shop' merger control. Thus the revisions to the Merger Regulation are expected to produce a more streamlined and improved system of referrals. In practice, however, this change means that more cases will be referred to the Commission as the key competition regulator. There are likely to be few cases arising through Article 4(4) requests. Where they will arise is when the companies concerned expect an Article 9 referral from a member state.

Once the jurisdictional competence of the EU has been established, the merger investigation can begin. It is the task of the DG Competition to identify and determine whether the proposed merger will have adverse effects on competition within the marketplace. The trickiest part of the investigation for DG Competition, and which replicates its difficulties with monopolies, lies in defining dominance. The concept is hard to pin down exactly and causes considerable contention among economists. This is more than just semantics, as the courts will determine the interpretation based on this wording. There were a number of recommendations made on this issue prior to the recasting of the Regulation (see Fitzpatrick 2005).

As of 1 May 2004 Article 2(3) of the Regulation reads as follows:

> A concentration which would significantly impede effective competition in the common market or in a substantial part of it, in particular as a result of the creation or strengthening of a dominant position, shall be declared incompatible with the common market.

The new wording does not fundamentally alter the existing dominance test as some might have wished, but it does place more weight on the 'impact' of the merger, and emphasizes more clearly that all post-merger scenarios where competition is impeded (and that result, for example, in higher prices, less choice for the consumer and less innovation) are going to be problematic. The explicit timetabling mechanism of the original Merger Regulation was maintained, although Regulation 139/2004 modified both time periods to provide an even more flexible timetable (see Box 6.2), to give the notifying parties more time to establish the compatibility of their merger with the common market.

BOX 6.2   The merger review timetable

Regulation 4064/89
Former: 1990–30 April 2004

Regulation 139/2004
Current: after 1 May 2004

Phase I
One month starting from day
of notification.
Extended to 6 weeks if
undertakings are offered
or a referral is requested.

Phase I
25 working days after
notification.
Extended to 35 working days if
undertakings are offered
or a referral is requested.

Phase II
An immediate four months to
carry out an in-depth
investigation.

Phase II
An immediate 90 working days
to carry out in depth
investigation;
+20 working days if requested by
the merging parties or by the
Commission;
+15 working days if companies
offering remedies after 54th day
of investigation.

Source: Derived and modified from DG Competition website: http://europa.eu.int/
comm/competition/mergers/cases/stats.html.

Phase I still involves a preliminary analysis which considers whether the Commission has jurisdiction; whether the matter could be referred to or from the member states; whether any problematic issues can be identified; whether all relevant materials and information been provided by the merging parties; and how much cooperation is required from the national authorities. The timing mechanisms have been altered slightly. DG Competition now has 25 days following formal notification to determine whether the merger falls within its jurisdictional thresholds. To this end it confers with other interested DGs and makes enquiries with third parties in an effort to determine whether the proposed merger raises any serious doubts as to its compatibility with the common market. At the end of the process DG Competition has three avenues open to it. It can proclaim the merger to be beyond the scope of the EU's jurisdiction; it can approve the merger on the grounds that it does not have any substantial effects on competition within the common market; or alternatively it can determine that the proposed concentration raises some serious questions as to its compatibility with the common market and decide that the case warrants closer scrutiny. If so, proceedings are opened for a more complex and lengthy second-stage (Phase II) investigation.

Phase II allows for an additional 90 working days of investigation. There is a degree of flexibility at this point and the Commission may, with the agreement of the notifying parties, extend the period of Phase II by a maximum of 20 working days (Article 10). If commitments are offered within the first 54 working days of Phase II, no extension will be permitted. It is also possible to extend the period of 90 working days during this stage of the investigative process under the so-called 'stop-the-clock' procedure. Here, the notifying parties are presented with a one-off opportunity to request an extension of no more than 20 working days, provided this request is made not later than 15 working days after the decision to initiate an in-depth inquiry. This last point in particular should be noted, for in addition to DG Competition and the merging parties, Phase II investigations always involve the Hearing Officer, other DGs, other firms and NGOs and consumer groups. It needs to be stressed that the shaping of the merger investigation and the final decision are the product of many contributing authors, expressing often quite different views on the merger (Burnside 2000:393). It is left for DG Competition to determine and reach its own conclusions.

At the end of that process, if it looks as though a conditional or negative decision is likely to be reached, a formal Statement of Objections is issued. This presents DG Competition's arguments and gives the parties to the merger two weeks to respond. There are three possible outcomes: the concentration may be cleared without attaching any conditions to it; it may be approved conditionally; or it may be prohibited. Unconditional clearances are relatively rare at this stage and there have been only 39 from 1990 to the end of January 2008, including *Boeing/Hughes Electronics*, which centred on a satellite business, and *Carnival/P&O* concerning cruise ships. In contrast, in the same time period 83 have been subject to some type of commitment. Only 20 have been prohibited outright and of these 3 have been overturned by the Courts. The lessons to be drawn from Phase II proceedings for merging parties are that there is a very good chance that cases that reach this stage will need alteration and/or commitments made by the parties; and, indeed, run a high risk of being prohibited.

Tweaked rather than radically altered, the new timetable will, it is hoped, prevent decisions being taken at the last possible moment when the Commission has almost run out of time. This revision to the Regulation reflects the Commission's concern over the speeding up of decision-making. Shorter investigations and speedier decisions benefit both sides, and both reduce the negative effect of a merger investigation on share prices and minimize the likelihood of rival and hostile takeover bids.

In terms of statistics, 3,696 proposed mergers were notified to the Commission between 1990 and January 2008 (of which 110 were subsequently withdrawn; see Box 6.3). The vast majority (some 3,178) were cleared as compatible by the end of Phase I during this same period. Phase II proceedings were opened on 176 occasions and only 20 of these were prohibited owing to the excessive market share and post-merger market dominance. These concerns were raised in the rejection of the notifications from *Volvo/Scania*, *GE/Honeywell* and *Saint-Gobain/Wacker-Chemie/NOM*. Significantly, the Commission has been equipped with additional investigative and fact-finding powers. Articles 11–13 of the revised Merger Regulation outline the Commission's substantive powers and these now include on-site inspection of books and records as well as powers to inspect and even seal business premises (Article 13(2)(d)). The previously existing possibility of asking for 'on-the-spot oral explanations' is refined, and the Commission is now entitled to ask 'any representative or member of staff for explanations on facts or documents relating to the subject matter and purpose of the inspection and to record the answers' (Article 13(2)(e)). In order to assist case investigations, fines for failing to respond to information requests from the Commission and for supplying incorrect or misleading information (which is requested in the revised version of Form CO or in response to a request for information) have been increased to a maximum of 1 per cent of the undertaking's aggregate turnover (Article 14(1)).

Periodic penalty payments not exceeding 5 per cent of the average daily aggregate turnover of the undertaking may be imposed for each working day of delay, in order to compel the undertaking to supply complete and correct information which the Commission had requested by decision (Article 15(1)). In *BP/Erdölchemie* from 2004 the Commission imposed a fine of

€35,000 on the applicants for omitting relevant information required under the CO form. At the time this constituted the highest fine possible, but now under the recast Merger Regulation fines can amount to 1 per cent of the turnover of the company concerned (see Merger Regulation, Articles 6(3) and 8(6)).

Accompanying non-legislative and innovative changes were introduced to complement Regulation139/2004. These sought to tackle some of the problems that had arisen in the past with regard to limited resources and the case analysis, and addressed in particular the soundness and suitability of the economic theories being used by DG Competition staff. The solutions involved the appointment of a Chief Economist, the use of 'devil's advocate' panels and the promotion of best practice. All three solutions are designed to ensure greater consistency and transparency within the decision-making process, so as to contribute to a more rigorous analysis that would stand up to external scrutiny and make the possibility of the Courts overturning the Commission's decision at best more unlikely and at worst – both from DG Competition's perspective – more difficult.

The role of the Chief Economist, Professor Damien Neven is to oversee, direct and provide much-needed independent economic expertise and guidance on methodological issues in the application of the EU competition rules. In addition to providing direct input into individual competition cases (in particular those involving complex economic issues and quantitative analysis), the Chief Economist is also charged with the development of general policy instruments and, when needed, will assist with cases pending before the Community Courts (Röller and Buiges 2005). In theory, the creation of this new post should ensure consistent and well-judged case argumentation. In this vein the more systematic use of 'devil's advocate' panels to strengthen internal scrutiny, and especially to provide guidance and expertise on economics and econometrics, should also facilitate the work and judgments of the Commisison. Under the more in-depth Phase II investigations the specific team dealing a case will submit their conclusions to a 'devil's advocate panel', whose members come mainly from Directorate A, to enable a 'fresh pair of eyes' to review the consistency of their approach.The changes to the EU merger regime were also accompanied by a number of draft notices, such as the Commission's adoption in December 2003 of its draft 'Best Practices on the Conduct of EC Merger Control Proceedings' (Commission 2003a). All efforts were designed to provide guidance on the day-to-day conduct of EC merger control and open the regime to greater consistency and clarity for the competition authorities, the undertakings and all other onlookers, but have they actually lived up to expectations?

Assessing merger policy: politics and political sensitivities

Since 1990 a genuine and autonomous merger regime has been constructed to deal with cross-border mergers in the European Union. The creation and evolution of such a full-blown European regime represents a major landmark in the process of European integration. It laid the foundations for the first coherent, European-level merger regime and clearly delineated responsibility between the national and supranational competition authorities. Positively, it has been acknowledged by the Commission as an administrative success story (Monti 2005). An effective pre-notification system, a thorough notification form and skilful handling of cases by high-calibre merger policy officials have been translated into a speedy and efficient regulatory regime which is often contrasted with the less positive experience in the restrictive practices and monopoly fields. However, the EU merger regime has always had its critics and these have included on occasions national competition authorities such as the German Federal Cartel Office (see Sturm 1996); firms whose merger plans have been rejected by the Commission; firms whose mergers have been agreed by the Commission but overturned by the Courts as in *SONY/BMG* in 2005; and academics and consumer groups that have been critical of the lack of transparency within the decision-making system (Neven *et al.* 1993). Concerns have been voiced that DG Competition has been rather 'trigger-happy' in its merger cases. There has also been criticism over DG Competition's combined role as case investigator, prosecutor, judge and jury. These issues are now considered.

Merger investigations are highly technical, encompassing both complex legal reasoning and economic analysis. There are always a number of conflicting issues in the examination of any merger. Some argue that mergers have a detrimental impact on the market in the longer term, and are critical of the short-termism that often drives the companies involved; others are suspicious about the accumulation of economic wealth in the hands of a small number

BOX 6.3   Statistical overview of mergers, 1990–January 2008

NOTIFICATIONS

Number of notifications	3696
Cases withdrawn (Phase I)	80
Cases withdrawn (Phase II)	30

REFERRALS

Article 4(4) request Form RS)	34
Article 4(4) referral to member state	31
Article 4(4) refusal of referral	0
Article 4(5) request (Form RS)	140
Article 4(5) referral accepted	132
Article 4(5) referral refused	4
Article 9 Requests for referral to member states	78
Partial referral	36
Full referral	31
Refusal of referral	4
Article 22 referrals to EU level	19
Referral	16
Refusal of referral	2

PHASE I DECISIONS

Article 6.1(a) – out of scope	52
Article 6.1(b) – compatible	3178
Article 6.1(b) – compatible under simplified procedure	1153
Figues included in 6.1(b) above	
Article6.1 b- compatible with commitments	158

PHASE II DECISIONS

Article 8.2 – compatible	39
Article 8.2 – compatible with commitments	83
Prohibition	20
Article 14 – Decisions imposing fines	8
Restore effective competition	4

Source: Commission at: http://europa.eu/comm/competition/mergers/statistics.pdf (accessed 25 February 2008).

of corporations; others still ponder the impact of mergers on, for example, employment; others again are more concerned about cases where the control of firms passes to overseas companies (Whish 2003:790–1).

All these issues together direct attention to the political sensitivities behind merger policy-making. There are five dimensions to the politics of merger control (see Box 6.4). These concern the disputes that take place between the national governments over how much control to delegate to the supranational level; the tensions between the national and EU jurisdictions over who should control particular cases; the clashes within the Commission's services and within the College of Commissioners; disagreements between rival companies and the Commission over the impact of specific mergers on particular markets; and contrasting interpretations of merger control between the EU regime and other non-EU competition regimes. Each aspect is now considered in turn.

BOX 6.4   Locating the politics of EU merger policy

Dynamic	Actors	Politics occur over
Construction of EU regime through to regulations	Member states	How much power should be delegated the EU level?
Tension between jurisdictions (Articles 9 + 22)	EU and national competition authorities	Who is best placed to deal with individual cases?
Clashes of policy preference	Commission services and European Courts	Decision making and divergent internal policy priorities
Disagreements over competitive conditions	Commission and proposed merging parties, consumer groups and third parties	Commission interpretations of competitive markets and dominance
Conflict and contrasting interpretations	EU and other international regimes, especially US	Differing views on impact of merger on competition

The construction of the EU Merger Regime

A study of EU merger policy needs to recognize the controversial nature for many member states of handing control, albeit initially limited in nature, through CD thresholds, to the supranational level. In many ways a principal–agency approach lends itself very much to the understanding why merger policy was delegated to the EC level (Doleys 2006). The relationship between cause and consequence in EU policy design and development is usually presented as the product of a bottom-up or a top–down process, where the impulse for change can emanate from the member states of the European Union, from the Commission, or from pressure from non-governmental (and primarily business) interests. Member State acceptance of the EU merger regime is a direct corollary and logical consequence of plans to complete the single market and can certainly be interpreted as a consequence of intergovernmental bargaining.

However, this interpretation is inadequate as an explanation of the origins of the EU merger regime, as it ignores the role played by actors within the business community, such as the European Roundtable of Industrialists (ERT) and the European Employers Confederation (Unice/BusinessEurope), who formed a coalition of interests with the European Commission to heap additional and arguably decisive pressure on national governments in favour of an EU system based firmly upon a level playing-field and a one-stop-shop facility. Two separate agendas were at work here. Each sought to shape the future political development of the policy. On the one hand, the Commission regarded the Council's decision to limit DG Competition's responsibilities as a temporary drawback; on the other hand, it appreciated that once a regime had been constructed it could later be reformed (that is, through the agreement of lower thresholds, as anticipated in the original Merger Regulation).

The tension between the national and supranational authorities

The creation of distinct jurisdictional zones and of a one-stop shop has not been unproblematic. Doubts about the European-level regulation of mergers existed in certain quarters from the outset, especially in Germany, focusing on the various criteria that might be applied across EU and national regimes and which might lead to tension over the authority best placed to tackle individual merger cases. The German competition authorities were concerned particularly about the degree to which pure competition reasoning could be undermined by the policy preferences of other DGs and Commissioners during the decision-making process. Put another way, the Federal Cartel Office was concerned about the possible politicization of merger cases. As discussed earlier, the original Merger Regulation had attempted to resolve this issue with the inclusion of Article 9 (the so-called German clause). Such requests were few in the early years of the regime. The first successful request was made in 1992 when the UK authorities were permitted to investigate the *Steetly/Tarmac plc* case that related to the brick and clay tile market in parts of England. In contrast, the Commission's decisions to reject the first four Article 9 applications from the German competition authorities intensified the unease within the Federal Cartel Office. The fifth attempt was successful only because the Commission had miscalculated the timetable mechanism and lost the ability to deal with the case itself as it was originally planned. Consequently, the *McCormick/CPC/Ostmann* case, which covered the German market for herbs and spices, was passed to the German authorities.

These initial experiences led Berlin to call for the creation of a new and truly independent European competition office (ECO) (Wilks and McGowan 1995a). With only lukewarm support from other member states and a much happier encounter with the Commission and Article 9 in the latter half of the 1990s, the ECO idea was dropped. The number of Article 9 requests has grown more rapidly in recent times and the Commission has guarded its competence in this area. By February 2008 the Commission had received 78 requests and granted full or partial referral in 67 cases. Most use of Article 9 is made (and maybe not so surprisingly) by both the British (see, for example, the partial referral in 2000 in *Interbrew/Bass*) and the German competition authorities (see the 2001 decision on *Shell/DEA*). As of the end of 2007 only four requests in total have been refused.

Another approach to referrals rests on Article 22(3) or the 'Dutch clause' that was originally designed to enable member state authorities who did not possess specific or substantive merger control legislation (as was the case in the Netherlands in 1989 and hence the name) to pass cases to the Commission for investigation where the proposed merger did not meet the CD thresholds. The original article was an adept attempt to secure legal certainty for the European (that is, EU and national) regime. Three of the first four referrals under Article 22 came from member states without merger legislation and the Commission subsequently issued prohibition orders against all three, namely *RTL/Veronica/Endemo* and *Kesko/Tuko* in 1996 and *Blokker/Toys 'R' Us* in 1997. However, by the end of 2005 with 26 (out of the EU 27) member states possessing their own domestic merger control legislation, Article 22(3) has lost much of its relevance. By the end of January 2008 it has only been used on 16 occasions. Because of awareness of such sensitivities, the revised Merger Regulation (Sufrin and Jones 2004:888) made it easier for member states to request referrals (under Article 4(4)) and it has been designed to facilitate such transfers. Caution will need to be applied carefully in future to ensure that the attraction of the one-stop-shop principle is not undermined. To this end the Commission has stepped up its cooperation and partnership with the national competition authorities within the European Competition Network (see Chapter 2). DG Competition accepts that national competition agencies should deal with cases where they are best positioned. It may grant referrals but it will still insist that the rules of the Merger Regulation are applied in all cases. Such steps are designed to dispel distrust; but problems still persist in sensitive areas, such as in the electricity and gas markets. Energy is currently the most controversial of all economic sectors because it throws up very sensitive questions about the ownership and control of national power supplies. The Commission is prepared to argue its corner against economic nationalism when energy (electricity and gas) bills are rising fast across Europe. Companies are looking to access new markets and merge national operations in an effort to cut costs and become pan-European power providers.

The proposed merger in 2006 between two of Europe's leading gas companies, namely Germany's E.ON and Spain's Endesa, illustrated the tensions. The Spanish National Energy Commission (CNE) had cleared the €26.9bn ($US34bn; £18bn) merger, albeit subject to some 19 conditions. The reaction of the Spanish government was on the one hand rather curious as it had earlier given its blessing to a bid for Endesa by the Spanish energy group Gas Natural; yet on the other hand it had concerns about the arrival of non-Spanish owners in the richly rewarding energy field. Nevertheless, the German company remained committed to the deal, although it objected to the regulator's caveats which sought to keep Endesa separate from its other operations, limit the firm's debt levels and keep up its current, and planned, levels of investments. E.ON was also informed that it was expected to sell some of Endesa's domestic businesses, including its one-third share in the Asco-1 atomic reactor, as well as some of its own coal-fired generating power plants; and commit to keeping gas supplies at previously agreed levels.

In 2006 the European Commission informed the Spanish energy agency that the Spanish government had broken EU merger rules in its handling of the takeover. This decision provides a clear illustration of Commission's determination to clamp down on economic nationalism. The Commission's case rested on two key issues. It argued, first, that Spain had illegally usurped the European Commission's power to impose conditions on mergers; and second, that the Spanish had imposed stringent conditions that contravened the free movement of capital and that these had to be lifted. E.ON welcomed the Commission's decision and immediately raised its takeover bid for the Spanish power company to €37bn ($US47bn; £25bn) in the wake of another potential bid for Endesa's shares from Acciona, a Spanish engineering and building group. This late bidder's arrival certainly surprised the markets and if successful, could have given it a say in future company development.

In late 2006 the Commission called for the Spanish government to withdraw the illegal conditions by 19 January 2007 and stated that failure to do so would lead the EU to initiate infringement proceedings against Madrid under Article 226 of the EC Treaty. This decision was a severe setback for the Spanish government which had been hoping to create a national champion in the energy sector to protect the industry from foreign takeover bids and it held its ground. Consequently, the case came before the European Court of Justice which ruled that Madrid had indeed infringed EU competition law by not withdrawing the conditions for E.ON's acquisition of Endesa. In the meantime the situation in the market had altered and E.ON's hopes of securing control of Endesa had faded when the Italian utility Enel unexpectedly bought almost 10 per cent of the Spanish company in what can be described as a raid on the markets. E.ON eventually dropped its EUR42 billion takeover bid for Endesa, and made a deal with Spanish building group Acciona SA (ANA.MC) and Enel SpA (EN), Italy's largest power utility, to carve up the company between them.

The European Commission's actions should serve as a major warning to any other EU member state which might be tempted to prevent flagship companies from falling into foreign hands.

Clashes within the Commission

There are some doubts as to whether there can be truly effective control mechanisms in the Commission as long as decision-taking lies in the hands of the European Commissioners. It seems that there remains the real possibility that any competition-orientated analysis within DG Competition could easily be overridden once the case comes before the more political College of Commissioners (McGowan and Wilks 1995). The history of EU merger control has indeed uncovered a degree of politicization on occasions. This was the case in the very first prohibition decision against *Aerospatiale-Alenia/de Havilland* in 1991. Here DG Competition was confronted by the proposed takeover of the Canadian turboprop aircraft manufacturer De Havilland by ATR, a Franco-Italian joint venture consortium led by Aerospatiale (France) and Alenia (Italy). Had the bid been successful, the joint venture would have given the French and the Italian firms around 50 per cent of the world market and just over 65 per cent of the EU market for commuter planes. In other words, it would have allowed the companies a market share far exceeding that of British Aerospace and Fokker, their main competitors. Both rivals opposed the merger, claiming that if it went ahead they would end up being pushed out of the market.

Sir Leon Brittan, Competition Commissioner at this time, opposed the merger on purely economic grounds, arguing that it would produce a dominant player in the market with very few competitors (Ross 1995:177–81). His position was challenged vociferously by DG Industry within the Commission, and by all four French and Italian Commissioners. The French and the Italian governments both supported the proposed merger. From the perspectives of Paris and Rome it would not only have facilitated the creation of a powerful global competitor, allowing for research synergies and economies of scale, but it would at the same time have a positive effect on employment. As a result, both governments put pressure on 'their' Commissioners to get the deal accepted. Moreover, Martin Bangemann and his team in industrial policy DG argued that the industrial advantages of the merger exceeded the drawbacks, rejecting DG Competition's market analysis and the free-market principles on which they based this analysis. Jacques Delors, then Commission President, who was sympathetic to the Franco–German arguments, also threw his support behind the merger. This left Brittan with a daunting task.

Fuelled by the conviction that he was right, the Competition Commissioner launched an intensive last-minute campaign to win the backing of his fellow Commissioners. It was unclear which side would win the debate in the College of Commissioners when even President Delors showed sympathy for the deal. However, in the end Brittan's arguments prevailed and the merger was prohibited, albeit narrowly by 9 votes to 7. The outcome angered the French government and the entire episode bore witness to the existence of conflicting national competition policy approaches, which appeared in microcosm within the Commission. In cases such as these, merger officials are frequently accused of taking an overtly political approach to decision-taking. It should be remembered, however, that it is the College of Commissioners, and not DG Competition, which is ultimately responsible for merger decisions. So even should the merger officials wish it so, there can be no guarantee that the competition criterion will override other policy considerations at the end of the day. Whichever constraints are placed on the College they are those that exist within the Merger Regulation itself, though there is a certain amount of leeway. Indeed, merger policy allows for a greater degree of political bargaining than some governments feel is tolerable. National interests and preferences, differing ideological approaches and the intensive lobbying of Commissioners by sectional interests can all influence and possibly even determine policy outcomes.

Disagreements: the relationship between business and the Commission

On looking at Box 6.3 it might seem that the initial and large number of clearances under Phase I (3178) and prohibition orders under Phase II merger investigation proceedings (20) from 1990 to the end of January 2008 may seem to raise questions about the credibility of European merger control. However, these statistics reveal little of the true picture and tell little about the significant level of interaction between the merging parties and DG Competition prior to any official notification of the proposed merger (and, for that matter, during the formal investigation). These informal discussions are encouraged by the Commission as they enable the merger network within DG Competition to identify and address in a cooperative manner possible difficulties that may arise from a merger. It is during these encounters that problems are often ironed out and disputes resolved. With the growing use of informal pre-notification discussions, DG Competition is often very aware of the details of a merger before any formal notification is made. This means that it has built up a great deal of expertise in judging what is and is not important in a notification. Indeed, contact between the business community and DG Competition is very much a core feature of competition governance. Although much has been written about the mobilization of general business interests at the EU level (see, for example, Greenwood *et al.* 1999; van Appeldorn 2002; Greenwood 2003; Coen and Dannreuther 2004) and their attempts to influence public policy outcomes, very little has been said specifically on the interactions between business and DG Competition as regards merger policy.

The revised 2004 Merger Control Regulation recognizes the importance of such contacts and has sought to make it easier for informal relations to take place. From the firms' perspective the relationship with EU competition officials is a crucial one, as what the merging parties really want from the process is complete clearance and no conditions. For any proposed merger the outcome that is sought is a green light to proceed. Firms operate to a 'game plan' in which they need to convince DG Competition of the merits of the merger and to convince the competition officials that there are no serious drawbacks to the deal. Phrased another way, companies seek to build a consensus and reach some form of accommodation with DG Competition, and to this end increasingly employ public affairs consultants (alongside their own teams of competition lawyers) who are familiar with the rules and procedures of the merger policy process and who are also able to make better use of the media to promote the benefits of the merger.

What is occurring here is a form of interest representation that is not too far removed from the customary policy-shaping activities familiar in other policy sectors. Consumer organizations and other business groups in the same sector as the proposed merger are keen to publicize their concerns to DG Competition and other parts of the Commission. Not surprisingly these are often extremely important in shaping the Commission's line on a merger and, as a consequence, such contacts between DG Competition and third parties are deeply resented by the merging parties. One recent example involved the German electronics giant Siemens, who successfully approached DG Competition over their concerns in the *Schneider/ Legrande* case. Such informal discussions may seem to suggest that the merger process lacks transparency. However, issues of business confidentiality make any form of total disclosure over who seeks access to DG Competition and why largely impossible.

Under the rules of the Merger Regulation the Commission's decision is not the final point in the process, as all firms have the right of appeal against a negative Commission decision to the Court of First Instance (CFI). For the first decade of the Merger Regulation relations between both EU institutions in Brussels and Luxembourg were largely cordial and far from contentious where mergers were concerned. This 'honeymoon' period came to an end after 2000 when the CFI struck down a series of Commission decisions in the *Airtours/First Choice*, *Schneider/Legrande* and *Tetra/Laval* cases. These decisions sent immediate shockwaves through DG Competition but for the business community they clearly opened up a real avenue and a means to challenge the Commission and were welcomed. Prohibitions or even clearances with conditions can have adverse effects on a company's standing and stock market value, as such outcomes are deemed evidence of failed business diplomacy, often culminating in the sacking of the negotiating team or changes in the governing board. Firms are more determined than ever to use the Courts where necessary.

Conflict and contrasting interpretations: the Commission and non-EU competition authorities

All restrictions on competition that may affect trade within the EU may actually originate from outside this geographical area. Therefore, given the reality that concentrations involving non-EU companies can have detrimental consequences for competition inside the EU, the question arises of how far the EU's jurisdiction extends. This leads us to consider briefly the complex and legal concept of extra-territoriality that is fast becoming an important aspect as globalization advances. The issue of who has jurisdiction is a problem, particularly in the control of mergers, when competition laws vary between states and when the different national authorities seek to enforce compliance with their own specific regimes.

The impact of EU merger policy is therefore felt far beyond Europe's borders, becoming particularly sensitive when the Commission's interpretation of a proposed merger is in direct conflict with that of other competition regimes, and most notably the

US authorities. Disagreements between the Commission and their American counterparts may be relatively rare, but when they do occur they become international news stories.

One such example is the infamous *Boeing–McDonnell Douglas* case from 1997. The dispute here centred on a merger between two American-owned aircraft producers and proved particularly contentious as the merger had been cleared by the US competition authorities in January 1997, even though initial concerns persisted about its impact on the aircraft construction market. Nevertheless, the Federal Trade Commission had allowed the merger to proceed in the hope that Boeing could help transform the fortunes of the uncompetitive McDonnell Douglas. Attitudes on the other side of the Atlantic differed greatly. DG Competition's main concern, and one that was widely shared by the EU member states, was that the European Airbus consortium should not be damaged by the arrival of a new and even more dominant presence in this market. More specifically, the Europeans objected to a substantial number of exclusive arrangements that sought to tie purchasers to Boeing for some twenty years. The politics behind this case were on display from the outset.

The then Competition Commissioner, Karel van Miert, made numerous statements to the media (and this was a rather unusual step to take during merger investigations) to voice the Commission's clear objections to the merger. The Commission's hostility towards the merger helped sour relations with the US government for most of 1997 and led to other highly prominent interjections. Al Gore, the US Vice President, threatened a trade war if the Commission moved to prohibit the merger while van Miert launched a counteroffensive, not only declaring that Boeing would be hit with very heavy fines if the merger was allowed to proceed but also suggesting that Boeing aircraft that entered EU space should be seized and impounded. As the Commission decision date drew closer even President Bill Clinton entered the arena to express his disquiet about the EU position. Ultimately, and at the eleventh hour, a deal was brokered between the Commisison and Boeing that allowed the merger to proceed, once many of the tying arrangements had been dropped.

A more recent example of high-level political intervention and controversy centred on the Commission's decision in 2001 to prohibit General Electric's takeover bid for Honeywell (see Morgan and McGuire, 2004). This case, the largest merger in recent business history and the first prohibition to involve just two US-based firms, was particularly sensitive, as this proposed merger had been given the green light by the American authorities and eleven other competition agencies. Its prohibition 'precipitated a torrent of criticism from the US accusing the Commission of arrogance, poor economics, outdated thinking and incompetent analysis' (Wilks 2005b:122). While Grant and Neven (Grant and Neven 2005) provide an excellent analysis of how the EU and US competition agencies used very similar empirical evidence but then reached very different conclusions, there is little doubt that beyond the economic analyses the political dimension was at play. This episode fuelled a public debate among American politicians and sections of the media and led to calls for US retaliation against EU companies. Merger decisions can have a substantial political impact. In order to overcome the dilemmas raised by different competition rules and regimes, states have sought to secure bilateral and multilateral international arrangements to create a framework at least to deal with common merger cases. Progress in this direction has been made but remains largely confined to mergers.

Conclusion

This chapter has shown merger policy to be the epitome of everything that is controversial about competition regulation. In so doing it has highlighted the sensitivities that underpin all Commission policies that regulate government–industry relations. With EU Council involvement in merger matters limited, politics is played out within the Commission, as national governments place direct pressure on 'their' Commissioner, raising considerably the stakes of merger outcomes. Decisions concern not only effects on European industrial structure, but end up as almost symbolic battles determining the ideological/national winners and losers in this aspect of European integration.

Sensitivities over the role played by the Commission in merger cases have raised important questions about the future development of merger control practice. Should the Commission be striving for a neutral, objective, rule-bound system of regulation which allows decision-takers only a limited discretion, or should officials be permitted a certain degree of flexibility when reaching merger decisions? And what sort of criteria ought to be used?

Should the encouragement of competition be the only consideration, or might other factors, such as European competitiveness, or
social and regional implications, be taken into account? In
European merger policy, the Competition Commissioners have
always been keen to play down the discretionary scope of the
merger rules, and have thus emphasized legal certainty over flexibility. In addition, they have tended to stress that the policy's effect
on European competition is always the deciding factor in merger
cases, denying that the Commission uses its merger powers for
other policy ends

At its heart the EU merger regime operates by demarcating the
borders between national and supranational control. It represents
one of the best examples of a federal policy (in all but name). It is a
policy in which the Commission seeks to strengthen its powers vis-
à-vis the member states in economic sectors such as banking. DG
Competition is also determined to put further pressure on potentially recalcitrant member state governments who are trying to
resist competition in the energy sector. For the immediate future,
resistance among EU governments may thwart the Competition
Commissioner's and DG Competition's ambitions, but their arguments are hard to ignore in the longer term. There are inconsistencies created within the single market when national authorities
determine merger cases, on the basis of divergent policy objectives,
particularly if their aim is to create national champions. For
example, in the banking sector the UK has prevented mergers
between the big banks, whereas France and Spain have been prepared to allow them.

Mergers will without a doubt remain politically contentious. The
revamped Merger Regulation and its accompanying measures have
been drafted in such a way as to ensure that DG Competition will
be able to provide clearer (economic) evidence to support its arguments. The new in-house scrutiny mechanisms are expected to help
achieve that objective, but clashes over which policy outcomes are
best are certain still to occur. The operations of EU merger policy
always seem subject to continuous revision. In April 2007, for
example, the Commission launched a public consultation on a
draft Notice on remedies acceptable under the Merger Regulation,
which required modifications to Regulation 139/2004. It will be
interesting to observe how the relationship between the Commission and the national competition authorities, on the one hand,
and the Commission and the Courts, on the other, develop in the

next few years. There does seem to be some discontent over the way EU mergers are handled, as well as issues over timetabling arrangements, appeals and the jurisdictional architecture. Some if not all of these issues will feature in the next review of the Merger Regulation scheduled for 2009.

Chapter 7

State Aid Policy

State aid control is arguably the most unusual of the EU's competition policies as it involves governments rather than firms. As a consequence it is extremely sensitive politically. By restricting the capacity of governments to intervene in their own economies, state aid policy sounds the death-knell of purely national industrial strategies. It does so by endowing the European Commission with the task of ensuring that subsidies granted in the EU are compatible with the single market. The logic of state aid control is that a firm gaining government support earns a potentially unfair advantage over its competitors (Commission 2007c). The argument that the Single European Market (SEM), and indeed European Monetary Union (EMU), are jeopardized by unchecked state aid is almost a truism. Even were all physical, regulatory and fiscal barriers to European trade to be removed, national subsidies would remain as one of the few protectionist and market-fragmenting instruments at the disposal of national and sub-national authorities. Yet there is no expectation that EU state aid policy will eliminate aid altogether – or even that this might be a desirable outcome. Rather, the policy's purpose is to protect the integrity of the single market and prevent subsidy races developing across the member states. Since 2000 and the introduction of the Lisbon Strategy, and particularly since 2005 when the ten-year Lisbon Strategy was re-launched midterm, state aid control has been justified in terms of the contribution it can make to industrial competitiveness. This emphasis is not entirely new, as state aid control has always been considered both a negative (prohibitive) policy and a policy contributing to more positive EU objectives, as in the case of services of general interest (Scott 2000).

This chapter provides an introduction to the EU's state aid policy, placing it firmly within the context of the internal market and the relaunched Lisbon Strategy, while highlighting the salience of the four themes which run through this book: modernization, Europeanization, decentralization and liberalization. It begins by identifying the legal instruments available to the European Commission and more specifically to DG Competition in its regulation of state aid, concentrating on the procedures that apply to this policy area and the way the Commission's aid control is organized. It is worth noting at this point that state aid procedures differ greatly from those that apply to the Commission's restrictive practices, monopoly and merger policies. The second part of the chapter focuses on policy evolution and policy content, first of all charting the development of the policy from its revitalization in the 1980s to 2008, and then reviewing in more detail the application of DG Competition's regional aid, sectoral aid and general and horizontal aid policies. The final section offers an assessment of the policy, focusing in particular on the politically controversial aspects of the regime and suggesting how state aid control might evolve in the future.

Organization, powers and decision-making

State aid policy is a rather unusual component of the EU's competition regime. It is, distinctively, a Commission-led supranational policy, which does not exist in any national context and conventionally is not considered part of domestic competition policy arrangements. The Commission itself calls its policy on state aid a 'worldwide unique system of rules' (Commission 2007c). Enforced in most cases by DG Competition, it has characteristics very different from the Commission's restrictive practices, monopoly and merger policies, not least in that the object of its rules and decisions are governments rather than firms.

From an organizational perspective, the inclusion of state aids control within DG Competition was a historical anomaly. When the DG was set up, it brought together not only what we now consider to be mainstream competition policies, but also policies on value added tax, European company law and European patent law, as well as on state aid. Of these latter policies all but state aid was transferred out of the Competition DG in 1968 (Hambloch 2007). The fact that state aid control remained within the DG has helped shape its pro-competition focus. For much of its history, state aid control was managed by a separate state aid directorate within DG Competition. However, since a major reorganization in 2003 (implemented incrementally between 2003 and 2005), the DG's state aid responsibilities have been integrated into directorates organized along sectoral/functional lines. This means, for example, that within Directorate A of DG Competition, Policy and Strategy, Unit A/3 deals with the policy and strategy dimensions of state aid control. Likewise in Directorate E, Markets and Cases IV: Basic Industries, Manufacturing and Agriculture, Unit E/3, deals with state aids and industrial restructuring (see Box 3.2). This new structure has been set up to encourage greater coherence across the DG, and across the policy, a response to the 'ghettoization' of state aid control in the earlier organigrams.

Alongside DG Competition, other DGs in the Commission have responsibility for state aid in sector-specific areas: transport and coal (DG for Energy and Transport), fisheries (DG for Fisheries and Maritime Affairs) and agriculture (DG for Agriculture and Rural Development). There also exist links to the officials of other DGs who have an interest in state aid, such as DG Regional Policy and a number of sectoral policy DGs.

As in other areas of competition policy, the decentralization of state aid control has been a recent topic of discussion, although as of 2008 little progress has been made in implementing recommendations. Yet state aid policy has always been enforced 'in close cooperation with the Member States' (Commission 2007c), with the EU regime placing organizational requirements on national (and indeed sub-national) governments from the early days of the policy. Some light was shed on this prior to the 2004 and 2007 enlargements when candidate countries had to set up state aid surveillance authorities to meet the Commission's pre-accession requirements. Moreover, since the publication of a Notice in 1995 (Commission 1995a), the Commission has been pushing for greater enforcement of state aid law by private actors in national courts; and it does seem in fact that the number of these cases is increasing. Domestic courts are also permitted to decide whether a state aid has been notified, and can grant relief (for example, demanding the repayment of the aid) in respect of non-notified aid. Nevertheless, exempting aid remains exclusively in the hands of the Commission (Commission 2007c). However, to push the agenda forward, in the 2005 State Aid Action Plan, which proposes reforms to the state aid regime (Commission 2005), the construction of a network of state aid authorities was suggested, echoing recent developments in anti-trust policy.

Defining state aid

The state aid regime comprises a system of Commission scrutiny over nationally granted state aid. Thus there is a paradox at the heart of the state aid regime: on the one hand the Commission has been empowered by the Treaty; but on the other, member states have the capacity to constrain the Commission. While this is often taken to mean that the Commission controls the granting of national subsidies, the word 'subsidy' does not do justice to the Commission's conception of a 'state aid'. 'State aid' is a more inclusive term, encompassing tax and interest relief, state guarantees and government holdings in companies, and the provision of goods and services by the state on referential terms, as well as straightforward financial assistance (grants). While the EEC Treaty was rather vague on what was and was not state aid, both the Commission and the European Courts have helped to clarify the kinds of support that fall under the state aid rules. The Treaty itself makes a distinction between aid 'conferred on a selective basis to undertakings by national public authorities' (Commission 2007c; Commission 2007d), which is prohibited, and aid to individuals or general measures (such as general taxation), which is not covered by the state aid rules. Thus to be subject to these rules, aid must involve the transfer of state resources (though the aid in question need not be transferred by the state authorities themselves). Further, it must be directed at certain firms; must at least threaten to distort competition; and (in the context of the Commission's rules) must affect interstate trade within the Union (Schrans 1973:173–8; Quigley 1988:242; Commission 2007d:3). Also, it must confer an economic advantage on the firms concerned that they would not otherwise have had. So a state aid might exist where a firm buys publicly owned land at less than the market price, for example (Commission 2007d:3). Small amounts of aid do not meet these criteria; thus under the *de minimis* rules, embodied in a Regulation in 2006, they are exempt (Commission 2006a). As the Commission puts it: 'the scope of Community State aid rules is wide (but not open-ended)' (Commission 2007d:4).

State aid is incompatible with the Common Market because of its distortive effects on competition and intra-Community trade (Commission 2007c). It is therefore considered a 'bad thing'. But if this statement told the whole story, the function of state aid policy would be merely to seek out existing aids, prohibit them, and prevent the grant of any new aid. That alone would not be a simple task. But the policy is even more complicated, as state aid may also be a 'good thing' on occasion. It may help to achieve the Treaty's market integration goals and reduce economic and regional disparities within the Union, or it may serve to complement other EU policies, such as cohesion and employment policy.

While the prohibition of state aid is confirmed in Article 87(1), formerly Article 92(1), within Title IV of the Treaty (Common Rules on Competition, Taxation and the Approximation of Laws), the potentially positive effect of aid control is acknowledged in the exemptions to the prohibitive rule. Article 87(2), formerly Article 92(2), provides clear-cut exemptions for certain aids: aid having a social character granted to individual consumers, or aid to make good damage caused by natural disasters or exceptional occurrences. However, the cornerstone of the Article 87 provision lies in its third paragraph. This provides for discretionary exemption, based on regional or sectoral criteria: where the aid contributes to a project of common European interest; where there is a serious disturbance in the economy; or which promotes culture or heritage conservation. There is also a clause which relates to aids to support 'certain areas of the Federal Republic of Germany affected by the division of Germany' (see Box 7.1 for the precise wording of the treaty provisions).

However, the curtness of these provisions leaves them open to interpretation both by the state aid officials in DG Competition and, subsequently, by the European Courts. As the treaty provisions allow for prohibition with one hand and exemption with the other, there is room here not only for flexibility in enforcing the policy, but also for a good measure of ambiguity as it places substantial discretion in the hands of the Commission. This may also allow political factors to enter state aid decision-making.

The procedural rules governing the enforcement of state aid policy are set out in Articles 88 and 89 of the EEC Treaty. Article 88(1), formerly 93(1), deals with 'existing aid': that is, aid already notified to and authorized by the Commission. It states that the Commission 'shall keep under review' all such aids and 'shall propose . . . any appropriate measures required by the progressive development or by the functioning of the common market'. In other words, there is no guarantee that aid which was approved in the past will be permitted indefinitely.

'New aids', by contrast, are to be notified to the Commission before they are implemented. Under Article 88(3), new aids must

BOX 7.1 State aid provisions of the Treaty of Rome

Article 87

1. Save as otherwise provided in this Treaty, any aid granted by a Member State or through State resources in any form whatsoever which distorts or threatens to distort competition by favouring certain undertakings or the production of certain goods shall, in so far as it affects trade between Member States, be incompatible with the common market.

2. The following shall be compatible with the common market:
   (a) aid having a social character, granted to individual consumers, provided that such aid is granted without discrimination related to the origin of the products concerned;
   (b) aid to make good the damage caused by natural disasters or exceptional occurrences;
   (c) aid granted to the economy of certain areas of the Federal Republic of Germany affected by the division of Germany, in so far as such aid is required in order to compensate for the economic disadvantages caused by that division.

3. The following may be considered to be compatible with the common market:
   (a) aid to promote the economic development of areas where the standard of living is abnormally low or where there is serious underemployment;
   (b) aid to promote the execution of an important project of common European interest or to remedy a serious disturbance in the economy of a Member State;
   (c) aid to facilitate the development of certain economic activities or of certain economic areas, where such aid does not adversely affect trading conditions to an extent contrary to the common interest;
   (d) aid to promote culture and heritage conservation where such aid does not affect trading conditions and competition in the Community to an extent that is contrary to the common interest;
   (e) such other categories of aid as may be specified by decision of the Council acting by a qualified majority on a proposal from the Commission.

Article 88

1. The Commission shall, in cooperation with Member States, keep under constant review all systems of aid existing in those States. It shall propose to the latter any appropriate measures required by the progressive development or by the functioning of the common market.

2. If, after giving notice to the parties concerned to submit their comments, the Commission finds that aid granted by a State or through State resources is not compatible with the common market having regard to Article 87, or that such aid is being misused, it shall decide that the State concerned shall abolish or alter such aid within a period of time to be determined by the Commission. If the State concerned does not comply with this decision within the prescribed time, the Commission or any other interested State may, in derogation from the provisions of Articles 226 and 227, refer the matter to the Court of Justice direct. On application by a Member State, the Council may, acting unanimously, decide that aid which that State is granting or intends to grant shall be considered to be compatible with the common market, in derogation from the provisions of Article 87 or from the regulations provided for in Article 89, if such a decision is justified by exceptional circumstances. If, as regards the aid in question, the Commission has already initiated the procedure provided for in the first subparagraph of this paragraph, the fact that the State concerned has made its application to the Council shall have the effect of suspending that procedure until the Council has made its attitude known. If, however, the Council has not made its attitude known within three months of the said application being made, the Commission shall give its decision on the case.

3. The Commission shall be informed, in sufficient time to enable it to submit its comments, of any plans to grant or alter aid. If it considers that any such plan is not compatible with the common market having regard to Article 87, it shall without delay initiate the procedure provided for in paragraph 2. The Member State concerned shall not put its proposed measures into effect until this procedure has resulted in a final decision.

> *Article 89*
>
> The Council, acting by a qualified majority on a proposal from the Commission and after consulting the European Parliament, may make any appropriate regulations for the application of Articles 87 and 88 and may in particular determine the conditions in which Article 88(3) shall apply and the categories of aid exempted from this procedure.
>
> *Source*: Consolidated Version of the Treaty Establishing the European Community, Official Journal C325/35, 24 December 2002.

not be granted before the Commission either takes a decision or else decides not to pursue the case. The procedure, as spelt out in the Treaty, is as follows: if the aid is likely to be illegal, DG Competition will open the investigative procedure outlined in Article 88(2), the so-called 'contentious procedure'. If it finds against the member state as a result of this investigation, a formal decision will be taken requiring the state to abolish or alter the offending aid. If the member state does not comply with this decision, or if it chooses to challenge it, the case may be brought before the European Courts.

Article 89, formerly Article 94, allows for the adoption of a procedural regulation by the EU Council. Any such regulation could only be issued on the basis of a Commission proposal and was to be approved by a qualified majority of member states in the Council, using the consultation procedure. Article 89 explains that such a regulation 'may determine the conditions in which Article 88(3) shall apply and the categories of aid exempted for this procedure'. In other words, this would be a Council 'enabling regulation', allowing the Commission to clarify its own rules within in the limits set by the Council at a later date. It was only in the late 1990s that the Commission eventually asked the Council to approve a regulation under this provision (Council 1999). Once approved in 1999, this allowed the Commission to issue its own implementing Regulation in 2004 (Commission 2004b). The content of this Regulation sets out the procedural requirements of the state aid regime. And as of 2007 the Commission was already proposing revisions to this Regulation (Commission 2007c).

Aside from the use of regulations, which is a particularly recent development in state aid law, the Commission has built up a large body of legislation (decisions) and soft law (taking the form of frameworks, guidelines and notices, for example), which has been supplemented by the European Court's expanding body of rulings on state aid. Regardless of particular reform initiatives, the continued construction and redrafting of this formal and informal state aid *acquis* is an ongoing process, which has as its objective the promotion of transparency, legal certainty and predictability for the policy's 'users'. As in other areas of competition policy, one might argue that the ultimate aim is for state aid policy to be self-regulating. Thus state aid law and policy aims to set out how public authorities are expected to behave when they consider granting preferential treatment (in the form of transfers of resources) to firms. However, evidence of this kind of self-regulation is yet to materialize and seems unlikely to do so in the foreseeable future.

Notification and non-notification

As noted above, the Commission's state aid policy relies on the prior notification of new or altered aids. This is an obligation placed on member state authorities. The obligation to notify is set out in Article 88(3) of the Treaty, which states that the Commission 'shall be informed, in sufficient time to enable it to submit its comments, or any plans to grant or alter aid'. However, as governments often see the state aid rules as constraints upon their capacity to pursue an independent industrial policy, it should come as no surprise to find an 'implementation gap' at this stage in the decision-making process, with non-compliance still one of the most persistent problems facing state aid officials. Although aid levels appear to be declining (see Box 7.3 below), the Commission still struggles to deal with the number of cases that exist.

The onus on governments to provide information to the Commission is problematic and it is not uncommon for member state authorities to look for loopholes in or to plead ignorance of the rules. However, member states also use state aid policy to justify their own domestic political agendas. Governments, keen to limit the flow of public expenditure, are adept at using DG Competition as a scapegoat and at blaming the Commission when state aid is cut (Smith 2000). Even so, it is clear that non-compliance will remain a problem as long as domestic political pressures weigh more heavily on governments than does the threat of Commission action. In other words, as long as governments see it in their interest to avoid applying the state aid rules in certain cases, the Commission will face an uphill struggle in its attempts to stem and redirect the flow of national subsidies.

As is also the case in other areas of DG Competition's work, the state aid staff within DG Competition is heavily dependent upon information gleaned from the financial press, from company reports, and from complaints made either by competitor firms, by member state governments, by consumer groups, or by consumers themselves. But uncovering a breach of the rules is only the first stage in the process. Dealing with that breach is the second; and this poses its own set of procedural challenges. Since 1990 a special procedure for dealing with non-notified aid has been in operation. This allows the state aid directorate to issue an interim order requiring the immediate suspension of the subsidy payment where a non-notified aid is identified (Slot 1990:751). The procedure also speeds up decision-making through the application of a series of strict deadlines. These changes are not without their practical difficulties however, as tight time-limits may lead the Commission to produce inadequately reasoned decisions.

Procedural breaches remain second-order infringements. As such, any failure to notify a procedural breach is not judged as seriously as the grant of an illegal aid, a substantive breach. Indeed, the European Court has stressed that aid cannot be deemed illegal simply because it has not been notified. The Commission still has a duty to investigate the case thoroughly, even though national judges do have the right to demand recovery of an aid on the grounds that it was not notified to the Commission. DG Competition has been critical of this line and it has long been pushing for powers which would require the repayment of non-notified aid, whether the aid itself was illegal or not (Winter 1993). Yet the Court has a point. If the penalties for non-notification are as tough as those for a breach of the aid rules, authorities granting aid which is likely to break those rules will have no incentive to notify. They would face the same penalties whether or not they informed the Commission.

Enforcement has always been one of the state aid regime's weak points. Without the kind of powers of investigation which characterize the anti-trust work of DG Competition, state aid officials have to find other ways of persuading or cajoling member states into abiding by the rules. Since the 1990s, it has placed a substantial emphasis on the recovery of illegal aid as a supplement to the state aid armoury. For example, in February 2008 the Commission requested that the Romanian authorities recover €27m from the motor vehicles company Automobile Craiova, paid to it as part of a privatization deal. In this case the Romanian authorities had imposed conditions of sale to ensure the maintenance of certain production and employment levels, accepting in return a lower sales price (Commission 2008a). This, the Commission deemed, constituted illegal state aid.

Another way the notification problem has been improved has been through the inclusion of a variety of specific non-notification requirements in the state aid frameworks, the latter being guidelines which cover particular categories of aid. This removed some of the less distortive aids, allowing officials to concentrate on the more important cases. Yet non-compliance has become so great a problem that the introduction of a compulsory system of notification was discussed in the 1990s, though given the already overstretched resources of DG Competition, this could cause more problems than it resolved, and has since disappeared from DG Competition's agenda.

The decision-making process

Once a state aid has come to the attention of DG Competition, the decision-making process proper can begin, though the procedures as set out in the Treaty provide only a loose framework to guide those involved. In practice, decision-making begins with an initial routine and informal investigation and is followed by the initiation, if appropriate, of a more formal and contentious procedure (see Box 7.2).

At the first stage, the *rapporteur*, who is the state aid official in charge of the case, has two months in which to determine whether the measure in question is in fact a state aid. If it is, he or she must then consider whether it is likely to fall under one of the Article 87 exemptions. This is a fairly straightforward assessment in the majority of cases, and most state aid is authorized at the end of the preliminary period of investigation. This aspect of state aid decision-making rarely gets much attention as it tends to be low-profile, routine and uncontroversial. Where there is clearly no case to answer, the aid is approved and the positive decision is pub-

BOX 7.2   State aid decision-making procedures

Stage	Action	Time limit	Possible outcomes
Stage 1: initial investigation	Questions posed by rapporteur: is the measure in question a state aid? If yes, does it fall under one of exemption provision?	2 months.	1. No case to answer. 2. Exemption provision clearly applies. 3. Need for further investigation.
Stage 2: 'contentious procedure' (in-depth investigation)	Letter to member state representatives; further investigation by Commission, including economic analysis; interested parties comment.	Reasonable length of time. usually no more than 6 months.	1. Negative decision.* 2. Conditional decision.* 3. Positive decision.

Note: *Recovery of aid may be requested.

lished in the EU's *Official Journal* ('C' Series). However, if the *rapporteur* feels that there is a case to answer, where there is doubt about the effects of the aid, or where further investigation is required before a judgment can be made, the more formal or 'contentious' Article 88(2) procedure is initiated. It should be stressed that a move to the second stage of the investigation is the exception rather than the rule. Even problem aid is more likely to be dealt with sooner rather than later. National authorities are told informally that an investigation is likely and will often agree to come to an informal settlement to avoid a lengthy investigation. It is clear that '[f]requently, the mere threat to open the procedure will induce a Member State to modify its proposal to make authorisation easier' (Caspari 1984:11).

If the initiation of the formal procedure is necessary, then an order, taking the form of a letter, is sent to the member state's representatives, allowing them to voice their opinion on the case. This second stage requires a much more in-depth appraisal of the state aid, in line with criteria set out in the Treaty, in the relevant case-law, and in the Commission's own frameworks and guidelines, which constitute its soft law infrastructure. Within these parameters officials use their discretion to weigh up the pros and cons of the aid in order to judge whether any 'compensatory justification' for it exists: that is, whether its benefits outweigh its anti-competitive effects (Mortelmans 1984). This 'compensatory justification' principle was confirmed by the European Court in the *Philip Morris (Holland)* judgment of 1980 (European Court 1980), in which the Court adopted what was essentially a pragmatic approach to state aid decision-taking by the Commission, confirming in the process the Commission's administrative discretion. The procedure at this stage is unambiguously adversarial. While informal discussions are the norm during the preliminary part of the decision-making process, this is not so once the contentious procedure is opened, as '[l]ong and tedious negotiations may weaken the credibility of the Commission' at this point (Hancher *et al.* 1993:240), and would deter national authorities from negotiating at the earlier stage.

In certain cases, where there is state ownership or where the aid forms part of a privatization deal, state aid officials apply another principle, the market economy investor principle (also known as the private market investor principle). This is particularly helpful when the Commission is trying to decide whether state aid granted to public undertakings constitutes a breach of the competition rules. The principle states that assistance is not considered to be illegal if the state body is acting as a private firm would: that is, guided by objectives of long-term profitability. To make this judgment, the Commission must examine whether there will be an acceptable return on the funds provided within a reasonable period of time. In 2008, for example, the Commission opened an in-depth investigation into state support of two German banks, IKB and Sachsen LB. These banks had begun to suffer financial difficulties as a consequence of their investment in the US sub-prime market. In the case of IKB, a state-owned bank, Kreditanstalt für Wiederaufbau (KfW), provided a market shield of around €9bn; in the case of Sachsen LB, a group of Landesbanken granted it liquidity assistance of around €17bn. While the German authorities claimed that the aid complies with the market economy investor principle, the Commission is keen to investigate this case further. At the time of writing, the investigation is ongoing (Commission 2008b).

While DG Competition must make sure that all parties directly involved in the case, including the firm in receipt of the aid, get a fair hearing and are kept informed of its progress, interested third parties, competitor companies for example, possess few rights. A very sketchy summary of the opening of the investigation is published in the *Official Journal* ('C' Series), but this Notice gives very little away for fear of betraying commercially confidential information. As such, it is often impossible for firms to know whether an investigation is likely to have any impact upon them, and whether they might play a part in the proceedings. As a result, third parties end up having to rely heavily on the European Court system to appeal decisions they feel are unjust. This all-or-nothing involvement is unsatisfactory, and tends to mean that competitors are reluctant to participate in state aid cases. An effort to improve the situation led to the provision of slightly more information in the original Notice and has meant that third parties are now sent copies of the Commission's decisions. Commission officials are keen to encourage competitors to come forward to help them construct a more complete picture of the market under investigation.

Where a formal decision is to be taken, this must be issued within a 'reasonable length of time', although it is for the DG to decide what this means in practice. The Commission is keen not to let the investigation drag on for longer than six months, although this timescale is not legally enforceable. The decisions at the end of the investigative process may be positive (possibly conditionally so) or negative. Negative and conditional decisions are published in the *Official Journal* ('L' Series), while positive decisions appear in the 'C' Series. In the former, the Commission may demand the recovery (repayment) of the aid. As noted above, this has become a powerful tool of sanction for the Commission since it was first used in 1983.

It is important for negative and conditional decisions to be adequately reasoned, as they often have to stand up on appeal. However, compared with the anti-trust side of competition policy, state aid decisions remain rather vague and short, even if there have been recent efforts to improve standards, especially as part of the 2005 reform package (discussed below). In the past, little if any attempt was made to undertake the kind of economic analysis required in an Article 81 or 82 decision. Where a market analysis was undertaken it tended to be rather general, providing little information on how the final decision was actually reached (Schina

1987:153). On a number of occasions, the European Courts have been critical of the Commission for failing in this respect, as have, not surprisingly, certain national governments.

The motives for taking a formal decision are arcane but important. This is arguably the most crucial part of the decision-making process. In the absence of a formal decision, cases cannot be appealed to the European Courts, and cannot therefore be used to clarify (or indeed challenge) existing state aid law and practice. In addition, the relatively high-profile nature of Commission decisions in this field tends to create controversy over both the general application of the state aid rules and the treatment of specific cases. These controversies highlight the Commission's role in administering the policy and play an important educational function directed at both national governments and the business community.

Towards a cohesive state aid regime

State aid control did not become a priority for the Commission until the late 1980s. Since then the Commission has clarified policy practice by means of various publications: communications, notices, frameworks, guidelines, letters to the member states and more recently regulations (Commission 2007d:4). In spite of the powers granted to it by the EEC Treaty, it was after 1968, with the completion of the customs union, that state aid control became relevant. Only with attempts to remove non-tariff barriers to trade did the eradication of unfair subsidization make any sense. Indeed, there were only two negative decisions in the 1960s, the first (*Ford Tractor Belgium*) in 1964 (Commission 1964); and the second, in 1969, relating to the textiles sector. While the accumulation of state aid case-law was a slow process, particularly when compared with developments in the restrictive practices (cartel) field, the experience gained in the early years of the policy was nevertheless invaluable, forming the foundation for the later, more coherent and effective policy.

Paradoxically, after 1973, recession made action on the state aid front both imperative and impossible. Unaccustomed to coping with high inflation, rising unemployment, falling demand and failing competitiveness, both industry and national governments turned to public expenditure to mitigate the negative effects of recession. With the state aid directorate unable to deal with the flood of aid notifications, and with member states in any case blatantly flouting the notification rules, there was little the Commission could do to stem the subsidy tide. Without access to information on the amount of aid being granted, and faced with governments that were far from cooperative, there was little hope at this stage of creating a policy that would have any impact upon market integration.

The revitalization of state aid policy over the course of the 1980s was part of that process of change that affected all aspects of European competition policy at the time. This allied market integration to liberalization, shaping the rhetoric and practice of state aid control. This new state aid policy was to be based on an understanding that without a full and accurate assessment of the aid granted in the Community, effective scrutiny and control of national subsidies would be impossible.

The establishment in 1985 of a Task Force on State Aids under the then Competition Commissioner, Peter Sutherland, marked the beginning of this new phase, though some initial steps had been taken by his predecessor, Frans Andriessen. The Task Force sought to review all aid granted in the Community in order to identify trends in subsidization. Its first set of findings, published in 1988 as the *First Survey of State Aids in the European Community* (Commission 1988a), presented a detailed inventory of Community state aid granted between 1981 and 1986. Although this was largely an exercise in data collection, the knock-on effect of the survey was far-reaching. The results made interesting reading, offering an insight into the member states' aid regimes. Some of the results were unexpected, though many served only to confirm prior assumptions. Across the board in 1988, aid made up approximately 10 per cent of public expenditure, though in some countries the proportion was closer to 20 per cent, amounting to, on average, between 3 and 5 per cent of GDP.

The inventory of aid led directly to a re-evaluation of the 'old' state aid policy. From 1989 Peter Sutherland's successor, Sir Leon Brittan, identified a number of common-sense priorities that warranted particular attention (Brittan 1989:12–14):

- *That the appropriateness of 'existing aid' should not be taken for granted*. By challenging aid approved by the Commission in the past, Brittan acknowledged flaws in the 'old' regime.
- *That the effectiveness of the policy must be improved*. Aid

schemes likely to have a particularly distortive effect on competition were to be dealt with as a matter of urgency in an attempt to direct and manage limited resources more effectively. Types of aid warranting special attention included general investment aid, export aid to third countries and aid to public sector firms.

• *That aid transparency must become a priority.* Brittan confirmed his preference for aid that was clearly identifiable and that had recognizable sectoral or regional ambitions that could be quantified. There was an understanding that aid transparency also meant that DG Competition had a responsibility to make its own policy more predictable and comprehensible, especially with reference to the criteria it was using to assess state aid cases.

Since 1988 a further eight surveys have been published, though these were discontinued in 2001, when they were replaced by the more transparent State Aid Register (of Commission decisions) and by the State Aid Scoreboard (see below), which was also expected to serve as a tool to encourage a greater degree of peer pressure than had been the case in the past. They became essential tools of state aid policy enforcement, used to inform broader policy developments, which in turn shaped individual decisions.

Partly as a consequence of highly publicized disputes, but also pushed by resource pressures, the question of reform re-emerged as an issue in the mid 1990s (Stuart 1996:331). In the first instance this focused attention on the adoption of a Council Regulation under Article 89, something which until that time DG Competition had resisted. However, as the Commission's state aid officials came to recognize their own weaknesses in dealing with state aid, they gradually came round to the idea. Thus a procedural Council Regulation was approved in 1999, followed by a Commission Regulation which came into force in 2004.

In 2001 a new initiative, the State Aid Scoreboard, was introduced. This was very much in line with the instruments used within the Lisbon Strategy to encourage best practice, and with the Single Market Scoreboard introduced in 1997 (see Table 7.1). However, it also harked back to the earlier aid inventory and the state aid surveys. Improving the quality of data available once again provided a spur to reform, not least as there was evidence of a quantitative kind to suggest that the Commission was losing the battle to control state aid.

Table 7.1   The trend in the level of state aid in the EU member states, 1997–2006

	1997	1998	1999	2000	2001	2002	2003	2004	2005	2006	Annual average 2001–02	Annual average 2004–06
EU25												
Total state aid less railways (€bn)								67.5	66.6	66.7		
As % of GDP								0.62	0.60	0.58		
Total state aid less agriculture, fisheries and transport (€bn)				48.0	50.5	56.8	52.0	47.5	47.3	47.9	53.1	47.6
As % of GDP				0.46	0.48	0.53	0.49	0.44	0.43	0.42	0.50	0.43
EU15												
Total state aid less railways (€bn)	98.9	66.1	57.1	59.1	62.3	65.6	57.0	61.7	60.9	61.1	61.1	61.2
As % of GDP	1.12	0.73	0.61	0.60	0.62	0.65	0.56	0.59	0.58	0.56	0.61	0.58
Total state aid less agriculture, fisheries and transport (€bn)	78.9	50.2	40.3	42.6	45.9	50.6	41.6	43.7	44.2	44.7	46.0	44.2
As % of GDP	0.90	0.55	0.43	0.43	0.46	0.50	0.41	0.42	0.42	0.41	0.46	0.42

Source: European Commission, State Aid Scoreboard © European Communities 1995–2008.

A more comprehensive reform was introduced eventually in 2005, with the introduction of the State Aid Action Plan (SAAP) presented by Commissioner Neelie Kroes (see Box 7.3). The SAAP's primary objective was to create a better fit between the Lisbon Strategy and the state aid rules by focusing on aid to support the competitiveness of EU industry, the creation of more sustainable jobs, social and regional cohesion and improving public services. Various measures were proposed under the Plan, all of which fell under four guiding principles: (i) less but better targeted aid; (ii) increased emphasis on economic analysis; (iii) more effective procedures including better enforcement; and (iv) shared responsibility between the Member States and the Commission (DG Competition 2007). The SAAP opened the way for a plethora of new texts, such as the new regional aid guidelines (discussed below), and is due for completion in 2009.

It should not be taken for granted, however, that the Lisbon Strategy will contribute to a strengthening of state aid control. After all, the competitiveness objectives within the Lisbon Strategy could provide a window of opportunity for those arguing in favour of a 'new interventionism', which revolves around support for innovation, competitiveness and employment (as opposed to the support of failing industries). Although few expect a return to the *dirigisme* of the past, this could challenge the primary pro-competition (and more neo-liberal) ethos of the state aid regime which has predominated since the mid 1980s. This point is further discussed below.

State aid reform was also important in light of the enlargement of the EU. Just prior to the introduction of the SAAP the state aid directorate had had to cope with the consequences of ten – later twelve – new member states joining the Union. A fair amount of progress on state aid had been made by the applicants prior to accession, as the state aid rules formed part of the core internal market requirements which had to be met prior to entry. As well as setting up surveillance authorities, applicant states had had to identify all of their 'existing aid'. In some countries, transitional arrangements had also been agreed with regard to fiscal aid schemes to attract foreign investment and measures to restructure domestic steel industries.

BOX 7.3 State aid roadmap: 2005–07

Modifications	2005/6	2007/8	2009
Substance	Road map for state aid reform 2005–09 Regional aid guidelines General Block Exemption (SME, Employment Training, R&D, de minimis, regional, environmental) Communication – interest rates Guidelines – R&D and Innovation Communication – short term credit insurance Communication – risk capital Decision and guidelines on the Services of General Economic Interest and transparency directive Guidelines – environment Framework on state aid to shipbuilding	Assessment/modification of the rescue and restructuring aid guidelines Notice on state aid in the form of guarantees Communication on direct business taxation Communication on state aid to public broadcasting Possible additional block exemption.	Assessment of the reform and review of existing state aid rules
Consultation documents	Communication on innovation	Consultation document on possible modification of Council Regulation (EC) no. 659.99 Consultation document on the different forms of aid	
Procedure	Internal best practices guidelines Promotion of state aid advocacy Increase monitoring of decisions and recovery Possible proposal for amendment of Council Regulation (EC) no. 994/98 (enabling regulation)	Possible proposal for amendment of Council Regulation (EC) no. 659/99 (procedural regulation) Notice on cooperation between national courts and the Commission in the state aid field	

Source: Commission, State Aid Action Plan, Less and Better Targeted Sate Aid: a roadmap for state aid reform 2005–09 (consultation document), COM (2005) 107 795, figure 1, p. 17 © European Communities 1995–2008.

Policy content

Although it is convenient to draw a thick line between the 'old' (pre-1980) and the 'new' state aid policy, the story of the evolution of state aid control turns out to be somewhat less clear-cut when we look at the component parts of the state aid regime. In all areas of policy, the seeds of the new policy were clearly identifiable in the policy that was constructed over the 1960s and 1970s. This is acknowledged in the sections below which examine the three main elements that together form the Commission's state aid policy: regional aid policy; sectoral aid policy; and horizontal aid policy.

Regional aid policy

Regional aid policy has its legal basis in Articles 87(3) (a) and (c) of the EEC Treaty. Article 87(3) (a) allows for an exemption to the aid prohibition if the aid is 'to promote the economic development of areas where the standard of living is abnormally low or where there is serious underemployment'. This provision was used to good effect at the time of the southern enlargement of the Community in the 1980s.

Article 87(3)(c) allows for aid to 'facilitate the development of certain economic activities or of certain areas, where such aid does not affect trading conditions to an extent contrary to the common interest'. This is a more wide-ranging catch-all provision which is open to a freer interpretation by state aid officials dealing with regional aid (Ballantyne and Bachtler 1990:12). It allows member states to assist regions that are judged disadvantaged when compared with national averages (Commission 2007d:5). The list of regions qualifying for exemption is decided by the Commission, on a proposal from national governments and justified by national criteria (Commission 2007d:5). However, state aid officials also have a fair amount of discretion in applying Article 88(3)(c), allowing a variety of different policy objectives to be pursued.

The need for a systematic check on nationally granted regional aid was mooted first in the 1960s as a response to what appeared to be a widening of disparities between the richer and poorer regions of the Community.

Over the course of the 1970s, the four regional aid principles were gradually embellished (Commission 1976, 1977, 1978,

1980). The rules were extended to cover the peripheral regions of the Community, and more helpful ways of measuring and evaluating aid were introduced. At the end of the 1970s, attention turned to two specific difficulties. The first involved the so-called *cumulation* issue. The concern here was over the unforeseen and unintended consequences of state aid. Regional aid, for example, may well have dramatic sectoral, environmental or social effects; and aid not intended to serve any regional end may still have a major impact on the regions. Despite some improvements made to notification practices since 1984, the difficulties involved in unpacking the cumulative effect of state aid remain.

A second problem related to the relationship between the Commission's cohesion goal (that is, the promotion of social and regional development objectives) on the one hand, and the objectives of DG Competition's state aid policy on the other. The interaction of the Commission's regional aid and regional development policies need to be considered at this point (Commission 1985b:126). The two policies are administered by different Commission DGs, namely DG Regional Policy and DG Competition, and coordination between them has long been problematic. Indeed, the inconsistencies apparent in the Commission's approach to European subsidies, as opposed to national and sub-national aid, also continued to preoccupy DG Competition into the 1990s and beyond. The reform of the Structural Funds in 1988 exacerbated the problem. Policy consistency was important not only for practical reasons; it also challenged assumptions about the EU's *raison d'être*, and more specifically questioned whether cohesion might in future take precedence over the competition goal (Frazer 1995:8, 12; Wishlade 1993:147).

While these fundamental questions remained unanswered, practical issues were resolved by means of an uneasy compromise. This involved a revision of the regional development maps used to assess the spread of European and national state aid, and which led to an investigation into the compatibility between the state aid rules and the schemes covered by the programming documents of the Structural Funds for 1994–9. DG Competition's regional aid policy continued to take a tough line on aid granted in the more developed (or central) parts of the Union.

New regional aid guidelines have been drafted to cover the budgetary period 2007–13. These are controversial in a number of respects. The 'old' member states grew concerned that they would prevent them from granting aid to their most disadvantaged areas, given that the focus of the guidelines was primarily on the new and poorer member states (Commission 2006b). This was understandable however in view of the 2004 and 2007 enlargements. Just prior to the publication of the guidelines the Commission also published a block exemption regulation simplifying procedures for approving regional investment aid (Commission 2006b).

Sectoral aid policy

The Commission's sectoral aid policy focuses attention on specific problem sectors and individual grants of aid within them. It has relied heavily on a 'framework' approach which involves the drafting of sectoral guidelines to spell out in some detail the type and scope of aid likely to be authorized. Guidelines have existed for the motor vehicles industry, synthetic fibres, shipbuilding, coal and steel, electricity (stranded costs), postal services, audio-visual production and broadcasting, as well as for agriculture and fisheries and finally transport. There are several functions performed by the framework approach. In publicizing the Commission's policy towards certain sectors, frameworks can help to clarify the criteria upon which the Commission takes its decisions. Frameworks are policy statements, and as such provide an insight into the thinking of the state aid directorate. They also allow the Commission to react to crises that afflict particular sectors. Where guidelines exist they were, at least initially, indicative of the informal policy-making approach common in the state aid domain. Since the 1990s 'the Court has clarified some, but by no means all, of the uncertainties surrounding the status of guidelines and frameworks in the area of state aids' (Hancher 1994). In some sectors regulations perform, or have in the past performed, a similar function, as we will see below.

The Commission has a general set of rules which relates to rescue and restructuring aid. However, it has also felt the need to develop policy for specific sensitive industrial sectors. In the motor vehicles sectors, the 1989 *Framework on Aid to the Motor Vehicle Industry* (Commission 1989) which was renewed several times in the 1990s, provides for the notification of all projects under an approved aid scheme. It also includes an assessment procedure for various types of aid, such as rescue aid, R&D and regional aid (Stuart 1996: 235). The aim has been to establish transparency in the motor vehicles industry and to impose a stricter discipline on firms in a sector that has long been characterized by close government—industry relations and huge injections of subsidy. In this instance DG Competition was reacting to problems in a sector which was considered highly sensitive by many member state governments, largely because of its employment potential, but also for symbolic reasons. Gradually, over time, the Commission used its framework approach to rein in subsidies to the car industry and to force it to abide by the aid rules, although this has not been an easy process.

Initially supplementing this Framework, a Multisectoral Framework which came into force in 1988 has set out rules for a number of sectors including motor vehicles with regard to grants of large investment aid. This was extended in 2001 for a year, and following a review was revised, with the current framework in place until 2009. The review, held in 2001, suggested that existing sectoral frameworks should no longer run in parallel, but should be integrated into the new Multisectoral Framework. This is indeed what happened. The aim was to address generic issues relating to industries facing serious structural problems. To this end it exempts from notification grants of investment aid under certain thresholds where the overarching aid scheme has already been approved in general terms by the Commission.

The Multisectoral Framework also applies to the synthetics fibres sector, another sensitive sector which has suffered from overcapacity over many decades. In 1996 the Commission drafted a Code on aid to the sector, extended to 2001, which gave the Commission some time to decide whether specific rules on synthetic fibres were really necessary (in view of the new Multisectoral Framework). This was very much the same procedure as existed in the motor vehicles case. The question was whether the revised Framework could substitute for the specific guidelines in these two sectors. This is indeed what happened when the revised Multisectoral Framework came into force in 2002.

A sector in which rather distinctive crisis measures have been used is shipbuilding (including ship repair and conversion). In this sector the Council has been able to enact legislation to reduce shipbuilding subsidies over a period of time. The input of the OECD has also been important in this sector at the international level (Hancher *et al.* 1993:125–34). The Commission Framework on shipbuilding (Commission 2003b) now substitutes for the last Council Regulation which expired in 2003 (Council 1998).

DG Energy and Transport, rather than DG Competition, is responsible for aid to the hard coal sector, the rules for which are governed by a Council Regulation (Council 2002). Like it the steel sector was originally covered by the European Coal and Steel Community Treaty, but with the Treaty due to expire in 2002, the Commission was keen to ensure continuity in the treatment of state aid to the industry. The rules which govern the steel industry are strict. Since 1993 rescue and restructuring aid has been deemed incompatible with the common market, and investment aid is now prohibited by the Multisectoral Framework. There are however more lenient though very specific provisions set out on closure aid, covering aid to support redundancy payments of steelworkers and aid where steel firms permanently cease production (Commission 2002b).

While the electricity sector, another sector overseen by DG Energy and Environment, is not the subject of a Commission Framework, there are specific rules governing state aid in the form of a 1996 (Council 1996) communication.

Like the utilities, the service sectors have been attracting Commission attention since the 1990s, when the Commission felt that there was scope for starting to inject competition into sectors that provided services of general interest. The banking and postal service industries for example have been subject to DG Competition scrutiny since the early 1990s, although progress has been relatively slow compared with other sectors largely because of the sensitivities of these sectors and the fact that they fall under the heading of services of a general economic interest (SGEI). In the postal services sector, for example, the Commission has made it clear that the state aid rules apply to postal services as a matter of principle. The 'Transparency Directive', agreed in 1980 (Commission 1980b) and which requires member states to provide information on the financial relationships with public undertakings, is particularly important in sectors such as these, as it allows the Commission to access the information it needs to take decisions. Of particular concern to the Commission, however, have been tax advantages granted to postal operators, which could potentially be used to cross-subsidize operations in sectors open to competition. However, the Commission found no evidence of cross-subsidization when called to take a decision on this matter, a finding supported by the Court of First Instance (Commission 1998).

The *Crédit Lyonnais* case was the first of its kind to affect the banking sector and has since been used as the benchmark for action on the rescue and restructuring of banks in difficulty (on a more recent UK banking case, see Box 7.4). In this case aid of approximately €610m granted by the French government was essential if the bank was to be saved from collapse. This put the Commission in a difficult position, but as in many aid cases, once a decision was taken not to allow the bank to fail the conditions attached to eventual approval were key. Thus the aid was approved, but only when the bank agreed to a number of concessions, including the selling off of a large part of its international network. The Commission has since claimed that this was crucial in setting a precedent for the banking industry. The line taken by the Commission was that there was no reason why the state aid rules should not fully apply to this sector, though its special characteristics would have to be taken into consideration. Critics have argued that this is a case where the market economy investor principle was not used as a criterion for Commission approval of the aid, and that political considerations were paramount.

Commission guidelines also govern cinematographic and other audio-visual works (Commission 2001b) and broadcasting. Aid

BOX 7.4 Northern Rock

On 5 December 2007, the Commission approved a package of aid measures from the UK government to the UK bank Northern Rock plc. The Commission had received details from the UK government on this case on 26 November 2007, and had effected an impressively quick turnaround within the initial investigative procedure – nine days – because of the emergency nature of the situation the Bank found itself in. The aid was dealt with as rescue and restructuring aid. The Commissioner, Neelie Kroes, reflected on the intensive contacts that had characterized the notification of the aid, and praised the UK authorities in this case for their 'good cooperation from the outset' (Commission 2007i). In February 2008, the UK government passed a law to nationalize the bank, necessitating another round of negotiations with the Commission. However, the case was made easier since the Northern Rock bank operated only within the confines of the UK market (*Financial Times*, 22 February 2008).

which relates to the marketing and the production of agriculture and forestry is covered by a Framework for the period 2007–13 (Commission 2006d). This makes it clear that agriculture is a special case.

It is perhaps ironic given the focus on DG Competition that one of the most controversial sectors receiving state aid in the past decade or so is one which falls beyond the control of the Competition DG. As in the case of coal and steel, the state aid rules for the transport sector are drafted and enforced by DG Energy and Transport. With recent trends towards liberalization, privatization and the restructuring of state-run or state-controlled industries, subsidies to railways, shipping firms and airlines have become especially controversial. In the road transport sector the general aid provisions of the Treaty apply for most kinds of aid, although there are exceptions for aid to transport equipment and the acquisition of road freight transport vehicles. Although the *de minimis* rules apply in this sector, the ceiling is reduced from €200,000 (see below) to €100,000. Where aid is over the latter amount, it is subject to the usual notification requirements. Sector-specific rules apply for rail, inland waterways, maritime transport and air transport.

In the case of the latter, the air transport industry has witnessed some of the most high-profile cases since the early 1990s, relating to the collapse of Sabena, the privatization of Olympic Airways and the last state aids to Air France. The Commission has been criticized for approving much of this aid on the basis of what looks very much like national pressure. However, there is no doubt that there has been a dramatic transformation in this sector since the late 1980s.

In the case of aid to Iberia, the Spanish carrier, an amount of 89bn pesetas in the 1990s was approved only because it was deemed by the Commission to be a normal commercial transaction in line with the Commission's 'market investor principle'. Likewise in the case of aid to Air France and the Portuguese carrier TAP, the Commission's approval was tied closely to efforts made by those airlines to restructure (Commission 1997b). The attention paid by the Commission to such cases reflects a changing attitude to national carriers over time however. In the past, airlines often received extremely preferential treatment and exemption from the competition rules. Guidelines issued in a 1994 Communication (Commission 1995b:185) responded to the emergence of a rather different industrial and political environment on subsidies. Even if many witnessing these cases saw quite a different trend in Commission behaviour which they believed reflected a more lenient approach to subsidization in these sectors, what became important was the conditionality attached to approval.

Horizontal aid

Despite the impression given in the section above, in most sectors there are no specific sectoral codes or frameworks; rather there are general cross-industry guidelines, which apply horizontally across the board to particular categories of aid. To clarify its policy on horizontal aid, the Commission has made full use of guidelines, frameworks and block exemption regulations, where it deems these will be useful, to set out the criteria which apply to categories of aid. The block exemption regulation tool is a relatively recent development resting on an enabling Council Regulation issued in 1998 (Council 1998b). As of early 2008 there are five such Regulations, on SMEs, employment, training, transparency in regional investment schemes, and *de minimis* (Commission 2007d). More broadly, rules exist in the following areas: aid for the rescue and restructuring of firms in difficulty; aid for small and medium enterprises; aid for research and development and innovation; aid for risk capital; aid for environmental protection; aid for services of general economic interest; aid to employment; and training aid (Commission 2007d:5).

An important set of rules deals with aid for the rescue and restructuring of firms in difficulty (Commission 2004c 2004d). These rules were originally developed back in 1979, with updated guidelines first issued in 1994. The Commission's line is clear: sectoral aid should do more than simply sustain the status quo. This usually rules out aid for production or operational purposes other than for a very short duration. In addition, rescue aid should not be used to pervert efforts to reduce capacity in crisis sectors and should be granted only where social problems are acute. Likewise, investment aid must not be granted if capacity is increased as a consequence. However, aid may be justified on the basis of a regional or social consideration if it is temporary (lasting no longer than six months), if it is a one-off grant, or if there is a restructuring plan attached to it ensuring the long-term viability of the firm receiving the aid. While general guidelines of this sort do not provide any legal certainty either for governments or for industry, they do help to suggest how state aid officials might act when confronted with a particular case. Even so, DG Competition is left with considerable room for manoeuvre when it comes to politically sensitive cases such as those involving industrial decline, restructuring and privatization. The rules were revised (still in the form of guidelines) in 2004 so as to clarify the existing guidelines, tighten up current practice and fill in some loopholes. They did not, however, substantially change the system already in place (Commission 2004a).

Another very important example of a horizontal aid framework is the Community Framework for Research and Development which was originally agreed in 1985, and revised in 1996 and 2006 (it is now the Community Framework for State Aid Research and Development and Innovation; Commission 2006e). Aid specifically directed at small and medium enterprises is also governed by a Commission Regulation. Also relevant for SMEs (though not exclusively so) are guidelines on aids of minor importance, so-called de minimis aid. There is a specific set of rules covering environmental protection, and in December 1995 the Commission agreed its *Notice on Employment Aid* (Commission 1995c).

Given DG Competition's desire to simplify the aids granted in the EU, it is hardly surprising that it has long been trying to inject transparency into the aid schemes notified to it (Brittan 1989). However, it has not tried to prevent governments from drafting their subsidization laws in a general form. Banning general aid schemes and clauses of a general nature in statutes would be politically difficult if not altogether impossible, since such schemes and clauses are often an essential part of national industrial policy. As sticking to the letter of the law in this area has not really been a political option, the Commission has sought to control the way general aid is applied, while at the same time remaining sensitive to national policy practice.

The use of Block Exemptions in a number of horizontal policy areas specified in an enabling Regulation in 1998 (Council 1998b) was said to be 'largely successful' in a review published in 2007 (Commission 2007f). From when the Block Exemptions were agreed in 2001, to 2007, around 1600 aid measures were exempted from notification. Based on the findings of this Review, the Competition Commissioner announced in 2007 that she would be proposing the introduction of a general block exemption regulation bringing all areas (that is, SMEs, R&D, employment and training) together in one piece of legislation and that this new Regulation would be widened in scope to include, for example, certain aspects of environmental aid.

Finally, the Commission has a specific policy designed to cope with the difficulties that arise in making judgments about state aid granted to services of general economic interest. This concerns economic activities that states decide are important and need to be provided to citizens where public intervention is the only way this is possible. The language of public compensation is used to describe these payments within the Commission's document, and this is clearly not considered state aid (according to the Court) where the aid is truly compensating firms for activities that would otherwise be uneconomic. To clarify the Commission's position and to draw on its experience, there is a Commission Framework and a Decision which can be used as guidance. The policy also draws on wider Commission documentation beyond the state aid field on services of general economic interest (see for example Commission 2003c).

Assessing state aid control

State aid policy, like other EU competition policies, is a Commission policy, the uniqueness of which lies in both its independence from the EU Council and European Parliament scrutiny, and the administrative discretion, which characterizes much of its decision-making. DG Competition has a degree of flexibility and discretion at various stages in the decision-making process: in deciding if a measure constitutes a state aid; in deciding if the aid is eligible for exemption (that is, in selecting the criteria on which a decision is taken); and in judging how the case ought to be pursued procedurally (Hancher 1994:134). However, in spite of its legal autonomy, it is certainly not in DG Competition's interest to be heavy-handed with national governments, as this could be counterproductive. One might even go so far as to say that 'the Commission is not always politically in a position to act in those areas in which it has the legal right' (Warnecke 1978:170).

EU state aid control has always been politically controversial. Yet political challenges in the past have tended to focus on individual cases subject to informal political influence. Since around the year 2000, while there have been many political challenges to the

Commission's authority in individual cases, there has also been in addition a concerted attempt to challenge the policy at a more fundamental level. These challenges have come from the older and larger EU member states, France and Germany in particular. There are a number of possible explanations for this. The weakness of the European economy and high unemployment rates in many European countries could explain a reluctance on the part of vulnerable member states to accept the EU's control in this area; or it could be a reflection of the weakening of the Commission. Another explanation points to the changing nature of governance within and by the EU, characterized by the use of softer instruments of policy management along 'new public management' lines, increasingly substituting for a more top–down, hierarchical kind of policy-making which is still largely how the state aid regime operates. Finally, these attacks might simply be a consequence of internal political agendas, personalities and with deal-making across the member states. In this light one way of understanding Commissioner Kroes's state aid reform plans of 2005 and beyond is as an attempt by DG Competition to undercut these challenges to the Commission's tough line on state aid by strengthening key elements of the policy at the very time of attack. This is essential as the number of cases the Commission has to deal with remains high (Table 7.2).

Table 7.2   Number of registered aid cases in 2005

Sector	Notified aid cases	Non-notified cases	Existing aid cases	Total
Agriculture	236	24	3	263
Manufacturing and services	350	36	14	400
Transport and energy	58	11	–	69
Fisheries	19	13		32
Total	663	84	17	764

Source: European Commission, State Aid Scoreboard 2007 © Euopean Communities 1995–2008.

So what form have these challenges taken? To answer this question it is necessary to point to what might be understood as a greater willingness on the part of national governments to challenge the Commission through a rarely used provision of the Treaty. Article 88 of the Treaty allows the Council to overturn a Commission state aid decision 'under exceptional circumstances'. This ostensibly gives the member states, acting unanimously, the final say in state aid decisions. However, until very recently it was little used.

In early February 2002:

> As the 20 Commissioners were preparing to vote on their officials' recommendation to ban tax breaks to road hauliers in France, the Netherlands and Italy, the governments of those three countries asked other Member States to overrule any ban even before it had been imposed. (Dombey and Guerrera 2002).

As the Council had three months to reach a decision, the Commission was left hanging, its authority undermined, though Dombey (2002a) claims that the Commission too was divided on this issue. Three months later almost to the day a decision was taken by the Council once Austria had agreed to follow the other 14 member states. According to the Financial *Times*, 'Brussels officials . . . [were] aghast at the horse-trading between member states on the issue' (Dombey 2002a). It was only after the Austrians received reassurances on a deal with Italy (one of the countries directly affected by the state aid decision) on heavy goods traffic transiting Austria that it agreed to make the vote unanimous (Dombey 2002a). The matter was complicated by the fact that the introduction of tax breaks followed mass protests against rising oil prices in September 2000, leading several member states to reduce fuel prices to quell the protests (Dombey and Guerrera 2002a). This eventually led the Commission to decide against pursuing the matter in the European Courts. After taking legal advice, a majority in the College of Commissioners, including the President and a number of 'heavyweight' Commissioners, felt that the Council could have made a strong case for the tax breaks constituting an 'exceptional circumstance', and that this was the point around which the case was likely to turn (Dombey 2002b).

The second case actually predated the first, and concerned aid granted to Portuguese pig-farmers in the 1990s. Here, once again, the Council had agreed to overturn two Commission decisions by a unanimous vote. But in this case the argument in support of the exceptional circumstances seemed much more tenuous, and the Commission decided to take the Council to Court over the decision, in the first legal challenge of its kind over a state aid matter (Guerrera and Mann 2002). It took almost two years for the European Court of Justice to rule on the case. Its judgment upheld the Commission's position, and seemed to confirm the Commission's pre-eminent position in state aid decision-making (Buck and Dombey 2004).

But it is not only through a more assertive use of Article 88 that the member states have challenged the Commission's authority. A further political challenge came and continues to come in the form of attacks on the Commission's post-2005 reform strategy. Although the Competition Commissioner did not need member state support for most of the state aid reforms it had initiated in 2005, it was politically difficult for her to implement them without member state approval (Buck 2005). Although the reform was supported in principle by the Council, there were a number of issues in which the Germans played a central role that demonstrated the latter's ability to build coalitions in support of what might be perceived by DG Competition as a weakening of the EU's state aid control by 'chipping away' at certain aspects which on first sight seem to lie at the margins of the Commission's policy. One instance of this came when a number of member states (Austria, France, Germany and UK) signed letters attacking the Commission's regional aid plans for not allowing the richer member states to support their poorer regions (see Fothergill 2006; Buck 2005).

Another instance occurred at the time of the introduction of new *de minimis* rules for state aid when UK and France joined Germany to oppose the Competition Commissioner's line. The governments involved wanted to extend the *de minimis* criteria to include what DG Competition considered to be non-transparent aid, namely loan guarantees. In this case Kroes agreed to review the matter, though the *Financial Times*, for one, argued that she should hold firm in resisting member state pressure (*Financial Times* 2007). At much the same time the German Presidency presented a report to the informal Competitiveness Council held in Würzburg on 26–28 April 2007, arguing for a softer line on state aid from the Commission, criticizing the slowness of its procedures and suggesting that new state aid rules should be introduced allowing the state aid maxima to be increased where non-EU countries had offered higher sums of aid to entice firms away from Europe. In this latter case, the German Presidency did not win the day and the proposal was not supported (Buck 2007). This was reflected in the report of the meeting which argued, rather, for increased efforts to support WTO and bilateral arrangements for state aid control involving third countries (Council Presidency 2007).

If relations between the Council and the Commission have at times been tense, the Commission–Court relationship has also been subject to certain stresses. As DG Competition's quasi-judicial procedure allows for the direct referral of cases to the European Court where governments are suspected of having breached the aid rules, the Commission–Court relationship has replaced the conventional Commission–Council relationship, though the European Court has frequently been criticized for siding too readily with the Commission in state aid cases. In the meantime it has been argued that:

> The Court, notoriously, has a long history of allowing the Commission to wave through state aids. The results have been entirely predictable: most Commissioners, being career politicians and viewing themselves as national representatives, tend to side with the home government. In state aid matters the Commissioners can be expected to prostitute themselves to political interests unless and until the Court requires otherwise. (Bishop 1995:331)

Although this assessment of the Court's role belies the political complexity of state aid decision-making, it is clear that it does reflect the European Court's cautious approach in state aid cases.

It seems clear then that in the past state aid officials have operated in an environment remarkably free from constraints. Using quasi-legal (or soft-law) instruments such as Frameworks, Notices and more general policy statements, DG Competition has even been able (or has been compelled) to fill in the gaps left by the European Court, the Council and the Parliament. It remains to be seen whether the increased use of Regulations will change this state of affairs. It must be emphasized, however, that it is the College of Commissioners and not DG Competition which is ultimately responsible for state aid decisions. The overtly controversial character of the policy, which former Director-General Caspari suggested was a consequence of the direct and unequal relationship between the member states and the Commission in this field (Caspari 1984), means that disagreements are frequent occurrences among individual Commissioners as well as among officials of the Commission's DGs. Where constraints *are* felt by DG Competition, these tended in the past to originate within and not outside the Commission – although this may be changing. The desired image of unity that the Commission tries to project is rarely convincing.

Conflicts have been much publicized, particularly in the financial press, and tend to emerge around three poles: around the balance between state interventionism and the free market, around multi-faceted national cleavages and around internal institutional constraints. In practice, the first two poles of conflict are usually blurred. They rest on the political views and ideological positions of individual Commissioners and on the extent to which they are placed under or subject themselves to national pressure. Votes in the College are taken on the basis of a simple majority and in confidence, although information on who voted for what is occasionally leaked, particularly in difficult cases. Whereas on the anti-trust side a pro-competition consensus was visible during the 1980s, on the state aid side if there was a consensus at all it was always more fragile.

Disagreements among DGs and Commissioners are nothing new, but intra-Commission disputes do show up remarkable policy inconsistencies (Schrans 1973:191). Where policies clash in their practical application, it is for the DGs or Commissioners themselves to argue that *their* policy line should take precedence. This is what happened when energy liberalization appeared on the Commission's agenda in the 1980s at the same time as DG XVII, now DG Energy and Transport, wanted to pursue a security of supply policy at the expense of introducing competition into the sector. The outcome was a compromise, although there are still tensions between the two DGs on this issue. Likewise, as noted above, DG Regional Policy and DG Competition have attempted to resolve conflicts between the grant of Community subsidies and the control of national aid by means of a rather unconvincing compromise.

In the 1991 *Renault* case the conflict was even more overtly political. DG Competition's decision to demand the repayment of aid granted conditionally to the French car company Renault by the French government received a great deal of publicity. The identification of a Delors–Brittan cleavage at the time, and the extensive lobbying undertaken by the then French Prime Minister, Michel Rocard, split any semblance of consensus on public sector aid within the Commission. Brittan was keen to take a tough line in demanding repayment to show that he was determined to implement the aid rules to the full. As such, he would not allow national pressures to influence the DG Competition line. Even so, he had to get the approval of a majority of the College of Commissioners, something he did ultimately manage to achieve (Thomas 2000: 127).

Conclusion

Disagreements of the kind identified above reflect the fact that the EEC Treaty was vague in defining its terms. But this

> should not cause surprise, for a satisfactory definition could be offered only as part of a broader conceptual framework for answering the central question of political economy: what is the proper relationship between the modern state and the market? (Harden 1990:100)

While the Treaty provides some guidance on this question, establishing broad parameters within which European states are expected to act, it certainly does not present a definitive EU model. The EU's state aid regime, like the wider competition regime, continues to evolve, reflecting not only internal policy and administrative dynamics, but also the wider context in which it operates – currently, that of the Lisbon agenda (with its emphasis on jobs and growth) as well as that of enlargement.

Although the Commission's state aid regime at times gives the impression of being the 'ugly duckling' (Ahlborn and Berg 2003: 41) or the 'Cinderella of the EU's Competition Policy' (Bishop 1995:331), it would be wrong to accept with grace its marginalization from the competition policy mainstream. State aid control may not be part of any conventional anti-trust framework, but it is an important component in DG Competition's competition armoury and the organizational reform of 2002–04 has sought to mainstream state aid policy within the DG. It is too early to say just how successful this has been, although there is some indication that state aid levels are decreasing (see Table 7.1 above). Moreover, export aid has virtually been eliminated; rescue aids, though permitted, are granted under much stricter conditions than in the past; and sectoral aid has declined, to be replaced by horizontal forms of aid that fit better with the EU's wider economic–industrial objectives.

Yet the fortunes of the state aid regime are mixed. It would not be overstating the case to claim that the Commission's state aid policy continues to be plagued by ambivalence and controversy. While the regime justifies its existence by claiming to promote competition, to encourage the operation of free and fair European markets and to create a level playing-field for European industry, it is intrinsically related to other EU policy objectives. The goals of environmental protection, regional development, employment promotion and international industrial competitiveness, to name but a few, may seem secondary objectives to many DG Competition-watchers, but they are nevertheless fundamental in tempering the neo-liberal rhetoric of the state aid directorate. They also lie at the heart of many of the political disputes over the grant of national aid. Yet if there seems to be some ambivalence here, we should not be surprised. After all, even the treaty provisions emphasize both the rule and exceptions to the rule. Nevertheless, this policy ambivalence strikes at the heart of persistent ideological debates about the role of the state, and, at European level, about the role of the EU in matters of industrial policy. It is no wonder that the policy is such a source of controversy.

Chapter 8

Theoretical Perspectives

Academic research on European integration has never been richer (Nelson and Stubb 2003; Wiener and Diez 2004). This book has added to this ever growing literature and has provided new insights into the history, the institutional actors, the main policy areas and the politics of EU competition policy. However, there remains one noticeable gap, which relates to the absence of non-economic theoretical perspectives on the policy's development. It is only in very recent times that such theoretical contributions have been made (see Büthe and Swank 2005; Doleys 2007; McGowan 2007). Indeed, the first edition of this book deliberately omitted discussion of theoretical approaches. Competition policy is far from being unique in its neglect of theory, however. Indeed, it is striking that many of the core EU market-related policies, such as agriculture, energy, fisheries and trade policy, not only remain marginal to the interests of many political science scholars and students, but have also been underdeveloped theoretically. This observation may be explained by the reluctance of some researchers to venture into highly complex policy arenas where economics, law and politics intermingle. It may also be a consequence of the decline of EU-focused public policy analysis since the late 1990s (Carter and Smith 2008).

There are a number of questions to address here. If a theory should be capable of asking meaningful questions about a given object (Rosamond 2005:238), then we might ask why competition rules were delegated to the EU level in the first place; why these rules became more powerful than the domestic rules; how we account for the policy's expansion; where we identify the pressure for adaptation and change in the regimes of both the existing and potential member states; and how internal EU developments impact on the wider international arena. This penultimate chapter sets out to encourage researchers working on EU competition policy to adopt more of a theoretical perspective when explaining policy integration.

So where and how do we begin to theorize EU policy-making? There has certainly not been a shortage of suggested explanations. These fall under a variety of headings, such as multilevel governance, international regime analysis, constitutionalization, the fusion thesis and policy networks. The usefulness of what might be deemed *en vogue* approaches (Schmitter 2004) is not explored here owing to space constraints but also because it is assumed that the starting-point for any theoretical debate about the dynamics of EU integration still must be the 'two families of integration theory' (Schimmelfenning and Rittberger 2006), intergovernmentalism and supranationalism, even if for some this might be considered an out-moded point of departure.

Theorizing competition policy is a challenging task, and this chapter cannot cover every possible approach. It is therefore intentionally selective and focuses specifically on the supranational family. At the outset we assume the reader's familiarity with a wider range of theoretical arguments, and equally do not rehearse the basics of the approaches applied here. These can be found elsewhere (see for example Wiener and Diez 2004; Cini 2006). This enables this chapter to concentrate on two potential applications which have been selected to encapsulate both 'older' and 'newer' phases of research within European integration studies. The first questions the suitability of neo-functionalism as a means of explaining developments in the evolution of EU competition policy. The second considers how far debates about Europeanization lend themselves to an understanding of the impact of policy upon member states' antitrust regimes.

But why choose these two? First, neo-functionalism has been selected because it is the first of the classical grand theories of regional integration (Haas 1958), which despite its mixed fortunes continues to remain relevant through its concept of spillover and by highlighting the role of elite supranational and European-level actors, such as the Commission and business interests. Moreover, it has undergone something of a renaissance since the mid 1990s. Second, recent interest in Europeanization (Featherstone and Radaelli 2003) lends itself well to the study of competition policy and enables us to identify, first, the extent to which policy convergence has taken place in this policy sector; and, second, the variables that help to explain this process (see for example Cini 2006).

This chapter maintains that by bringing specific policies under the spotlight it might be easier to recalibrate existing theories.

We stress at the outset, however, that it is not our intention to set up straw men to knock down. We wish to start a discussion about theorizing competition policy. To this end the chapter is divided into two main sections. The first identifies the relevance of neo-functionalist theory, the second the concept of Europeanization. Moreover, it should be emphasized strongly that we are not advocating a particular stance or trying to adopt a specific position on each of these approaches, but simply asking how valuable they might be to the study of European competition policy.

Can neo-functionalism account for supranational competition governance?

Neo-functionalism placed emphasis on the key agents of change in the early years of the European integration process. These agents were identified as technocratic elites, politicians, supranational interest groups and other lobbies. According to Haas:

> political integration is the process whereby political actors in several distinct national settings are persuaded to shift their loyalties, expectations and political activities to a new centre, whose institutions possess or demand jurisdiction over pre-existing national states. The end result is a new political community, superimposed over the existing ones. (Haas 1958:16)

This supranational activity was understood to unleash a self-reinforcing dynamic that culminated in further and deeper integration, a process labelled 'spillover'. This is without doubt the most widely recognized concept within neo-functionalism. Haas clearly attributed an expansive logic to the process of European integration (Haas 1968:283–317).

The establishment of the EEC in 1958 shifted the focus of regional integration from the narrower confines of coal and steel to a much wider policy agenda, most notably concerning the eradication of internal tariffs; the realization of a common subsidized agricultural sector; the search for a European-level transport policy; and the construction of competition rules. The European Commission played an important role in this process. However, Haas admitted that at the time 'social scientists were less interested in the substantive activities and achievements of these organizations than in the theories seeking to explain the success of regional integration' (Haas 2004:xiii). It is possible this prevented the recognition of some real and significant steps in economic and political integration.

The EEC Treaty clearly saw competition policy as a means of promoting European integration as well as a way to secure economic growth and protect consumer welfare. The original six EEC member state governments agreed to pass responsibility for this policy to the new supranational institutions. This transfer (or delegation) seemed uncontroversial, since this was a policy area of which most member states had little direct experience.

Once created, the supranational competition regime started to develop its own dynamics and trajectory. This was initially a slow process. The competition regime needed time both to bed in, understand and appreciate its powers and capabilities and to realize its potential (see Table 8.1). It had also to watch how its policies and decisions were interpreted by the European Court. This temporal perspective on public policy development is all too readily overlooked in academic writings, particularly in neo-functionalist accounts. The macro-level narrative of the EU's development in the 1960s most often suggests a slowdown, helping some authors to write off neo-functionalism, even where a more meso-level policy focus might suggest otherwise.

Yet the evidence in support of a neo-functionalist account should be examined a little more closely. In the field of competition, the Directorate General for competition was set up in 1960, and throughout the 1960s and 1970s it slowly accumulated experience resting on a growing body of case-law, while also developing norms and values that were disseminated within the Commission and to the wider competition policy community.

Haas developed his spillover thesis by hypothesizing that 'group pressure will spill over into the federal sphere and thereby add to the integrative impulse' (Haas 1958:xiii). This interpretation is a challenge to intergovernmentalism and in particular to the view that supranational institutions will always remain weak because they lack sufficient resources and popular support to expand their power base. The European competition regime was certainly deficient in both, but over the course of a few decades DGIV (now DG Competition) nevertheless made good use of its limited staff and prioritized its main areas of interest, before gradually extending its

Table 8.1   Tracing the expansive development of EU competition policy

	1957	1960s	1970s	1980s	1990s	2000+
Restrictive practices	0	1	2	3	4	4
Abusive monopolies	0	1	1	2	2	3
Mergers	0	0	0	0	4	4
Liberalized utilities (telecoms, energy, postal services)	0	0	1	2	4	4
State aids	0	1	2	2	3	3

Scale coding:
0, no EU competence;
1, EU competence but mostly dormant (with cartels);
2, EU competence slowly developing;
3, EU competence and active;
4, EU competence and very active.

activities across all aspects of the competition domain. In addition, the DG was constantly devising measures (such as the imposition of ever higher financial levies for infringing the competition rules) to speed up case investigations and to focus the day-to-day workload of its staff on the most pressing cases.

Thus, the reforms to the competition regime which came into effect in 2004 could be interpreted as part of or even perhaps the end of an ongoing process, anchoring the supranational character of competition governance. These developments are in line with neo-functionalist premises to the extent that the ethos of the EU competition regime gradually began to impact upon existing domestic regimes (see also below on Europeanization). Any assessment of European competition policy has to acknowledge the centrality of the European Commission as a credible, autonomous, quasi-judicial and policy-making institution that wields substantial power over both private businesses and member state governments. At the same time, its activities have often proven contentious, and the Commission has responded to criticism by amending and redefining its policy, and by regular internal restructuring and revised procedural initiatives. DG Competition's success owes much to its acceptance by the business community. This has formed the basis of its legitimacy. The Commission has also sought to disseminate more extensive information to the public on why it pursues competitive conditions and how such outcomes benefit the consumer. Few EU citizens may access, for example, the very impressive and revamped (in November 2006) DG Competition website, but a brief exploration of the site will reveal how, why and where the competition authorities have conducted their activities. Few will be unimpressed by the vast number of household names in a range of sectors (from Cadbury Schweppes to Carlsberg, from Sony to Nintendo, from British Airways to Air France and from Boeing to Airbus), that have fallen foul of the EU's competition rules.

Subsuming Commission officials, an epistemic community (van Waarden and Drahos 2002) of competition lawyers and economists, business leaders and national competition officials are constantly engaged in discussions about competition norms and values. Each group pursues its own distinct interests. Thus the Commission (and the Courts) provide political opportunity structures for such actors, including those that, if neo-functionalist logic holds, favour market integration. Exchanges occur both formally and informally at conferences (for example, the Competition Day Conference that is now held under each EU Presidency) and specialist competition policy/law conferences (as organized, for example, by the American Chamber of Commerce in Brussels). This very much fits the mould of elite integration and is exactly the kind of engagement that is to be expected given the technicalities of competition law and economics. So could an alliance of Commission and business interests, national officials and competition experts impose their will on national governments and help to push integration forward? The deliberations over merger policy (see Chapter 6) provided an illustration of exactly how pressure may be exerted on the member states in support of a further delegation of powers to the EU level.

Responsibility for handling cross-border mergers had been a notable omission from the EEC Treaty. But how can we explain the agreement of a Merger Control Regulation in 1990 from a theoretical perspective? One avenue might be to present the final agreement in the Council as a clear illustration of intergovernmental bargaining. Another avenue for exploration lies primarily in an alliance between the Commission and the business community. The latter had become increasingly concerned about the rules, or the lack of them, in some member states and the varying approaches towards mergers being taken. Confusion abounded. Business sought a level playing-field and a one-stop shop for proposed mergers. This compelled the more recalcitrant states to back down in their opposition to regulation in this field.

This episode may be viewed as an example of Haas's argument that regional integration takes place when societal actors, in 'calculating their interests, decided to rely on the supranational institutions rather than their on governments to realise their demands' (Haas 2004:xiv). It was also assumed that this acceptance or need for supranational responsibility would strengthen the Commission's legitimacy claims.

Indeed, if spillover is conceived of in terms of 'an expansive logic of sector integration' which has ramifications, not only for particular sectors, but also across sectors, then competition policy makes for a fascinating case-study. Although the EEC Treaty had earmarked action in a range of anti-competitive activities from the outset, the Commission placed most of its energies in its early decades on restrictive practices, with a more limited involvement in monopolies. However, by the mid 1980s, competition regulation had begun to tackle the much thornier and politically controversial issue of state aid. Moreover, it subsequently acquired responsibility for mergers and began to focus its energies on injecting competition into the public utility sectors. Phrased another way, not only have the parameters of EU competition policy been extended over the years, but the policy has also come to impact on other industrial sectors that in the past were shielded from the competitive process. The belief in competitive markets (see Figure 8.1) thus led to demands for further sectoral integration.

Moreover, sweeping changes have occurred across the utility sectors such as in postal services and in the banking and insurance industry. Yet such horizontal developments remain controversial and specific initiatives have encountered resistance in some member states. One of the most publicized examples was the dispute over the so-called Bolkestein Directive in 2005/06. This Directive sought

Figure 8.1   Competition policy as spillover into other sectors

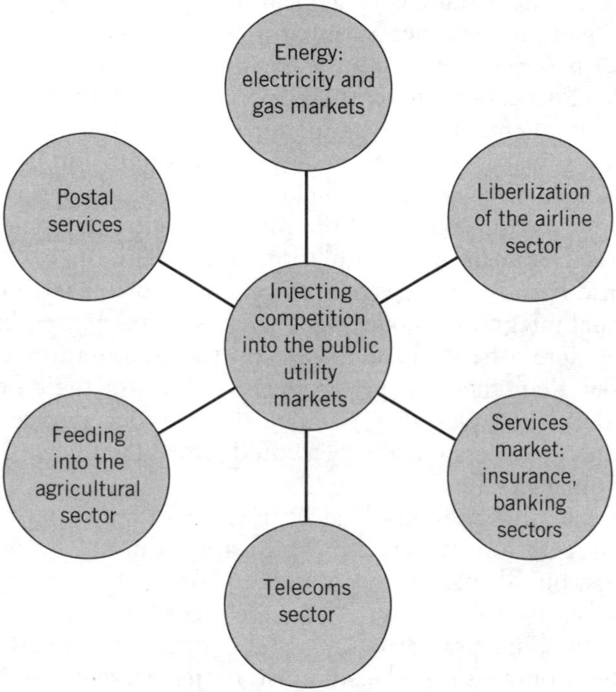

to open up the services markets to greater competition. Vocal opposition was strongest in France and Spain and led to sizeable demonstrations in both countries and violent arguments in the Council and the European Parliament. Yet the fact that a consensus was ultimately reached between those two institutions illustrates the potency of the competition logic.

Even if neo-functionalism no longer carries much weight as a macrotheory of European integration, it may still have analytical purchase as a midrange theory applicable to the development of individual sectors. (This applies mainly to the policy areas outlined in the treaties that are central to the realization of the internal market.) However, more work needs to be done in applying, in a rigorous fashion, neo-functionalist concepts to such policy cases – and indeed to competition policy. We have taken only a small step here in suggesting one theoretical avenue that could be explored.

Exploring Europeanization

Another potentially illuminating way of explaining developments in EU competition policy draws on the growing literature on Europeanization (Olsen 2002; Featherstone and Radaelli 2003). Within the political science literature most authors focus on the impact of the European Union on domestic actors and structures (Dyson and Goetz 2003). This is the way we use the term in the section below. A few authors, however, do recognize the EU as only one form of Europeanization (Wallace 2000). There may still be little in the way of a universal definition of Europeanization (Buller and Gamble 2002; Olsen 2002) but this should not prevent us from identifying concepts which might be applied to our competition case. For example Harmsen and Wilson (Harmsen and Wilson 2000) have identified eight different types of Europeanization in the literature and these include new forms of European governance, policy isomorphism, modernization, national adaptation and the reconstruction of identities. Some of these will be referred to below.

The Europeanization of EU restrictive practices policy

The EU cartel regime (see Chapter 4) developed incrementally after 1958 as the Commission became more aware of and comfortable with its powers. Over time the EU rules seem to have altered the perceptions and approaches of the national competition regimes towards cartels. The realization that cartels threatened to undermine the EEC's ambitious plans to create a genuine common market led the founding member states to include provisions for a European cartel regime in the EEC Treaty (see Box 8.1). This was remarkable given that most of these states had no domestic anti-trust legislation at this time.

The EU regime gradually came to shape and impact upon domestic systems created by the member states. The transformation or assimilation process can be explained as the product of both voluntary and coercive pressures. In the case of the former, this comprised direct policy convergence with Article 81 to bring national norms and practices into line with those of the EU. Developments in Italy and the Netherlands in the late 1980s and early 1990s exemplify this voluntary approach as these states had not possessed any substantial domestic legislation prior to the

BOX 8.1 Europeanization dynamics in EU cartel policy

Dynamic	Process	Actor involvement
Construction	Creating European regime.	Member state governments.
Assimilation	Increasing similarity of national policy with the 'European' model.	Domestic actors.
Collision	Conflict can occur in the multilevel system.	EU and domestic decision-making.

Source: Adapted from Lodge (2002a).

setting up of the EEC. By the end of 1998, some 8 (of the then 15) national authorities were already in a position to apply Article 81 directly. The EU rules also impacted, however, more interestingly on those member states that already had domestic competition regimes. The rationale behind the most recent revisions to domestic competition policy both in Germany (see Lodge 2002) and the UK (Green and Robertson 1999; Cini 2006) readily illustrate the assimilating tendencies, although other forces may also be at work (for example, US influence). This means that

> companies which had hitherto turned a blind eye to obligations under EU national law either because they were not relevant, were not understood, or worse, were unlikely to be detected, will now find that EU rules have permeated into national competition law. (Nazerali 1998:82–3)

Assimilation has also taken the form of a more coercive process, which can be deemed 'forced Europeanization'. This was in evidence in the requirement for all potential EU states to put in place the appropriate competition machinery as one of the essential preconditions for EU accession. Successive waves of EU enlargement not only have expanded the reach and scope of EU governance but also have exported policy values, perceptions and norms to all potential member states.

By the end of the 1990s the European cartel arena had been transformed. Interestingly, both the British and the EU authorities had almost simultaneously initiated plans for reforming cartel policy. The assimilation process, in relation to both Articles 81 and 82, was further facilitated through Regulation 1/2003. As explained in Chapter 3, this allows member state authorities to judge cartel cases, with specific reference to the EU rules.

The Commission's willingness to allow the national authorities greater involvement in competition enforcement reflected a much-improved relationship between the two sets of actors, demonstrating how far the Commission had come since its initial decentralization drive was first outlined in the early 1990s. So-called 'mimetic' and 'professionalization' triggers are in evidence here. The former rest on greater interaction between competition officials at both the national and supranational levels, and have more recently been enhanced through the European Competition Network (ECN) (see Chapter 3). The ECN provides a forum estab lished to facilitate cooperation across national and supranational arenas, allowing the actors involved to iron out inconsistencies in the application of the policy. Its establishment should be seen as a further attempt, and part of a wider agenda, to encourage international cooperation, of which the virtual International Competition Network, established in 2001, remains the best example.

This assimilation of national models in line with the EU model greatly facilitates the operation of a genuine decentralized cartel policy. It also reflects a Europeanization of policy that is built on an acceptance at both the national and EU levels of common rules. From a policy development perspective the decentralization of the EU rules is of further significance because it enables the national authorities to become fully evolved in the further development and refinement of EU competition law. Moreover, the Commission's willingness to allow the national authorities the power to grant exemption has freed its hands, enabling staff in DG Competition to focus their activities on more serious breaches of the competition rules.

Despite the improved relationships between the EU and national competition authorities and the direct applicability of Article 81, the potential for conflict and collision still persists. The best example is to be found in the recent reforms to domestic competition legislation in the United Kingdom which although providing evidence of Europeanization also reflect a degree of divergence, demonstrated most clearly in the 2002 Enterprise Act. This marks a new departure by criminalizing participation in so-called 'hard-core' cartels. More specifically, as is the practice in the United States, this facilitates the handing down of prison sentences of up to five years, as well as the imposition of hefty personal fines for anyone engaged in such activity. This major shift was not welcomed by the business community but, rather, reinforced the UK Labour government's determination to rein in cartels at a national level and also internationally by fostering cooperation. The next logical stage is an agreement on extradition. In short, on the one hand British policy illustrates a clear case of assimilation with EU policy, but on the other hand it also reflects the influence of other regimes, especially that of the US. In this case there appear to be limits to Europeanization. However, there may also be opportunities here, as domestic reforms could offer a way of uploading values and policy content to the European level. Europeanization should not be viewed as a unidirectional impulse, despite our earlier rather top-down definition of it. Rather, it operates at both national and supranational levels and this is its strength and attractiveness as a (meta)theoretical approach. As such the study of EU cartel policy looks like it could provide an interesting illustration of Europeanization in action.

Europeanization and EU merger control

The evolution of EU merger policy (see Chapter 6) likewise lends itself to Europeanization interpretations and provides evidence of both 'bottom-up' and 'top-down' approaches. We suggest here that the Europeanization of merger policy can best be understood and analysed under three key headings: construction, establishing distinct jurisdictional boundaries, and reinforcement. All three are considered briefly, but the first question that arises is who was responsible for constructing the merger regime.

While the Merger Regulation was implemented only in 1990, its introduction echoed earlier debates on anti-trust in the EEC. As already noted above, the EU merger regime could be interpreted as the outcome of intergovernmental bargaining and member state acceptance of the need for a European solution to cross-border mergers. However, the preferences of the business community, represented by the European Roundtable of Industrialists (ERT) and the European Employers' Confederation (formerly Unice, now

BusinessEurope), were also important in so far as they lobbied actively for a Regulation.

Having recognized or been forced to recognize the need for an EU-wide merger policy, all that remained was for the Council to determine and construct the rules of an EU regime and, more specifically, to set clear jurisdictional boundaries that demarcated where the responsibilities of the member states and the European Commission lay. The process of reaching agreement on the Merger Regulation was always going to prove rather fraught. Consequently, the Commission's proposal was watered down by the Council to restrict the Commission's responsibilities. However, the Commission accepted this decision as a temporary drawback and realized that once a merger regime had been constructed, it could be further reformed at a later date. The key for the Commission and the business community was getting the EU merger rules onto the books.

If the 1989 Merger Regulation defined the Commission's powers and conferred competence on the Community, then Regulation 139/2004, which updated the Regulation, has reinforced the objectives in the original text with regard to the Commission's powers and on jurisdictional boundaries. This has been greeted relatively enthusiastically as an attempt to modernize existing practice. Against the backdrop of these developments a case can be made not only that there has been a become Europeanization of EU merger policy, but also that the interested parties, who form the competition policy (epistemic) community, have themselves undergone a process of Europeanization (see Box 8.2).

From the firm's perspective, the relationship with the EU's competition officials is a crucial one, as the merging parties are selfishly seeking complete clearance and to avoid any attached conditions. Firms operate to a 'game plan' in which they need to convince DG Competition's officials of the merits of the merger and that there are no serious drawbacks to the deal. Companies therefore seek to reach some form of accommodation with DG Competition and to this end employ (alongside their own teams of competition lawyers) public affairs consultants who are familiar with the rules and procedures of the merger policy process. They also use the media to promote their merger. Indeed the way the media are used both by the merging parties and by the Commission during merger investigations is undervalued and greater consideration in future competition policy research needs to be accorded to what often

BOX 8.2   Europeanization dynamics in EU merger policy

Dynamic	Process	Actor involvement
Construction of EU merger regime through Regulation 4064/89	Creating European regime and subject to political wrangling	Member state governments, non-governmental actors
Establishing distinct jurisdictional boundaries	Division of European/national competence through Community Dimension (CD) thresholds	European Commission, national competition authorities, business groups
Reinforcement of supranational competition governance through Regulation 139/2004	Reaffirmation of a European jurisdiction plus the corrective measures to make for more effective handling Referrals to EU level under Article 22	Commission, national authorities, business groups, lawyers

Sources: Adapted from Lodge (2002); McGowan (2005).

amounts to a 'sophisticated press management strategy' (Heim 2003:77).

What is occurring here is a form of interest representation and lobbying that is similar to the customary policy-shaping activities familiar in other policy areas. This may is perhaps to be expected from the parties concerned, but consumer organizations and other business groups in the same sector as the proposed merger are also usually keen to advance their interests to DG Competition and other parts of the Commission. There is some evidence to suggest that the media and lobbying activities that take place at the time of proposed mergers really do affect outcomes, but more research is needed to confirm this.

In both the restrictive practices and the merger fields there is a great deal of potential for applying concepts found in the Europeanization literature, as well as particular definitions of Europeanization, as a way of focusing attention on certain aspects of the development of the EU's competition regime. While there is more work to be done here, as in the neo-functionalist case, some of the groundwork has already been done by otherwise examining Europeanization from a policy content or policy process perspective. Scholars of competition policy should draw on this literature in designing and developing their own research agendas.

Conclusion

A political research agenda on a policy area such as competition policy, where most of the research undertaken is by lawyers and economists, demands a theoretical perspective drawing on existing political (and perhaps sociological) theories. Without such a perspective, there is a danger that political scientists, themselves immersed in the legal and economic literatures, forget what it is they were planning to do at the outset. Theories of politics – or in our case, of European integration – offer a reality check for researchers, allowing them to ask questions so far ignored in the existing literature, and which might otherwise be dismissed as irrelevant.

In this chapter we have questioned, in a rather tentative way, whether there might be some scope for drawing on European integration theories to inform our understanding of European competition policy. At this point, we accept that our ambitions are rather limited. In selecting neo-functionalism and Europeanization it was not our intention to get bogged down in claims and counter-claims about the suitability of each. Instead, this chapter has deliberately opted to leave the discussion open-ended. It is our hope that this chapter will inspire researchers to contemplate and take forward our initial idea – or even indeed to respond to it in a less positive manner. We will watch with interest.

Chapter 9

Conclusions

This chapter highlights the most important developments, trends and issues in the field of EU competition policy. In it we return to discuss the four themes identified in the introduction – modernization, Europeanization, decentralization and liberalization – but will also address other issues of relevance, particularly where these are not discussed at length in the chapters above.

Modernization and decentralization: policy and organizational reform

Policy reform has long preoccupied everyone interested in the regulation and operation of the European competition regime. Two member states have been at the forefront of the reform debate. UK governments have in the past favoured the status quo and have, as such, opposed the transfer of further enforcement powers to the Commission. This was very much in line with their general approach towards European integration. By contrast, German governments have been the most vocal critics of the EU's competition regime, calling loudly for a depoliticization of enforcement and the injection of a large dose of transparency into the decision-making process. In their criticisms of the EU system, both UK and German governments have each demonstrated a touching commitment to, and defence of, their own national competition regimes, even where, in the case of the former, they have been willing to engage in domestic reforms on their own initiative.

However, calls for reform have come from many quarters, and not just from national governments. While some of these have involved substantive issues, others have reflected concerns over resource constraints and administrative overload, which were expected to intensify after the 2004 enlargement. DG Competition had long claimed that it had insufficient resources with which to enforce its policy effectively. While in the 1990s it compared in size

214

to the German Federal Cartel Office and the UK Office of Fair Trading, it has a much larger market to contend with and an enormous workload. With the backlog of cases becoming a permanent feature of policy enforcement from the early 1960s on, the Commission has had to prioritize its decision-taking. This has meant that DG Competition activity has been largely reactive, driven by notifications and complaints. The way it has reacted to cases put before it has shaped the policy's evolution, though this approach clearly has its limitations. Indeed it has been said that 'the chief continuing weakness of . . . [DG Competition] . . . in the enforcement of competition policy is that its inadequate resources both in financial terms and in numbers of officials, have prevented it from ever completely digesting the workload' (Goyder 1993:493).

Since the early 1990s, Article 81 and 82 cases presented the biggest challenge, as more efficient procedures were already in place under the Merger Regulation after 1990, and the state aid backlog was never such a contentious issue. DG Competition continued to be a victim of its own success. The speed with which it was able to take merger decisions served only to focus more attention on DG Competition's rather poorer record in restrictive practices and monopoly cases.

As a consequence, it came as no surprise that the modernization agenda, proposing the reform of European competition policy, should seek to tackle these issues. The most striking initiative within the modernization has been the withdrawal of the notification requirement from firms and the removal of DG Competition's exclusive right to exempt agreements under Article 81(3). This has been replaced by an automatic exemption for firms, who must now conduct their own self-assessment on the basis of criteria which the Commission or National Competition Authorities would themselves use, and which is explained at length in published guidelines. Thus, the new system got rid of the old ex ante system, and introduced a system of ex post control. It is no exaggeration to talk of this as constituting a 'revolution' in policy enforcement, which allows DG Competition to concentrate on its most important cases and to be more proactive in using enforcement to develop further its policy.

Although the modernization label has tended to be used only with reference to the Article 81 reform, this does not mean that other aspects of European competition policy – namely merger control and state aid policy – have stagnated since the 1990s; far from it. Following a review conducted in 1989, the Commission produced a Green Paper in 2002 on a revised Merger Regulation. This was agreed by the Competitiveness Council in 2003 and has since come into force (2004). It contained a number of new procedural, substantive and jurisdictional reforms to the earlier version. In the case of state aid, proposals to kick-start (once again) an activist state aid policy were initiated a little later in 2005 with the introduction of the State Aid Action Plan (SAAP).

Policy reform has been accompanied by organizational reform. There have been many of these in DG Competition's history. But the most recent, which was introduced between 2002 and 2004, was dramatic, affecting the DG as a whole. It constituted an attempt to integrate almost all the constituent parts of European competition policy, instituting a functionally based structure of four sector-based directorates which was intended to enable joined-up thinking and policy-learning across monopoly, mergers and state aid policy. It also responded to a need to rationalize staff resources in view of the impending enlargement of the EU, which was expected to increase DG Competition's workload by around 40 per cent. The maintenance of a separate cartel directorate was also an important signal as to the priority to be given in future to this aspect of European competition policy, reflecting a similar preference given to the pursuit of certain cartel cases in the US anti-trust regime (Wigger 2008).

In the past, critics of the Commission's competition policy often pointed to the legal formalism which characterized its decision-taking. In other words, it was argued that the Commission tended to define success in terms of legislative outcomes, and undertook its analysis based solely on the letter of the law. Those who criticized this approach claimed that the neglect of economic analysis and policy outcomes was extremely dangerous – economic realities rarely equate with legal frameworks and doctrines. This was more than just an academic debate. If the Commission's policy sends out the wrong signals to firms, and firms react by altering their behaviour in line with Commission policy, the impact on European competition and competitiveness could be dramatic. It is for this reason, and as a result of pressure from the Courts, that since the late 1990s the Commission has been employing more economists, and incorporating into its policy the latest economic thinking on competition regulation. In practice, increasing emphasis is now placed on efficiency reasoning and short-term consumer welfare (Wigger 2008) in both cartel and merger decisions, emulating key aspects of the US anti-trust approach. Here, cartels are deemed the worst of all anti-competitive offences and are subject to priority action. Economic analysis of a microeconomic kind now drives the policy.

A key innovation to support this policy shift has been the appointment of a Chief Economist. This position was created to provide the DG with guidance on economics and econometrics in the application of the competition rules, both in terms of general policy developments and instruments, and in specific cases. It was expected that the views of the Chief Economist would carry some weight where cases were appealed to the European Courts. The first to hold this position was Lars-Hendrik Röller, replaced in mid 2006 by Damien Neven.

Decentralization and Europeanization: from delegation to network governance

The Commission's modernization agenda saw decentralization as a key element of the reform; and decentralization, not least in view of the impending enlargement(s), demanded a process of Europeanization. This took two forms. First, it involved the adaptation of domestic competition regimes – both those of existing member states (on a voluntary basis), and those of the pre-2004/2007 applicant states (in a rather less voluntary manner, given that they were intent on meeting EU criteria for membership). Second, it involved what the Commission referred to as the construction of a common competition culture across the EU. This is less about an institutional convergence and more about cultural or ideational convergence. In other words, its objective is to instil in all relevant players common understandings and interpretation of European competition rules.

Modernization is closely associated with an enhanced process of decentralization. Decentralization initiatives by DG Competition predate the most recent reforms. However, since 2003, the drive to decentralize the policy has become more than just desirable; it has become a key component of the new European regime. Central now are the National Competition Authorities (NCAs), which become more important players in the competition regime.

Domestic courts too are also seen increasingly as having a crucial role to play. Together the NCAs and domestic courts are now able to apply Article 81(3) and exempt agreements directly, for the most part without recourse to DG Competition.

The creation of this network of enforcement was a strategy to resolve certain long-standing difficulties for DG Competition. It has some potential, but it is not risk-free. That it is set up at a time when twelve new EU members are coming to terms with a new system could cause problems, jeopardizing the coherence of that system should national authorities fail to take decisions in a manner compatible with EU rules and norms. Moreover, there has been some concern among the business community, for example, that the changes could diminish rather than enhance legal certainty, since it might be difficult to be certain about the validity of decisions. It was also clear that the reforms shifted the resource burden of competition regulation to the level of the firms.

One solution to this potential problem came in the form of the European Competition Network (ECN). The ECN was established to provide an arena for policy learning and the exchange of ideas among officials involved in the regulation of competition within the member states. It also has a more practical purpose which is to engage in information exchange and the investigation of cases. Decisions are taken about which national jurisdiction has responsibility for a case. In practice, the first authority to open a case tends to keep it (Wilks 2007). Where there are more than three countries likely to be affected, the case goes to DG Competition. On the whole the ECN operates virtually through the DG Competition website (with no private access however), though there are also meetings from time to time (see Chapter 3).

Recent studies have used principal–agent theory to model EU competition policy (Wilks 2005a; Doleys 2007). These studies seem to build on earlier ones which conceptualize the EU's competition regime as a 'regulatory state' (Majone 1993). Taken to its natural conclusion, a regulatory conception of the regime could see the hiving off of some of DG Competition's functions to an agency outside the Commission. The most radical initiative of this kind was the proposal to create a European Cartel Office (ECO). In the 1990s this attracted attention from both practitioners and from the media, and the proposal found supporters among the most senior of national actors. This was by no means a new idea at the time, however, having been discussed as early as 1965. The idea reappeared at the end of the 1980s when revived by Sir Sidney Lipworth, the former head of the UK Monopolies and Mergers Commission, when it was feared that the EU merger regime might become too politicized, and that competition criteria within the regime might end up taking second place to short-term political considerations.

The creation of an ECO would have implied the transfer of responsibilities for competition policy away from the Commission to a new autonomous agency. The attraction of this agency would have rested in its independence from both national and Commission control. Governmental interference, it was argued, would be minimized, decision-making procedures would be open to greater scrutiny, sectional lobbies would have less of a say over policy, and DG Competition would be less likely to be accused of playing prosecutor, judge and jury at one and the same time.

The proposal was in essence a German one, although it also found support in other quarters. Its main proponents were the German competition authority, the Bundeskartelamt (BKartA), and the German Economics Ministry. This governmental support led to the issue being given an airing during the 1996–97 Intergovernmental Conference, although no changes were agreed at the 1997 Amsterdam summit. Not surprisingly, the model for the ECO would have been the Berlin-based BKartA. Its underlying rationale would have been the promotion of competitive markets in a system in which the competition criterion would have overridden all other policy considerations. Political and social influences would, as a result, be reduced to a minimum (McGowan 2005).

Since the end of the 1990s the Cartel Office idea has waned in importance and because it was not included as part of the Commission's modernization plans, attention has turned to other issues. In a sense one might see the decentralization agenda as a substitute for the creation of a Competition Agency. This decentralization agenda operates on a different model of governance, however, which has more to do with the construction of networks than with the reinforcement of clear dividing lines between principals and agents.

Thus, the EU competition regime has been subject to a process of Europeanization. This has led to the adaptation of member state institutions and legal frameworks in a non-linear process of convergence, bringing them loosely into line with EU rules and norms. There is no assumption here that what we will end up with are policies that mimic each other in any perfect sense; rather the aim is the formation of a grouping of competition systems, each compatible with the others and with the EU-level regime. The way this change is encouraged by the Commission is non-coercive. Just as the relationship between principal and agent was a prerequisite for Europeanization, Europeanization would seem to be a prerequisite for the next stage in the competition regime's evolution: towards a form of network governance.

Yet delegation remains a useful point of departure for understanding the EU-level regulation of competition, not least as it points us towards two crucial questions about the policy: how to decide on division of responsibilities or competencies between the EU and national authorities; and how to balance legal certainty against the discretionary and political dimensions of competition regulation. The question of 'who does what?' is a perennial problem for competition regulators. One way of managing the division between EU and domestic competencies is quantitatively. The concept of a 'threshold' has become the means to this end as embodied in the so-called *de minimis* rules. These establish the thresholds under which the competition provisions do not apply. In the state aid case, the *de minimis* rules, formerly contained within a Notice, have recently been included in a Commission Regulation. Clauses in the Merger Control Regulation also allow for the transfer of cases from one level to another under certain specified circumstances, so that qualitative as well as quantitative elements can come into play.

These qualitative distinctions can blur as much as they separate the two levels of competence. Ultimately, where it matters, DG Competition has pre-emption rights and is able to claw cases back to the EU level.

For firms to work within a legally defined framework of rules, they must be able to know and understand the law. Legal certainty is not a luxury as far as they are concerned. An unpredictable policy may mean that firms are prevented from being law-abiding, as an ad-hoc policy approach implies that conduct which is legal one day may well be illegal the next. It is in the Commission's own interest, therefore, to develop a clear and transparent policy, one which will induce law-abiding behaviour on the part of the business community.

There are a number of different components which contribute to the legal certainty objective. One of the most obvious is decision-making speed. Under the old (pre-2003) system, long delays in dealing with cases, especially those that fall under Articles 81 and 82, meant that firms were often expected to exist in a sort of limbo for the two or three years during which the Commission was conducting its investigation and the Courts made their judgments. The implications were considerable for the firms involved, and that seemed particularly unfair where there was ultimately no case to answer. The modernization reform has done away with these long delays, but may have substituted one form of uncertainty for another. A second component involves Commission explanations of its policy in areas where case-law and legislation are not explicit. Where there is room for manoeuvre on the part of the Commission, officials are often keen to publish explanatory Notices, Frameworks and Guidelines. More recently, Green and White Papers have been produced for consultation purposes in advance of new Commission proposals. The DG Competition website is impressively comprehensive if also somewhat intimidating.

However, despite a proliferation of documentation of this kind, the Commission remains rather ambivalent when it comes to clarifying its own internal decisional processes. It is keen not to draw for itself a policy straightjacket which would ultimately undermine the flexibility which is considered essential for effective competition control. This desire to avoid constraints can often be at odds with the business community's demands for transparency. Recognizing that both objectives are important, the Commission has little alternative but to seek out a balance between the two.

European competition policy is unique in the autonomy that it grants the Commission, and the discretion allowed its officials during the decision-making process. Yet the policy's administrative flexibility is something of a double-edged sword. On the one hand, a flexible policy may be adaptable and free from pernicious rigidities. On the other hand, the potential for arbitrary and non-accountable decision-taking is likely to be substantial. Discretion in the hands of competition officials is legitimate to the extent that it rests on a firm treaty base and on subsequent secondary legislation. The treaty provisions are themselves open to a wide interpretation, however, and Regulation 1/2003, with the other procedural competition rules still, places substantial powers in the hands of the DG Competition staff. These include the power to investigate cases on the ground and the right to decide cases informally. It is down to the European Courts to keep the Commission in check. Yet the

European Courts have tended to confirm rather than constrain the discretionary capacity of the competition regulators, even though it is acknowledged that administrative discretion does not exist in a vacuum, but occurs within fairly well-defined legal margins. The Courts have been a good deal less tolerant of Commission reasoning since the late 1990s, however, though this has been more about the quality of DG Competition's economic analysis, and of the evidence it provides to the Courts, than about the exercise of its discretion.

The increasing use of informal decision-making tools, such as comfort letters and informal undertakings, as a quick way of settling non-controversial cases, infers an incremental and unchecked extension to DG Competition's discretionary scope. The Courts have very little input in these cases as these 'decisions' are neither judicable nor legally binding, at either European or national level. Both the Commission and the firms subject to these arrangements may see the advantages of a more informal approach to decision-making, but the likely impact on the accountability and legitimacy of the policy must also be taken into consideration.

Arguments for policy reform have often found their justification in the perception that the European competition regime is highly politicized. It is often claimed that the policy allows for a political input into the decision-making process, introducing non-competition criteria into European-level decisions. For those who would prefer to see a more stringent economic–legal basis at the heart of the policy, concern is less about the discretionary capacity of DG Competition officials and more about the deals that get done within the College of Commissioners.

Although ostensibly independent, Commissioners frequently act according to nationally defined preferences and interests. Ideological as well as national imperatives are important in accounting for these differing political perspectives. During the 1970s, for example, Commissioner Davignon's interventionist industrial strategies undermined rather weak attempts to apply the competition rules coherently. In the 1980s, Jacques Delors and the more interventionist Commissioners in the College frequently crossed swords with the likes of Peter Sutherland or Sir Leon Brittan who tended to take a more liberal line. Merger policy and state aid control are the aspects of the competition regime most prone to these disputes and it is in these areas that the debates over politicization are most intense.

Politicization is possible only thanks to the flexibility legally allowed the Commission during the decision-taking process. This is not unrelated to the issue of discretion discussed above. However, the question is less one of official discretion, and has more to do with the autonomy of the Commission vis-à-vis the other European institutions: that is, it is really about institutional balance. With the EU Council and the European Parliament having only marginal roles to play, competition policy is defined and developed incrementally and almost exclusively through Commission decision-taking and policy statements, and through the gradual accumulation of case-law. The fact that the Commission's role is largely an executive one might suggest that these accusations of politicization are without foundation. But, since in this instance the Commission is really acting as policy-maker and decision-taker, as well as detective, prosecutor, judge and jury, the Commission invariably becomes the focus of all political activity.

However, to say that the Council and the Parliament are largely excluded from competition decision-making does not mean they do not have influence. This is especially so for the member states. Their influence will be transmitted through individual (national) Commissioners in some cases; or via the President and the Competition Commissioner in others. Through both channels, member states seek to influence both individual competition cases, where they have an interest, and the general thrust of the policy – particularly during episodes of reform.

Liberalization: competition v. competitiveness revisited

In the 1980s and the early 1990s, the history of European competition policy was read as a shift from interventionist industrial policy, in which national champions continued to be promoted, to a neo-liberal agenda associated with privatization and liberalization. The Commission's liberalization agenda focused on injecting competition into sectors that had previously – for various reasons – been exempt from the competition rules. The sectors included covered those seen as important in terms of national prestige: for example, the motor vehicles sector, as well as others sometimes referred to as natural monopolies where structural and historical reasons existed for an absence of competition. These latter sectors fall mainly under the heading of 'services of general economic interest' (or SGEIs)

It may well be that the neo-liberal character of the post-1980s period has been exaggerated, as what we are really talking about during this time is a shift towards the injection of competition into previously closed policy domains. Although this was clearly ideological, it did not go as far as it might have in a practical sense because of the opposition of certain national governments and industries. However, using the policy to achieve objectives other than competition has certainly been frowned upon by those advocating a neo-liberal approach, and this is clearly the mainstream view among DG Competition and the epistemic community around European competition policy.

Since the late 1990s there has been some questioning of the pro-competition orthodoxy, and even some evidence that competition policy is being challenged by other policies, with objectives that may at times conflict. This is not to say that competition policy is in any way in decline, just that it may not be as high on the list of industrial/business objectives for governments and the EU as other policies and policy objectives. Why and from where these challenges have emerged is open to question. One argument is that the arena for ideas about the role of the state has been opened up through the anti-globalization lobbies in and since the 1990s. These demonstrated that for those feeling uncomfortable with the neo-liberal ideology, particular as applied to the global economy, there was an alternative, or perhaps several alternatives – even if at times those alternatives were neither as well articulated nor as clearly defined as the neo-liberal orthodoxy.

One might question moreover whether this orthodoxy was in fact so orthodox. Voices from France, in particular, would suggest otherwise, with neo-liberalism viewed as an Anglo-Saxon ideology imported upwards to the European level. These voices eventually received a sympathetic hearing from France's president, Nicolas Sarkozy, elected in 2007. Even if it is unclear at this point whether he is really prepared to step beyond a rhetorical condemnation of the EU's pro-competition ethos, an early indication of his stance (whether heartfelt, or purely on pragmatic grounds) was his removal, with tacit support by the German Presidency at the time, of the competition objective from the Treaty of Lisbon as approved by the EU's Heads of State and Government Summit in June 2007.

It would seem, however, that the shift may have begun before Sarkozy's election. The Lisbon Strategy, particularly in the form it took after 2005, has emphasized the importance to the EU of competitiveness and more sustainable employment. A cursory examination of the DG Competition website provides instances of the frequent assertion that these objectives go hand in hand with the promotion of competition. But is this always the case? Competition and competitiveness as objectives are not always compatible. Even if there is no suggestion of a return to the dirigisme of the 1970s, there is scope for a new interventionism by the EU and by its member states to promote EU competitiveness, which may see competition as a means to that end on some occasions, but not on others. Using the language of hierarchy, the question of which takes precedence – competition or competitiveness – needs to be addressed. Given the pervasiveness of the Lisbon Strategy, the answer may be competitiveness. Yet, if Lisbon is more about rhetoric than about practical policy initiatives (at least when it comes to initiatives only loosely attached to the Strategy), then the answer is not so clear-cut. Moreover, not everyone agrees that a new interventionism is on the horizon. Wigger (2008), for example, argues that the modernization agenda pursued by DG Competition constituted a deepening of the neo-liberal turn dating originally from the mid 1980s, and that continuity or a deepening of the 1980s neo-liberal agenda is the order of the day.

International cooperation and the centrality of the EU–US relationship

Globalization pressures demand that regulators need also to tackle competition policy issues internationally. This is difficult to do, and relatively little headway has been made in multilateral fora. International organizations do have a role in competition policy. The OECD has a Competition Committee comprising the leaders of the world's competition authorities and is supported by a Competition Division which produces analysis for publication. It also organizes the OECD Global Forum on Competition, which includes business and consumer representatives, bringing them together with competition officials in annual meetings with the aim of engaging in a policy dialogue. The WTO too has been involved in competition matters. This was one of the so-called 'new issues' which were introduced following the Singapore Ministerial Council in 1996 and which led to the establishment of a working group to examine the relationship between trade and competition. However, by July 2004 the WTO's General Council had agreed that this would not be part of the negotiations in the Doha Round, and since then the working group has been inactive. The failure of an attempt to forge hard competition rules at the international talks was largely due to the fact that the US did not support the initiative. Rather, they pushed for a softer form of multilateral cooperation, culminating in a new initiative, the International Competition Network (ICN), which was set up in 2001. The ICN exists virtually as a network of anti-trust authorities to promote procedural and substantive convergence and cooperation. It does not engage in rule-making, but where conclusions are reached by its working groups, they issue 'Recommendations' or 'Best Practices'.

Efforts to deal with international issues bilaterally have been more successful. The EU and the US are by far the key players – the 'giants' of competition policy from a global perspective. This image of the two regimes provides an interesting lens through which to assess the EU's economic power (something which is done more frequently drawing on the experience of trade policy). The relationship between the EU and the US regimes has been characterized in large by a spirit of cooperation. However, there have also been tensions over disagreements in the handling of cases. The two regimes are not identical, and what concerns the EU does not always worry the US. One example of such a disagreement can be found in one of the Microsoft cases (as discussed in Chapter 4). When the Court of First Instance ruled against Microsoft in September 2007, the US Assistant Attorney General for Antitrust within the Department of Justice, Thomas O. Barnett, made a pronouncement that the decision could harm consumers and threaten innovation and competition. The response of the Competition Commissioner, Neelie Kroes, was swift, criticizing Barnett and making the point that the EU would never interfere in judgments within the US jurisdiction, as he had done in the case of the EU.

The future of European competition policy

There is no doubt that European competition policy is one of the Commission's flagship policies. It is perhaps a shame from the EU's perspective that successes in this policy domain are little known outside certain financial, legal and academic circles. Despite its flaws, the policy has withstood the test of time and has matured into a cohesive and increasingly comprehensive competition regime. Based on a system of supranational regulation which shows the extent to which the Commission can play an active, assertive and indeed at times an independent role within the EU, and a powerful role vis-à-vis the United States, it has become an example of how the Commission can increase the scope and depth of its competence, using its own as well as the European Court's resources. Yet despite the Commission's relative detachment, in this policy area, from the more conventional European policy process, which relies on EP and Council legislation, it is still dependent on the EU governments for its position of relative autonomy. The Commission can act independently in competition matters (in policy-making, as well as decision-making), but it does so within a framework and in a policy environment determined by the good-will of the member states, and based on an underlying consensus about the merits of competition and the necessity of European-level competition policy.

From the analysis at the start of this chapter, it seems clear that the Commission will face numerous challenges as it seeks to improve its competition enforcement over the next decade or so. In summary, these challenges fall into two broad categories. On the one hand, there are the challenges of effectiveness. These question DG Competition's capacity to cope with the enormous case responsibilities while remaining focused on policy outcomes. The main issue is, as ever, that of resources. But the prioritization of cases, the decentralization of enforcement and the increasing use of economic analysis in investigations – in sum the modernization – are also important. On the other hand, however, there also exist challenges of democracy. With the legitimacy of the policy now frequently called into question, in part owing to the exclusion of the Council and the EP from the competition policy process, efforts to inject more accountability, or at least more transparency, into competition policy are likely to continue to preoccupy Commission staff. Managing the political-discretionary input into decision-making will also be part of this second challenge.

Ultimately, it is the relationship and balance between the challenges of effectiveness and democracy that will shape how European competition policy evolves in future. This evolution is not just an internal matter, a process of navel-gazing by DG Competition or Commission staff, but is dependant on external factors, such as national perceptions about the function of competition policy, and the often unpredictable character of the international political economy. So while it has been possible in this chapter to identify some of the difficulties likely to face the European competition regime in its sixth decade, just what the policy might look like in, say, 2015 or 2020 is at this point left entirely to the reader to speculate upon.

Guide to Further Reading

There is a substantial literature on European competition policy. Most of this is written by economists and lawyers, and may not always be easy reading for those outside those specialisms. However, there is a growing literature on European competition policy within political science and European Studies.

The best point of departure is of course our own text. However, readers may also wish to get a feel for the policy by referring to DG Competition's website at http://ec.europa.eu/comm/competition/index_en.html This is an essential source of factual information on the legislation, as well as containing important non-legislative documents and policy statements. There is access from here to all the cases and decisions of the Commission and the Courts; information on the structure of, and personnel within DG Competition; and almost daily updates of the latest news and developments. This website is complemented by the Commission's *Annual Competition Policy Reports* and its quarterly *Competition Policy Newsletter*, which can also be accessed from the site. For greater analysis we direct readers to the following works which we have placed under the headings used to structure this book.

Overview

For a general overview of the EU competition policy regime readers might consult Wilks (2005a and b) and Wilks and McGowan (1996). Although a little outdated now, Amato (1997) provides a great insight into the politics of competition policy. Goyder (2003), Monti (2007), Jones and Sufrin (2008) and Whish (2003), provide much deeper but excellent coverage of all aspects of competition law. Bishop and Walker (2002 with new edition pending) and Motta (2004) provide very informative economic interpretations. The reports from the House of Lords (1993, 2002) contain invaluable insights and analyses of the workings of European competition policy, presented in an accessible fashion. There are a number of specialized competition policy journals, for example, the *European Competition Law Review* and the *Journal of Competition Law and Economics*.

History

Gerber (1998) has provided excellent narrative of the themes and developments in European competition policy. See also Wigger (2008). Goyder (2003) still provides an excellent starting point for anyone interested in the history of DG Competition. Doern and Wilks (1996) still serve as a good starting point for an examination of national competition regimes. Historians such as Leucht (2008); Seidel, (2007, 2008) and Warzoulet (2006) are now entering this particular arena, shedding invaluable light on aspects of the origins of the EU regime, drawing on archival data sources.

Institutions

McGowan and Wilks (1995) provide an initial starting point for discussion of the EU competition regime. Readers should also see Monti (2007) for discussions of decentralization and enforcement; and Hofmann (2006) for an in depth analysis of procedure. For further information on the European Competition Network, see Wilks (2007).

Restrictive practices

Whish (2003), Goyder (2003) and Jones and Sufrin (2008) provide extensive coverage of restrictive practices and the issues that arise under Article 81. Ododu (2006) focuses specifically on this article. For an excellent discussion of how European cartel policy has evolved over the last century see Harding and Joshua (2003). For further discussion of the most recent developments in the EU context see McGowan (2005) and McGowan (forthcoming, 2009).

Monopolies

This may be the least accessible policy area for non-lawyers and economists but there are a number of places to start investigating this aspect of the policy. Readers should see Jones and Sufrin (2008) or/and Goyder (2003), who provide a good and in-depth overview, as do Van den Bergh and Camesasca (2006).

O'Donoghue and Padilla (2006) also fuse economics and law for very informative insights into monopoly policy. Motta (2004) provides a much more economics-based analysis. For information on more recent debates on the reform of Article 82, see Kroes (2005) and Sher (2004).

Mergers

On merger policy there is a growing literature. One of the best and extensive legal accounts can be found in Navarro *et al.* (2005), but see also Cook and Kerse (2006), Goyder (2003) and Weitbrecht (2005). For more political perspectives on the evolution of merger policy see Bulmer (1994), Doleys (2006), McGowan and Cini (1999) and see also Buch-Hansen (2008).

State aids

A number of the standard law texts (though not all) include chapters on state aid, alongside other aspects of competition law. Biondi *et al.* (2004) provides in-depth coverage and analysis of the law from a wide range of perspectives. There are a number of articles of interest, not least Cremona (2003), who looks at state aid and enlargement. From a more political or institutional perspective, Smith (1996 and 2000) provides an excellent introduction to the evolution of the policy. Cini (2001) discusses the soft law perspective. For those interested in regional state aid, one need look no further than the excellent work of Fiona Wishlade (for example, Wishlade 2008).

Theoretical perspectives

Theorizing EU competition policy within the literature on EU integration studies and political science debates in general is a relatively new endeavour but work is appearing and readers should access Büthe and Swank (2005), Doleys (2007), Lehmkuhl, (2008) and McGowan, L. (2007).

References

ABA (2005) 'The European Competition Network: What It Is and Where It Is Going', American Bar Association Section on Antitrust Law Brown Bag Program, 19 April, at: http://www.abanet.org/antitrust/source/07-05/Jul05-ECNBrBag7=28f.pdf

Ahlborn, C. and Berg, C. (2004) 'Can State Aid Learn From Antitrust? The Need for a Greater Role for Competition Analysis under the State Aid Rules', in A. Biondi, P. Eeckhout and J. Flynn (eds) *The Law of State Aid in the European Union* (Oxford University Press).

ALDE (2006) Competition Policy Paper, October, at: http://www.alde.eu/fileadmin/files/Download/CompetitionPolicy_EN1_web.pdf

Amato, G. (1997) *Antitrust and the Bounds of Power* (Oxford: Hart).

Areeda P. and Turner, D. (1975) 'Predatory Prices and Related Practices under Section 2 of the Sherman Act', *Harvard Law Review* 88(4):697–733.

Ballantyne, E. and Bachtler, J. (1990) *Regional policy under Scrutiny: The European Commission and Regional Aid,* European Policies Research Centre, University of Strathclyde Research Paper no. 9 (Glasgow).

Barry, N. (1989) 'Political and Economic Thought of the German Neo-liberals', in A. Peacock and H. Willgerodt (eds) *The German Social Market* (Basingstoke: Macmillan).

Berghahn, V. R. (1986) *The Americanisation of West German Industry* (Leamington: Berg).

Bernini, G. (1983) 'The Rules on Competition', *Thirty Years of Community Law* (Luxembourg: Centre Européen des Consommateurs).

Biondi, A., Eeckhout, P. and Flynn, J. (eds) (2004) *The Law of State Aid in the European Union* (Oxford University Press).

Bishop, S. (1995) 'State Aids: Europe's Spreading Cancer', *European Competition Law Review* 16(6):331–3.

Bishop, S. and Walker, M. (2002) *The Economics of EC Competition Law: Concepts, Application and Measurement,* 2nd edn (London: Sweet & Maxwell).

Braun H.-J. (1990) *The German Economy in the Twentieth Century* (London: Routledge).

Brittan, L. (1989) 'A Bonfire of Subsidies? A Review of State Aids in the European Community', *European Access* no. 3:12–14.

Brittan, L. (1990) 'The Law and Policy of Merger Control in the EEC', *European Law Review* 15(5):351–7.

Brittan, L. (1994) *Europe: The Europe We Need* (London: Hamish Hamilton).

Brodley, J. and Hay, D. (1981) 'Predatory Pricing: Competing Economic Theories and the Evolution of Legal Standards', *Cornell Law Review* 66: 738–803.

Buch-Hansen, O. (2008) 'Rethinking the Evolution of European Merger Control: A Critical Political Economy Perspective', PhD Thesis, Copenhagen Business School.

Buck, T. (2005) 'Brussels State Aid Reform Proposal Could Lead to Big Job Losses, Say Governments', *Financial Times*, 1 February.

Buck, T. (2007) 'Germany Urges Relaxation of EU Subsidy Rules', *Financial Times*, 25 April.

Buller, J. and Gamble, A. (2002) 'Conceptualising Europeanisation', *Public Policy Administration* 17(2):2–24.

Bulmer, S. (1994) 'Institutions and Policy Change in the European Communities: The Case of Merger Control', *Public Administration* 72(3):423–44.

Burnside, A. (2000) 'Governance of EC Merger Control – Bumps in a Level Playing Field', in *EC Merger Control: Ten Years On, Papers from the EC Merger Control 10th Anniversary Conference*, EC/IBA:381–403.

Büthe, T. and Swank, G. (2005) 'The Politics of Antitrust and Merger Review in the European Union: Institutional Change and Decisions from Messina to 2004', Working Paper, Mimeo, Duke and Stanford Universities.

Carter, C. and Smith, A. (2008) 'Revitalizing Public Policy Approaches to the EU', *Journal of European Public Policy* 15(2):263–81.

Caspari, M. (1984) 'State Aids in the EEC', Reprinted from the *Annual Proceedings of the Fordham Corporate Law Institute* (New York: Matthew Bender).

Caspari, M. (1987) 'The Aid Rules of the EEC Treaty and their Application', speech delivered in Florence, 14–15 May.

Cini, M. (2001) 'The Soft Law Approach: Commission Rule-making in the EU State Aid Regime', *Journal of European Public Policy*, 8(2):192-207.

Cini, M. (2008) 'The Europeanisation of British Competition Policy', in I. Bache and Jordan, A. (eds) *The Europeanization of British Politics* (Basingstoke: Palgrave).

Cini, M. (ed.) (2006) *European Union Politics* (Oxford University Press).

Clark, J. M. (1940) 'Toward a Concept of Workable Competition', *American Economic Review* 30(2):241–56.

Coen, D. and Dannreuther, C. (2004) 'Differentiated Europeanisation: Large and Small Firms in the EU Policy Process', in K. Featherstone and C. Radaelli (eds) *The Politics of Europeanization* (Oxford University Press).

Commission (1964) *Ford Tractor Belgium*, Negative Commission Decision no. 64/651/CEE, 28.11.1964.

Commission (1966) 'Memorandum on the Concentration of Enterprises in the Common Market', *EEC Competition Series 3* (Brussels).

Commission (1976) *Fifth Report on Competition Policy 1975* (Luxembourg).

Commission (1977) *Sixth Report on Competition Policy 1976* (Luxembourg).

Commission (1978) *Seventh Report on Competition Policy 1977* (Luxembourg).

Commission (1979) *Eighth Report on Competition Policy 1978* (Luxembourg).

Commission (1980a) *Ninth Report on Competition Policy 1979* (Luxembourg).

Commission (1980b) *Commission Directive No. 81/723/EEC of 25 June 1980 on the Transparency of Financial Relations between Member States and Public Undertakings as well as on Financial Transparency within Certain Undertakings* (Transparency Directive).

Commission (1981) *Tenth Report on Competition Policy 1980* (Luxembourg).

Commission (1982) *Eleventh Report on Competition Policy 1981* (Luxembourg).

Commission (1984) *Thirteenth Report on Competition Policy 1983* (Luxembourg).

Commission (1985a) *Completing the Internal Market: White Paper from the Commission to the European Council,* COM (95) 310 (Luxembourg).

Commission (1985b) *Fourteenth Report on Competition Policy, 1984* (Luxembourg).

Commission (1988) *First Survey of State Aids in the European Community* (Brussels).

Commission (1989) Community Framework on State aid to the Motor Vehicles Industry, *Official Journal* C123, 18 May.

Commission (1992) *Twenty-First Report on Competition Policy 1991* (Luxembourg).

Commission (1993) *Twenty-Second Report on Competition Policy 1992* (Luxembourg)

Commission (1994) *Twenty-Third Report on Competition Policy 1993* (Luxembourg).

Commission (1995a) Commission Notice on the cooperation between the Commission and the courts of the EU Member States in the State aid field, *Official Journal* C312/8.

Commission (1995b) *Twenty-Fourth Report on Competition Policy 1994* (Luxembourg).

Commission (1995c) Guidelines on aid to Employment , *Official Journal* C334 of 12.12.95:4.

Commission (1996) *Green Paper on the Review of the Merger Regulation,* COM(96) 19 final (Brussels).

Commission (1997a) *Green Paper on Vertical Restraints in EC Competition Policy,* COM(96) 721 final (Brussels).

Commission (1997b) *Twenty-Sixth Report on Competition Policy 1996* (Luxembourg).

Commission (1998) 'Notice from the Commission on the Application of the Competition Rules to the Postal Sector and on the Assessment of Certain State Measures Relating to Postal Services', *Official Journal* C39, 6.2.1998:2–18.

Commission (2000) *Report from the Commission to the Council on the Application of the Merger Regulation Thresholds,* COM(2000) 399 final, Brussels, 28.6.2000.

Commission (2001a) *Green Paper on the Review of Council Regulation (EEC) No. 4064/89,* COM(2001) 745/6 final.

Commission (2001b) *Commission Communication: Certain Legal Aspects Relating to Cinematographic and Other Audio-Visual Works,* COM(2001) 534 final, 26.9.2001.

Commission (2002a) 'Regulation 1400/2002 on Vertical Agreements and Concerted Practices in the Motor Vehicle Sector', *Official Journal* L203/30.

Commission (2002b) 'Notice on Immunity from Fines in Cartel Cases', *Official Journal* C45 19.02.2002.

Commission (2003a) *Best Practices on the Conduct of EC Merger Control Proceedings*, DG Competition, at: http://ec.europa.eu/comm/competition/mergers/legislation/proceedings.pdf

Commission (2003b) 'Framework on State Aid to Shipbuilding' 2003/C 317/06, *Official Journal* C317, 30.12.2003.

Commission (2004a) *Joint Statement of the Council and the Commission on the Functioning of the Network of Competition Authorities*, at: http://ec.europa.eu/comm/competition/ecn/joint_statement_en.pdf

Commission (2004b) 'Commission Regulation (EC) no. 794/2004 Implementing Council Regulation (EC) no. 659/1999 Laying Down Detailed Rules for the Application of Article 93 of the EC Treaty', *Official Journal* L140, 30.4.2004:1–134.

Commission (2004c) 'Community Guidelines on State Aid for Rescuing and Restructuring Firms in Difficulty', *Official Journal* C244 of 1.10.2004: 2–17.

Commission (2004d) 'Commission Adopts New Rules Governing Aid to Firms in Difficulty', MEMO/05/172 of 7.07.2004

Commission (2005) 'State Aid Action Plan, Less and Better Targeted Aid: A Road Map for State Aid Reform 2005-08' (Consultation Document), SEC (2005) 985.

Commission (2006a) *Report on Competition Policy 2005*, SEC(2006) 761 final.

Commission (2006b) 'Commission Regulation (EC) no. 1998/2006 of 15 December 2006 on the application of Articles 87 and 88 of the Treaty to *De Minimis* Aid', *Official Journal* L379 of 28.12.2006.

Commission (2006c) 'State Aid: Commission Adopts New Regional Aid Guidelines', Press Release, IP/05/1653.

Commission (2006d) 'The Commission Adopts New Rules on State Aid in Agriculture', Press Release, IP/06/1697, 6 December 2006.

Commission (2006e) 'Community Framework for State Aid Research and Development and Innovation' *Official Journal* C323, 30.12.2006.

Commission (2007a) *Report on Competition Policy 2006*, COM(2007) 358 final.

Commission (2007b) 'Networks', at: http://ec.europa.eu/comm/competition/ecn/index_en.html

Commission (2007c) *Draft Revised Commission Notice on the Application of Articles 87 and 88 of the EC Treaty to State Aid in the Form of Guarantees*, 18 July, http://ec.europa.eu/comm/competition/state_aid/reform/draft_guarantee_notice_18072007) en.pdf

Commission (2007d) *Vademecum. Community Rules on State Aid*, revised 15 February.

Commission (2007e) 'State Aid Control. Overview', at: http://ec.europa.eu/comm/competition/state_aid/overview/index_en.cfm, consulted 11 September.

Commission (2007f) *Proposal for a Commission Regulation Amending Regulation (EC) no. 794/2004 Implementing Council Regulation (EC) no. 659/1999 Laying Down Detailed Rules for the Application of Article 93 of the EC Treaty*, at: http://ec.europa.eu/comm/competition/state_aid/reform/procrules_notif_en.pdf

Commission (2008a) 'State Aid: Commission Requests Romania to Recover €27 Million Unlawful Aid from Automobile Craiova', Press Release, IP/08/315, 27/2/2008.

Cook, C. J. and Kerse, C. S. (2006) *EC Merger Control*, 4th edn (London: Sweet and Maxwell).

Coppel, J. (1992) 'Curbing the Ruling Passion: A New Force for Judicial Review in the European Communities', *European Competition Law Review* 13(4):143–8.

Council (1968) Regulation 1017/68 'Agreements in Road and Inland Waterways', *Official Journal* spec. edn 302.

Council (1986) Regulation 4056/86 'Liner Conferences in the Maritime Sector', *Official Journal* L378/14.

Council (1997) Council Regulation (EC) no. 1310/97 of 30 June, *Official Journal* L180, 9.7.97.

Council (1998a) *Council Regulation (EC) 1440/98 on State Aid to the Shipbuilding Industry*, 29 June.

Council (1998b) *Council Regulation (EC) No. 994/98 on the Application of Articles 92 and 93 of the Treaty Establishing the European Community to Certain Categories of Horizontal State Aid* (State Aid Enabling Regulation).

Council (1999) Regulation No. 659/1999 of 22 March 1999 Laying Down Detailed Rules for the Application of Article 93 (now 99) of the EC Treaty. *Official Journal* L 83/1, 27.03.1999:1–9.

Council (2003) *Council Regulation 1/2003 of 16 December 2002 on the Implementation of the rules on Competition Laid Down in Articles 81 and 82 or the Treaty* (Modernization Regulation).

Council (2007) 'Success through research – informal Council Competitiveness – Research', Summary by the President, Würzburg, 26–27 April, at: http://www.bmbf.de/pub/rat_wettbewerbsfaehigkeit_schlussfolgerungen_en.pdf

Council/EP (1996) *Directive 96/92/EC Concerning Common Rules for the Internal Market in Electricity*, 19 December.

Cownie, F. (1986) 'State Aid in the Eighties', *European Law Review* 11(4):247–69.

Cremona, M. (2003) 'State Aid Control: Substance and Procedure in Europe Agreements and the Stabilisation and Association Agreements', *European Law Journal* 9(3):265–87.

Davidson, L. (2005) 'The New EC Merger Regulation – Guaranteeing the Effectiveness of the Architecture of Separate Jurisdictional Zones', unpublished paper.

Doern, G. B. and Wilks, S. (1996) 'Introduction', in G. B. Doern and S. Wilks (eds) *Comparative Competition Policy: National Institutions in a Global Market* (Oxford: Clarendon).

Doleys, T. (2006) 'The Origins of EU Merger Control: Insights from Agency Theory', paper delivered as the ECPR Third Pan European Conference on EU Politics at Bilgi University, Istanbul, 21–23 September.

Doleys, T. (2007) 'Managing the Paradox of Discretion: Commission Authority and the Evolution of EU State Aid Policy', paper presented at the

37th Annual UACES Research Conference, University of Portsmouth, 3–5 September.

Dombey, D. (2002a) 'Defeat for Brussels over Haulier Tax', *Financial Times*, 4 May.

Dombey, D. (2002b) 'Brussels Rejects Action over State Aid Revolt', *Financial Times* 15 May.

Dombey, D. and Guerrera, F. (2002) 'Little Noticed Treaty Clause May Curb Monti's Power', *Financial Times* 18 February.

Downes, T. A. and MacDougall, D. S. (1994) 'Significantly Impeding Effective Competition: Substantive Appraisal under the Merger Regulation', *European Law Review* 19(5):286–303.

Dyson, K. and Goetz, K. (2003) *Germany, Europe and the Politics of Constraint* (Oxford University Press).

Featherstone, K. and Radaelli, C. *The Politics of Europeanization* (Oxford University Press).

Financial Times (2007) 'Controlling State Aid', editorial, 20 July.

Fishwick, F. (1993) *Making Sense of Competition Policy* (London: Kogan Page).

Fitzpatrick, E. (1995) 'Articles 85 and 86: Control of Restrictive Practices and Abuses of Dominant Positions', in L. Davidson, E. Fitzpatrick and D. Johnson (eds) *The European Competitive Environment* (Oxford: Butterworth-Heinemann).

Fothergill, S. (2006) 'EU State Aid Rules: How the European Union is Setting the Framework for Member States', Own Regional Policies', paper prepared for the RSA Conference, Leuven, June.

Fox, E. (1981) 'The New American Competition Policy', *European Competition Law Review* 2: 439–51.

Frazer, T. (1995) 'The New Structural Funds, State Aids and Interventions on the Single Market', *European Law Review* 20(1):3–19.

Gerber, D. J. (1998) *Law and Competition in Twentieth Century Europe: Protecting Prometheus* (Oxford: Clarendon).

Goyder, D. G. (1988) *EEC Competition Law* (Oxford: Clarendon).

Goyder, D. G. (1993) *EC Competition Law*, 2nd edn (Oxford: Clarendon).

Goyder, D. G. (2003) *EC Competition Law*, 4th edn (Oxford: Clarendon)

Grant, J. and Neven, D. (2005) 'The Attempted Merger between General Electric and Honeywell: A Case Study of Transatlantic Conflict', *Journal of Competition Law and Economics* 1(3):599–633.

Graupner, F. (1973) 'Commission Decision-Making on Competition Questions', *Common Market Law Review* 10(3):291–305.

Green, N. and Robertson, A. (1999) *The Europeanisation of UK Competition Law* (Oxford: Hart).

Greenwood, J. (2003) (ed.) *The Challenge of Change in EU Business Associations* (Basingstoke: Palgrave).

Greenwood, J., Strangward, L, and Stancich, L. (1999) 'The Capacity of Euro Groups in the Integration Process', *Political Studies* 47(1):127–38.

Guerrera F. and Mann, M. (2002) 'EU Members Face Brussels', Legal Action', *Financial Times* 27 February.

Haas, E. B. (1958) *The Uniting of Europe: Political, Social and Economic Forces 1950–1957* (Stanford University Press).

Haas, E. B. (2004) 'Introduction: Institutionalization or Constructivism?', in *The Uniting of Europe: Political, Social and Economic Forces 1950–1957*, 3rd edn (University of Notre Dame Press).

Hambloch, S. (2007) 'Competition Policy in the EEC in the 1960s', paper presented at the Workshop on European Competition Policy, 1930–2005, Sorbonne University, Paris, 14–15 September.

Hancher, L. (1994) 'State Aids and Judicial Control in the European Community', *European Competition Law Review* 3:134–50.

Harding, C. and Joshua J. (2003) *Regulating Cartels in Europe* (Oxford University Press).

Harmsen, R. and Wilson, T. M. (eds) (2000) *Europeanization, Institution, Identities and Citizenship* (Atlanta, GA: Rodopi).

Hawk, B. E. (1985) *United States, Common Market and International Anti-Trust: A Comparative Guide* (New York: Harcourt Brace Jovanovic).

Heim, H. (2003) 'Problems and Process: European Merger Control and How to Use it', *Journal of Public Affairs* 4(1):73–85.

Hofmann, H. C. H. (2006) 'Negotiated and Non-Negotiated Administrative Rule Making: The Example of EC Competition Policy', *Common Market Law Review* 43(1):153–78.

Holmes, P. and Sydorak, A. (2006) 'Rivalry and Co-operation in European Competition Policy: Towards a Global Competition Cartel', paper delivered as the ECPR Third Pan European Conference on EU Politics at Bilgi University, Istanbul, 21–23 September.

Hölzler, H. (1990) 'Merger Control', in P. Montagnon (ed.) *European Competition Policy* (London: Chatham House/RIIA).

House of Lords (1982) *Competition Practice*, Select Committee on the European Communities, Eighth Report, session 1981/2 (London: HMSO).

House of Lords (1993) *Enforcement of Community Competition Rules*, Select Committee on the European Communities, Report with Evidence, HL 7 (London: HMSO).

House of Lords (2002) *The Review of the EC Merger Regulation*, Select Committee on the European Union, HL Paper 165 (London: HMSO).

Hunter, A. (1969) 'Introduction', in A. Hunter (ed.) *Monopoly and Competition* (Harmondsworth: Penguin).

Jacqué, J. P. and Weiler, J. H. H. (1990) 'On the Road to European Union – a New Judicial Architecture', *Common Market Law Review* 27:185–207.

Jones, A. (1993) 'Woodpulp: Concerted Practice and/or Concerted Parallelism', *European Competition Law Review* 14(6):273–8.

Jones, A. and Sufrin, B. (2004) *EC Competition Law*, 2nd edn (Oxford University Press).

Jones, A. and Sufrin, B. (2008) *EC Competition Law*, 3rd edn (Oxford University Press).

Kamamoto, D. (2003) 'European Antitrust Chief Is No Shrinking Violet', CNET News Blog, at: www.news.com/8301-10784_4-9881416-7.html

Kerse, C. S. (1988) *EEC Antitrust Procedure* (London: European Law Centre).

Kon, S. (1982) 'Article 85, para. 3: A Case for Application by National Courts', *Common Market Law Review* 19(4):541–61.

Korah, V. (1980) 'Concept of a Dominant Position within the Meaning of Article 86', *Common Market Law Review* 17:395–414.

Korah, V. and Lasok, P. (1988) 'Philip Morris and Its Aftermath', *Common Market Law Report* 25(2):333–68.

Korah, V. and Rothie, W. A. (1992) *Exclusive Distribution and the EEC Competition Rules: Regulations 1983/83 and 1984/84* (London: Sweet & Maxwell).

Kroes, N. (2005) 'Preliminary Thoughts on Policy Review of Article 82', speech delivered to the Fordham Corporate Law Institute, New York, 23 September.

Kroes, N. (2006) 'More Private Antitrust Enforcement through Better Access to Damages: An Invitation for an Open Debate', at the Conference on Private Enforcement in EC Competition Law: The Green Paper on Damages Action, Brussels, 9 March.

Kroes, N. (2007) 'Assessment of and Perspectives for Competition Policy in Europe', speech made at the Celebration of the Fiftieth Anniversary of the Treaty of Rome, Barcelona, 19 November.

Lehmkuhl, D. (2008) 'On Government, Governance and Judicial Review: The Case of European Competition Policy', *Journal of Public Policy* 28(1): 139–59.

Leucht, B. (2008) 'Transatlantic Policy Networks and the Creation of a European Antitrust Law, 1950–1', in W. Kaiser, B. Leucht and M. Rasmussen (eds) *Origins of the European Polity: Transnational and Supranational Integration, 1950–72* (London: Routledge).

Lodge, M. (2002) 'Varieties of Europeanisation and the National Regulatory State', *Public Policy and Administration* 17(2):43–67.

Lugard, H. H. P. (1996) 'Vertical Restraints under EC Competition Law: A Horizontal Approach', *European Competition Law Review* 17(3): 166–77.

Maher, I. (2002) 'Competition Law in the International Domain: Networks as a New Form of Governance', *Journal of Law and Society* 29(1):112–36.

Maher, I. (2006) 'The Rule of Law and Agency: The Case of Competition Policy', Chatham House Working Paper, IEP WP 06/01.

Majone (ed.) (1993) *Regional Institutions and Governance in the European Union* (London: Praeger).

Maudhuit, S. and Soames, T. (2005) 'Changes in EU Merger Control: Part 3', *European Competition Law Review* 26(3):144–50.

McGowan, L and Wilks, S. (1995) 'The First Supranational Policy of the European Union: Competition Policy', *European Journal of Political Research* 28(2):141–69.

McGowan, L. (1994) 'Half-Baked Rather than Whole-Hearted: Competition Policy in Germany', *Debatte* 2(1):128–49.

McGowan, L. (2000) 'At the Commission's Discretion: Fining Infringements under the EU',s Restrictive Practices Policy', *Public Administration* 78(3):639–56.

McGowan, L. (2005) 'Europeanization Unleashed and Rebounding: Assessing the Modernisation of EU Cartel Policy', *Journal of European Public Policy* 12(6):986–1002.

McGowan, L. (2007) 'Theorising European Integration: Revisiting Neofunctionalism and Testing Its Suitability for Explaining the Development of EC Competition Policy?', European Integration Online Papers II(3), at: http://eiop.or.at/eiop/index.php/eiop/article/view/2007_003a/46.

McGowan, L. (forthcoming, 2009) *The Antitrust Revolution in Europe* (Cheltenham: Elgar).

McGowan, L. and Cini, M. (1999) 'Discretion and Politicization in EU Competition Policy: The Case of Merger Policy', *Governance* 12(2): 175–200.

Merkin, R. and Williams, K. (1984) *Competition Law: Antitrust Policy in the UK and the EEC* (London: Sweet & Maxwell).

Metcalfe, L. (1996) 'The European Commission as Network Organization', *Publius: The Journal of Federalism* 26(4):43–62.

Michelmann, H. (1978) *Organisational Effectiveness in a Multinational Bureaucracy* (Farnborough: Saxon House).

Monti, G. (2007) *EC Competition Law* (Cambridge University Press)

Monti, M. (2000) 'Fighting Cartels Why and How?', speech to the Third Nordic Competition Policy Conference, Stockholm, 11–12 September.

Morgan, E. and McGuire, S. (2004) 'Transatlantic Divergence: GE Honeywell and the EU's Merger Policy', *Journal of European Public Policy* 11(1):39–56.

Morgan, E. J. (2001) 'A Decade of EC Merger Control', *International Journal of the Economics of Business* 8(3):451–73.

Mortelmans, K. (1984) . 'The Compensatory Justification Criterion in the Practice of the Commission in Decisions on State Aids', *Common Market Law Review* 21(3):405–34.

Motta, M. (2004) *Competition Policy: Theory and Practice* (Cambridge University Press).

Mulvey, S. (2007) 'Profile: Neelie Kroes', *BBC News*, 17 September, at: http://news.bbc.co.uk/2/hi/europe/6998300.stm

Navarro, E., Font, A, Folguera, J. and Briones, J. (2005) *Merger Control in the EU* (Oxford University Press).

Nazerali, J. (1998) 'Plus ça change, plus c'est la même chose', *Business Law Review* 19(4):84–5.

Neale, A. and Goyder, D. G. (1980) *The Antitrust Laws of the United States of America*, 3rd edn (Cambridge University Press).

Neven, D., Nuttall, R. and Seabright, P. (1993) *Mergers in Daylight: The Economics and Politics of European Merger Control* (London: Centre for Economic Policy Research).

O'Donoghue, R. and Padilla, A. J. (2006) *The Law and Economics of Article 82* (Oxford: Hart).

Odudo, O. (2006) *The Boundaries of EC Competition Law* (Oxford University Press).

Olsen, M. (2002) 'The Many Faces of Europeanisation', *Journal of Common Market Studies* 40(5):921–52.

Pardolesi, R. and Renda, A. (2004) 'The European Commission's Case against Microsoft: Kill Bill?', *World Competition* 27(4):562–3.

Parisi, J. (2005) 'A Simple Guide to the EC Merger Regulation of 2004', *The Antitrust Source*, at: www.antitrustsource.com

Peeperkorn, L. (2001) 'New Notice on Agreements of Minor Importance (de minimis Notice)', *Competition Policy Newsletter*(1): February.

Peters, B. G. (1992) 'Bureaucratic Politics and the Institutions of the European Community', in A. Sbragia (ed.) *Euro-politics: Institutions and Policymaking in the New European Community* (Washington, DC: Brookings).

Pheasant, J. (2006) 'Damages Action for Breach of the EC Antitrust Rules: The European Commission's Green Paper', *European Competition Law Report* 27(7):365–81.

Phlips, L. (1983) *The Economics of Price Discrimination* (Cambridge University Press).

Pope (1993) 'Some Reflections on Italian Flat Glass', *European Competition Law Review* 14(4):172–6.

Quigley, C. (1988) 'The Notion of a State Aid in the EEC', *European Law Review* 13(4):242–56.

Reynolds, M. J. and Anderson, D. G. (2006) 'Immunity and Leniency in EU Cartel Cases: Current Issues', *European Competition Law Review* 27(2):82–90.

Röller, L-H. and Buigues, P. A. (2005) 'The Office of the Chief Competition Economist at the European Commission', at: http://ec.europa.eu/dgs/competition/officechiefecon_ec.pdf

Rosamond, B. (2000) *Theories of European Integration* (Basingstoke: Macmillan).

Rosamond, B. (2005) 'The Uniting of Europe and the Foundation of EU Studies: Revisiting the Neofunctionalism of Ernst B. Haas', *Journal of European Public Policy* 12(2):237–54.

Ross, G. (1995) *Jacques Delors and European Integration* (Cambridge: Polity).

Schimmelfennig, F. and Rittberger, B. (2006) 'Theories of European Integration', in J. Richardson (ed.) *European Union: Power and Policy-Making* (Abingdon: Routledge).

Schina, D. (1987) *State Aids under the EEC Treaty: Articles 92–94* (Oxford: ESC).

Schmitter, P. C. (1969) 'Three Neofunctional Hypotheses about International Integration', *International Organization* 23(1):297–317.

Schmitter, P. C. (2004) 'Neo-Neofunctionalism', in A. Wiener and T. Diez (eds) *European Integration Theory* (Oxford University Press).

Schrans, G. (1973) 'National and Regional Aid to Industry under the EEC Treaty', *Common Market Law Review* 10:175–8.

Scott, C. (2000) 'Services of General Interest in EC Law: Matching Values to Regulatory Technique in the Public and Privatised Sectors', *European Law Journal* 6(4):310–25.

Seidel, K (2007) 'Establishing an Economic Constitution for Europe: DG IV and the Origins of a Supranational Competition Policy', paper presented at the 37th Annual UACES Research Conference, University of Portsmouth, 3–5 September

Seidel, K. (2008) 'DG IV and the origins of a supranational competition policy establishing an economic constitution for Europe', in W. Kaiser, B. Leucht and M. Rasmussen (eds) *Origins of the European Polity: Transnational and Supranational Integration, 1950–72* (London: Routledge).

Shapiro, C. (1995) 'Aftermarkets and Consumer Welfare: Making Sense of Kodak', *Antitrust Law Journal* 63(2):483–512.

Sher, B. (2004) 'The Last of the Steam-Powered Trains: Modernising Article 82', *European Competition Law Review* 25(5):243–6.

Slot, P. J. (1990) 'Procedural Aspects of State Aids: The Guardian of Competition versus the Subsidy Villains', *Common Market Law Review* 27:741–60.

Smellie, R. (1985) 'Competition Policy in the EC: A Conference Report', *Government and Opposition*, 18(3):267–90.

Smith, M. P. (1996) 'Integration in Small Steps: The European Commission and Member State Aid to Industry', *West European Politics* 19(3):563–82.

Smith, M. P. (2000) 'Autonomy by the Rules: The European Commission and the Development of State Aid Policy', *Journal of Common Market Studies* 72(3):380–423.

Sosnick, S. H. (1958) 'A Critique of Concepts of Workable Competition', *Quarterly Journal of Economics* 72(3):380–423.

Stuart, E. G. (1996) 'Recent Developments in EU Law and Policy on State Aids', *European Competition Law Review* 4:226–39.

Sturm, R. (1996) 'The German Cartel Office in a Hostile Environment', in G. B. Doern and S. Wilks (eds) *Comparative Competition Policy: National Institutions in a Global Market* (Oxford: Clarendon).

Swann, D. (1983) *Competition and Industrial Policy in the European Community* (London: Methuen).

Temple-Lang, J. (1977) 'The Procedure of the Commission in Competition Cases', *Common Market Law Review* 14(2):155–73.

Temple-Lang, J. (1979) 'Monopolisation and the Definition of 'Abuse', of a Dominant Position under Article 86 EEC Treaty', *Common Market Law Review* 16:345–64

Temple-Lang, J. and O'Donoghue, R. (2002) 'Defining Legitimate Competition: How to Clarify Pricing Abuses under Article 82EC', *Fordham International Law Journal* 26:83–162.

Thomas, K. P. (2000) *Competing for Capital: European and North America in a Global Era* (Washington DC: Georgetown University Press).

Tsoukalis, L. (1993) *The New European Economy*, 2nd edn (Oxford University Press).

Van Appeldorn, B. (2002) 'The European Round Table of Industrialists: Still a Unique Player', in J. Greenwood (ed.) *The Effectiveness of EU Business Associations* (Basingstoke: Palgrave).

Van Damme, E. E. C., Larouche, P. and Müller, W. (2006) 'Abuse of a Dominant Position: Cases and Experiments', TILEC Discussion Paper No. 2006-020, at SSRN: http://ssrn.com/abstract=925626

Van den Bergh, R. J. and Camasasca, P. D. (2006) *European Competition Law and Economics: A Comparative Perspective*, 2nd edn (London: Sweet & Maxwell).

Van Gerven, W. (1974) 'Twelve Years of EEC Competition Law (1962–73) Revisited', *Common Market Law Review* 11(1):38–61.

Van Waarden, F. and Drahos, M. (2002) 'Courts and (Epistemic) Communities in the Convergence of Competition Policies', *Journal of European Public Policy* 9(6):913–34.

Vickers, J. (2006) 'Market Power in Competition Cases', paper presented at the BIICL Conference on the Reform of Article 82, London, 24 February.

Von der Groeben, H. (1961) European Parliamentary Debates, 19 October, *Economic Journal* 73(289):54.

Wagner, K. (1956) *Die Diskussion uber ein Gesetz gegen Wettbewerbsbeschrankungen in Westdeutschland nach 1945* (Zurich: Polygraphischer).

Wallace (2000) 'Europeanization and Globalization: Complementary and Contradictory Trends', *New Political Economy* 5(3):369–82.

Warnecke, S. J. (1978) *International Trade and Industrial Policies: Government Intervention and an Open World Economy* (London: Macmillan).

Warzoulet, L. (2006) 'La France at la mise en place de la politique de la concurrence communautaire (1957-64)', in E. Bussiere, M. Dumoulin and S. Schirmann (eds), *Europe organisée, Europe du libre-échange. Fin XIXe siècle – Années 1960, PIE-Peter Lang*: 175–201.

Warzoulet, L. (2007) 'At the Core of European Power: The Origins of Competition Policy (1957–64)', paper presented at the Workshop on European Competition Policy, 1930–2005, Sorbonne University, Paris, 14–15 September.

Weatherill, S. (1989) 'EEC Competition Law: Complaining to the Commission', *The Company Lawyer*, 10(3):47–51.

Weatherill. S. and Beaumont, P. (1995) *EC Law*, 2nd edn (Harmondsworth: Penguin).

Weiler, J. (1993) 'Journey to an Unknown Destination: A Retrospective and Prospective of the European Court of Justice in the Arena of Political Integration', *Journal of Common Market Studies* 31(4):417–46.

Weitbrecht, A (2005) 'EU Merger Control in 2004: An Overview', *European Competition Law Review* 26(2):67–74.

Whish, R. (1989) *Competition Law*, 2nd edn (London: Butterworth).

Whish, R. (2000) 'Regulation 2790/1999: The Commission's New Style Block Exemption for Vertical Restraints', *Common Market Law Review* 37(4):887–924.

Whish, R. (2003) *Competition Law*, 5th edn (London: Butterworth).

Wiener, A. and Dicz, T. (2004) *European Integration Theory* (Oxford University Press).

Wigger, A. (2008) 'Competition for Competitiveness: The Politics of the Transformation of the EU Competition Regime', PhD Thesis, Free University of Amsterdam.

Wigger, A, and Nölke, A. (2007) 'Enhanced Roles of Private Actors in EU

Business Regulation and the Erosion of Rhenish Capitalism: The Case of Antitrust Enforcement', *Journal of Common Market Studies* 45(2): 487–513.

Wilks, S. and McGowan, L. (1995a) 'Disarming the Commission: The Debate over a European Cartel Office', *Journal of Common Market Studies* 33(2 pp. 259–74.

Wilks, S. and McGowan, L. (1996) 'Competition Policy in the European Union: Creating a Federal Agency?', in G. B. Doern and S. Wilks (eds) *Comparative Competition Policy: National Institutions in a Global Market* (Oxford: Clarendon).

Wilks, S. (1996) 'The Prolonged Reform of United Kingdom Competition Policy', in G. B. Doern and S. Wilks (eds) *Comparative Competition Policy: National Institutions in a Global Market* (Oxford: Clarendon).

Wilks, S. (2005a) 'Agency Escape: Decentralisation or Dominance of the European Commission in Competition Policy', *Governance* 18(3):113–39.

Wilks, S. (2005b) 'Competition Policy', in H. Wallace, W. Wallace, and M. Pollack (eds) *Policy-Making in the European Union* (Oxford University Press).

Wilks, S. (2007) 'The European Competition Network: What Has Changed?', paper presented at the European Studies Association Conference, Montreal, 17–19 May.

Winter, J. A. (1993) 'Supervision of State Aid: Article 93 in the Court of Justice', *Common Market Law Review* 30:311–39.

Wishlade, F. (1993) 'Competition Policy, Cohesion and the Co-ordination of Regional Aids in the European Community', *European Competition Law Review* 14(4):143–50.

Wishlade, F. (forthcoming, 2008) 'Competition and Cohesion – Coherence or Conflict? European Union Regional State Aid Reform Post-2008', *Regional Studies* .

Woolcock, S. (1989) 'European Mergers: National or Community Control?', Royal Institute of International Affairs Discussion Paper no. 15 (London).

Zweifel, T. (2003) 'Democratic Deficits in Comparison: Best (and Worst) Practices in European, US and Swiss Merger Regulation', *Journal of Common Market Studies*, 41(3):542–66.

Index

abuse (of dominant position)   99, 100–1,
    108, 111–19, 123
acquis communautaire   8
Advisory Committee   136
Aerospatiale/Alenia/de Havilland case
    135, 154
Air France case   188
Airtours/First Choice case   138, 139, 157
Akema   76
AKZO   114–16
Alliance for Liberals and Democrats for
    Europe   133
American Chamber of Commerce   96
Andriessen, F.   31, 177
anti-competitive practices   9, 11
anti-trust regime   12, 13
    United States   12, 13
Article 1   140
Article 2   128, 132, 142
Article 3 (f) [3 (g)]   17
Article 4   141, 148
Article 8   136–7
Article 9 ('German clause')   134, 151
Article 11   90
Article 14   145, 148
Article 14   145
Article 22   148, 149
Article 23 (Regulation 1/2003)   109
Article 23 ('Dutch clause')   134, 151
Article 81   130
Article 82
    monopoly policy   98–102, 106, 108,
        109, 110, 112, 117, 118, 120–1,
        122, 123–6
    merger policy   129
Article 85 [81]   10, 16, 17, 18, 33, 34,
    35, 36, 65, 67, 69–7, 86, 90, 93, 98
Article 86 [82]   10, 16, 17, 18, 22, 30,
    33, 34, 35, 36, 98–102
Article 87   34
Article 90 [86]   17, 27, 122
Article 92 [87]   166, 167, 182
Articles 92–94 [87–89]   17, 36
Article 93 [88]   166, 168, 193
Article 94 [89]   169
Article 226   153
Article 296   134
Astra Zeneca case   120

Atlas Phoenix venture   81
Austria   193
Automobile Craiova   172

Bangemann, M.   145
Barnett, T. O.   226
BAT and Reynolds case   130
Belgian Wallpapers case   29, 56
Belgium   18
Bitumen   85, 87
Block Exemption Regulations   21, 71–4,
    76, 78, 190
    Motor Vehicles Block Exemption
        Regulation   60
Boing/Hughes Electronics   144
Boing/McDonnell Douglas merger case
    46, 158
Bolkestein Directive   205
BP   87
BP/Erdölchemie case   145
BPB Industries plc   106
British Airways   69, 130
British Caledonian   130
British Polythene Industries   94
British Telecommunications   81, 105
Brittan, L.   31, 33, 35, 40, 154, 177–8,
    197, 222
Bundekartellamt   137

cabinets   48
Canal +   81
Canal Digital   81
Carnival/P & O case   144
cartels   5, 63–4, 75–6, 89–97, 207–10,
    217
    Cartels Directorate   89
Cast Iron and Steel Works case   82
Central and Eastern Europe   35
CFK case   95
Chicago School   12, 32
Chief Economist   146, 217
Chrisso Corporation   86
civil code   18
Clinton, B.   158
College of Commissioners   46–7, 136,
    154
Colonna Report   25

Commercial Solvents   118–19
Commissioners   45–6, 222
Common Agricultural Policy   18
Common External Tariff   24
community dimension   132, 138, 141
Community Framework for Research and
    Development   190
Community Framework for State Aid
    Research and Development
    innovation   *see* Community
    Framework for Research and
    Development
Compagne Maritime Belge Transports
    102, 106
Competition Commissioners   31, 45
concentration process   5
Concert venture   81
Confederation of British Industry   96
consumer protection   4
consumer welfare   3, 4
Continental Can case   56, 102, 104, 129
Coppel, J.   56
Council of Ministers   20, 21, 72
Court of First Instance   54, 57–9, 94–5,
    138, 139
Crédit Lyonnais case   187
cumulation issue   183

Davignon, Commissioner   222
de minimis rule   68, 101, 165, 194, 220
decentralization   8, 35, 38, 214–23
    of competition policy   60, 61
Delors, J.   154–5, 222
Deltafina   94
Deutsche Telekom   81, 117, 120
'devil's advocate' panels   146
Directorate
    A (Policy and Strategic)   50, 52, 89,
        146, 164
    B (Markets and Cases I: Energy and
        Environment)   50, 52, 134
    C (Markets and Cases II: Information,
        Communication and Media)   50,
        52
    D (Markets and Cases III: Financial
        services and Health-related
        markets)   50, 52
    E (Markets and Cases IV: Basic
        Industries, Manufacturing and
        Agriculture)   50–1, 52, 164
    F (Markets and Cases V: Transport,
        Post and other services)   51, 52
    G (Cartels)   51, 52, 89, 216
    H (State Aid)   51, 52
    R (Registry and Resources)   51, 52

Director-General   49, 50, 51–2, 202
discriminatory pricing   111, 112–13
Doern, G. B.   3
dominance   99, 101, 102–11, 123, 128
DP AG (Parcels) case   115

E.ON   152–3
Eastern Europe   *see* Central and Eastern
    Europe
Ehlermann, C.D.   49
Endesa   152–3
Enterprise Act (2002)   14, 37, 210
Euratom Treaty (1957)   55
European Bureau of Consumers' Unions
    72
European Cartel Office   44, 218–19
European Coal and Steel Community
    11
    Court   55 (*see also* European Court of
        Justice)
    Treaty   16, 128
European Competition Act (1956)   18
European Competition Office   151
European Competition Network   38,
    59–61, 90–1, 94, 209, 218
European Court of Justice   21, 25, 27,
    28, 30, 33, 54, 55–7, 94–5, 104,
    107, 121, 128, 130
European Courts   7, 41, 54–9, 66, 94–6,
    135, 221–2
    see also Court of First Instance;
        European Court of Justice
European Economic Community   11, 55,
    128
    Treaty (1957)   10, 16, 17, 18, 57, 65,
        121, 125, 128, 202
    state aid policy   165–9, 197
    see also Articles
European Employers' Confederation
    95–6, 150, 210
European enlargement   37–8
European Free Trade Association   35
European integration   8
European Monetary Union   162
European Parliament   41, 42, 223
    Committee on Economic Monetary
        Affairs   42
European Round Table of Industrialists
    87, 96, 150, 210
Europeanization   7–8, 200, 207–13,
    217–23
exclusive dealing agreements   111–12
exclusive distribution   21
Exclusive Distribution and Purchasing
    Regulation   21

exclusive purchasing 21
Exxon 138

Far East 32
Football World Cup decision 108
Form CO 134–5
Framework on Aid to the Motor Vehicle
Industry 184–5
France 18, 129
merger policy 137, 154
state aid policy 194, 196–7
France Télécom 81
French Court Appeal 60
Motor Vehicles Block Exemptions
Regulations 60
Friedman, M. 32

Gema case 120
General Electric case 158–9
General Motors case 114
geographical market 105
Germany 14, 15, 18, 208, 214, 219
merger policy 128, 129, 134, 137,
150
National Socialism 14
ordo-liberal School 14
state aid policy 167, 174, 194–5
GlaxoSmithKlein 132, 138
Glaxo Wellcome 132, 138
Gore, A. 158
Goyder, D. G. 56, 89
Grant, J. 159
Green Papers 78–9, 97, 137, 140
Groeben, H. von der 21, 65
Grundig–Consten 22, 55

Haas, E. B. 201, 202, 205
Harmsen, R. 207
Hoechst 86
Hoffmann–La Roche (Vitamins) case
29, 75, 102, 104, 106
horizontal agreements 5, 74–6
horizontal price-fixing 84
horizontal restraints 65
HOV-SVZ/MCN case 113

Iberia case 188
Iberia/GB Airways case 69
IBM case 30, 109
ICI 76
IKB 174
industrial concentration 25
industrial policy 24, 25, 26, 28
Internal Market and Consumer Protection
Committee 133

International Competition Network 96,
209, 226
Italian Flat Glass case 58, 91, 102
Italy 18, 207–8
merger policy 154

Japan 6
joint ventures policy 80–2
Jösten draft 15

Kodak judgement 116
KONE 92–3
Kroes N. 40, 46, 63, 93, 111, 125, 187,
192, 194, 226

Law Against Restraints of Trade (1957)
15
legal service 47–8
Leniency Notice 86–7, 97
Leucht, B. 16
liberalization 8, 122, 223–5
Lipworth, S. 219
Lisbon Agenda *see* Lisbon Strategy
Lisbon Strategy 39, 162, 180, 225
Lowe, P. 49
Lucite 76
Luxembourg 18

market economy investor principle 174
market integration 4, 24
market power 103, 105–9
market share 106, 107
market-sharing agreements 5, 84
McCormick/CPC/Ostmann case 157
MCI Corporation 81
merger 131, 140
Merger Control Regulation 17, 33, 34,
40, 52, 127, 131, 132, 134, 135–6,
137, 141, 156–7, 211
merger policy 5, 6, 33, 127–61, 204–5,
210–13, 216
origins of European merger control
128–31
Merger Task Force 134, 136, 138, 139
Methacrylates decision 75
Microsoft case 47, 109–11, 118, 120,
123, 226
Miert, K. van 40, 45, 46, 137, 158,
160–1
Mitsubishi Elevator Europe 92
MMO2 (Telefonica O2 Europe) 81
Mobil 138
modernization 7, 36, 214–17
Monnet, Jean, Memorandum 16
Monochloroacetic Acid case 93–4

monopoly   2
monopoly policy   5, 6, 22–3, 98–126
Monti, M.   40, 45, 139
Motor Vehicles Block Exemption
    Regulation   60
Multisectoral Framework   185, 186

Napier Brown/British Sugar case   115
National Competition Authorities   41,
    59, 89–90, 217–18
national courts   41, 59
national expert   53–4
NEC   81
neo-functionalism   200, 201–6
  'spillover' process   201, 205, 206
Netherlands   18, 207–8
Neven, D.   146, 159, 217
'new' competition policy   34
new public management   7
Nintendo case   77
non-tariff barriers to trade   24
Northern Rock case   187

Official Journal   136, 173, 175
oligopoly   5
Olympic Airways case   188
one-stop-shop principle   142, 152
Organisation for Economic Co-operation
    and Development   225
Otis   92–3

Paris Summit   26
per se rule   66
Philip Morris (Holland) case   31, 174
Philip Morris/Rothmans judgment   33
Plasterboard case   117–18
Plastic Industrial Bags case   94
Polypropylene case   66, 82
Portugal   193–4
predatory pricing   5, 114, 116
price-fixing   5
private market investor principle   *see*
    market economic investor principle
Prodi, M.   36
product market   103–4
Prokent/Tomra case   120
PVC case   58, 82

qualified majority voting   43
Quinine case   82
Quinn Barlo   76

rapporteur   172–3
Reagan, R.   13
rebates   111–12

refusal to supply   111–12, 118–19
Regulation 1/2003   63, 70, 88–9, 99,
    109, 123
Regulation 17   18–19, 20, 27, 36, 39, 99
Regulation 139/2004   142, 143, 146,
    211
Regulation 4064/89   140, 143
relevant market   102, 103–5
Renault case   196–7
restrictive practices policy   5, 6, 21,
    63–97, 207–10
  assessment   82–9
Rocard, M.   197
Röller, L. H.   217
Romania   172
Russia   35

Sabena case   188
Sachsen LB   174
Schaub, A.   49
Schindler   92
Schneider/Legrande case   138, 139, 156,
    157
science and technology policy   25
Sealink/B & I Holyhead case   119
Secretariat-General   47–8
Seidel, K.   39–40
services of a general economic interest
    (SGEIs)   6, 186, 223–4
Shell   85
Sher, B.   122, 124
Sherman Act (1890)   12, 16
Siemens   156
Single European Act   55, 57
Single European Market   4, 162
  'new' competition policy   32, 33
Single Market Programme   33
Smith, A.   2, 11
SmithKleinBeecham   132, 138
Soda Ash case   35, 95
Solvay case   95
SONY   81
Spain   152–3
'spillover' process   201, 205, 206
state aid policy   22–3, 33, 52, 162–198,
    216
  Action Plan   164, 180–1
  assessment   191–7
  content   182–91; horizontal aid policy
      189–91; regional aid policy
      182–4; sectoral aid policy   184–9
  decision-making process   172–6;
      notification and non-notification
      170–2
  definition   165–70

state aid policy – *continued*
  organization, powers and decision-
    making 163–76;
  treaty provisions 165–9
Steetly/Tarmac plc case 157
stop-the-clock procedure 144
Structural Funds 183
subsidiary principle 8
Sutherland, P. 31, 33, 35, 40, 45, 177,
    222

T-Mobile 81
TAP case 188
Task Force on State Aids 177
Teleno Broadband 81
temporal market 103, 105
Tetra/Laval case 138–9, 157
Tetra-Pak case 35, 106, 113, 116–17
Thatcher, M. 14
ThyssenKrupp 92–3
traité-cadre 128
traité-loi 128
Transparency Directive 186
tying agreements 111–12, 117–18
  see also exclusive dealing agreements

unfair pricing 111–12, 113–17
United Brands case 104, 105, 107,
    113

United Kingdom 13, 14, 37, 208, 210
  Enterprise Act (2002) 14, 137
  Labour government 14, 210
  merger policy 128, 129, 137
  state aid policy 194
United States 12, 24, 32, 66, 114,
    158–9, 210, 226
  anti-trust regime 12, 13
  Chicago School 12, 32
  Federal Trade Commission 158
  restrictive business practices 13
  Sherman Act (1890) 12, 16
  Supreme Court 13

vertical agreements 5, 76–80
vertical restraints 65
Virgin/British Airways case 106–7
Vitamins case 75
Völk v. Vervaecke ruling 68
Volkswagen case 77

Wanadoo Interactive case 116
Whish, B. 76, 101, 106, 108, 138
White Papers 32, 130
Wigger, A. 225
Wilks, S. 3, 61
Wilson, T. M. 207
Woodpulp case 58
World Trade Organization 225–6

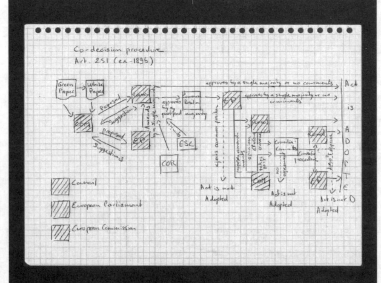